Philosophy of Perception

The philosophy of perception investigates the nature of our sensory experiences and their relation to reality. Raising questions about the conscious character of perceptual experiences, how they enable us to acquire knowledge of the world in which we live, and what exactly it is we are aware of when we hallucinate or dream, the philosophy of perception is a growing area of interest in metaphysics, epistemology, and philosophy of mind.

William Fish's *Philosophy of Perception* introduces the subject thematically, setting out the major theories of perception together with their motivations and attendant problems. While providing historical background to debates in the field, this comprehensive overview focuses on recent presentations and defenses of the different theories and looks beyond visual perception to take into account the role of other senses.

Topics covered include:

- The Phenomenal Principle;
- Perception and hallucination;
- Perception and content;
- Sense data, adverbialism, and idealism;
- Disjunctivism and relationalism;
- Intentionalism and combined theories;
- The nature of content;
- Veridicality;
- Perception and empirical science;
- Nonvisual perception.

With summaries and suggested further reading at the end of each chapter, this is an ideal introduction to the philosophy of perception.

William Fish is Senior Lecturer in Philosophy at Massey University, New Zealand.

Routledge Contemporary Introductions to Philosophy

Series editor: *Paul K. Moser*, Loyola University of Chicago

This innovative, well-structured series is for students who have already completed an introductory course in philosophy. Each book introduces a core general subject in contemporary philosophy and offers students an accessible but substantial transition from introductory to higher level college work in that subject. The series is accessible to nonspecialists, and each book clearly motivates and expounds the problems and positions introduced. An orientating chapter briefly introduces its topic and reminds readers of any crucial material they need to have retained from a typical introductory course. Considerable attention is given to explaining the central philosophical problems of a subject and the main competing solutions and arguments for those solutions. The primary aim is to educate students in the main problems, positions, and arguments of contemporary philosophy rather than to convince students of a single position.

Classical Modern Philosophy
Jeffrey Tlumak

Classical Philosophy
Christopher Shields

Continental Philosophy
Andrew Cutrofello

Epistemology
Second edition
Robert Audi

Ethics
Harry Gensler

Metaphysics
Second edition
Michael J. Loux

Philosophy of Art
Noël Carroll

Philosophy of Biology
Alex Rosenberg and Daniel W. McShea

Philosophy of Language
Second edition
Willam G. Lycan

Philosophy of Mathematics
Second edition
James R. Brown

Philosophy of Mind
Second edition
John Heil

Philosophy of Perception
William Fish

Philosophy of Psychology
José Bermudez

Philosophy of Religion
Keith E. Yandell

Philosophy of Science
Second edition
Alex Rosenberg

Social and Political Philosophy
John Christman

Philosophy of Perception

A Contemporary Introduction

William Fish

Routledge
Taylor & Francis Group

NEW YORK AND LONDON

First published 2010
by Routledge
711 Third Avenue, New York, NY 10017

Simultaneously published in the UK
by Routledge
2 Park Square, Milton Park, Abingdon, Oxon OX14 4RN

Routledge is an imprint of the Taylor & Francis Group, an informa business

© 2010 Taylor & Francis

Typeset in Garamond by Prepress Projects Ltd, UK

Library of Congress Cataloging in Publication Data
Fish, William, 1972–
Philosophy of perception : a contemporary introduction /
William Fish.
p. cm. — (Routledge contemporary introductions to philosophy
Includes bibliographical references.
[etc.]
1. Perception (Philosophy) I. Title.
B828.45.F57 2009
121'.34—dc22
2009036467

ISBN 10: 0-415-99911-1 (hbk)
ISBN 10: 0-415-99912-X (pbk)
ISBN 10: 0-203-88058-7 (ebk)

ISBN 13: 978-0-415-99911-3 (hbk)
ISBN 13: 978-0-415-99912-0 (pbk)
ISBN 13: 978-0-203-88058-6 (ebk)

For Freya, Anya, and Finlay

Contents

Acknowledgments   xi

1   Introduction: Three key principles   1
    Overview   1
    Three key principles   3
    Conclusion   9
    Questions   9
    Notes   9

2   Sense datum theories   11
    Overview   11
    The Phenomenal Principle and misleading experiences   11
    Sense data and the Common Factor Principle   13
    The time lag argument   15
    Sense datum theory formalized   16
    Sense datum theory and the two hats   18
    Sense datum theory and the Representational Principle   23
    The sensory core theory   23
    Percept theory   24
    Sensory core theory, percept theory, and the two hats   27
    Metaphysical objections to mental objects   29
    Questions   30
    Notes   30
    Further reading   31

3   Adverbial theories   33
    Overview   33
    Adverbialism   36
    Adverbialism and metaphysics   37
    The many property problem   39
    The complement objection   43
    Adverbialism and the two hats   44
    Questions   47

	Notes	47
	Further reading	48
4	**Belief acquisition theories**	**51**
	Overview	51
	Perception as the acquisition of beliefs	52
	Belief acquisition theory and the two hats	54
	Perception without belief acquisition	56
	Perception, belief, and our conceptual capacities	59
	Acquiring new concepts	61
	Blindsight	63
	Questions	63
	Notes	63
	Further reading	64
5	**Intentional theories**	**65**
	Overview	65
	Varieties of intentionalism	66
	Theories of perceptual content	71
	How do experiences get their contents?	77
	Representationalism and the two hats	78
	Questions	82
	Notes	82
	Further reading	85
6	**Disjunctive theories**	**87**
	Overview	87
	The causal objection	89
	Epistemological disjunctivism	91
	Disjunctivism about metaphysics	91
	Disjunctivism about content	92
	Disjunctivism about phenomenology	94
	Naive realism	96
	Disjunctive theories of hallucination	98
	Disjunctivism and illusion	104
	Disjunctivism and the two hats	106
	Questions	108
	Notes	109
	Further reading	110
7	**Perception and causation**	**113**
	Overview	113
	The causal theory of perception	118
	Questions	121

Notes   121
Further reading   123

8   Perception and the sciences of the mind   125
Overview   125
Theoretical paradigms and their underlying assumptions   126
Important phenomena   128
Perception, cognition, and the phenomenal   134
Color vision and color realism   140
Questions   145
Notes   145
Further reading   146

9   Perception and other sense modalities   149
Overview   149
Individuating the senses   149
Touch, hearing, taste, and smell   157
How distinct are the senses?   161
Questions   162
Note   163
Further reading   163

References   165
Index   175

Acknowledgments

Thanks to everybody I've talked philosophy of perception with over the years—there really are too many of you to mention individually, but I'm very grateful to you all. Particular thanks are due to my recent graduate philosophy of perception class: Rhys Burkitt, Malcolm Loudon, Justin Ngai, Louise Nicholls, Hayden Shearman, Jeremy Smith, and Marcel Zentveld-Wale, who, over the course of a semester, worked through a draft of this book with me. I am also very grateful to Ned Block, Alex Byrne, Tim Crane, Dave Chalmers, Stephen Duffin, Kati Farkas, Heather Logue, Stephen Hill, Susanna Schellenberg, and two anonymous readers, who provided me with valuable advice and suggestions at various stages of the project. I am indebted to them all for their input. Thanks also to the *Journal of Consciousness Studies*, for permission to reproduce the synesthesia pop-out figures; Random House, for permission to reproduce the picture of the vase-face illusion; *Behavioral and Brain Sciences*, as well as Alex Byrne and Dave Hilbert, for permission to reproduce the cone sensitivity and metamer graphs; and the Hackett Publishing Company for permission to reproduce the opponent-processing schematic and graph. Finally, thanks to Beth, for all of her support, and to my children—Freya, Anya, and Finlay—who make it all worthwhile. This book is dedicated to them.

1 Introduction

Three key principles

Overview

In this chapter we begin by introducing the *two hats*: two "tests" for an adequate philosophical theory of perception. These are the epistemological hat, which focuses on perception's role of providing us with information about the external world, and the phenomenological hat, which focuses on the conscious aspects of visual experiences.

The remainder of the chapter then considers three important principles by which philosophical theories of perception may be distinguished from one another. The Representational Principle states that all visual experiences are representational. The Phenomenal Principle states that if I am consciously aware of a property then a bearer of that property must exist for me to be consciously aware of. The Common Factor Principle states that indiscriminable veridical perceptions, hallucinations, and illusions have an underlying mental state in common.

Over the course of this book, we will be thinking philosophically about our capacity for *sense perception*—our capacity to perceive the world by means of our sense organs.[1]

If one is of a scientific bent, one might wonder just what the role of *philosophical* theorizing about perception is: isn't empirical science in the process of discovering what the nature of a visual experience is and what is going on when we perceive? The relationship between the philosophy of perception and the associated sciences of the mind will be discussed in more detail in Chapter 8 but, for now, let us simply note that philosophical thinking about perception has a remit that is somewhat broader than that of the sciences.

Whilst philosophers are indeed concerned with many of the questions that motivate empirical investigators—questions of how our capacity to perceive is related to our brains, bodies and environment, for instance—philosophical theories of perception are also explicitly fashioned to take more philosophical

considerations into account. Two considerations that are of particular importance for the philosopher of perception are the following:

> *Phenomenology*: Perceptual experiences are paradigmatically *conscious*
> experiences: they have a *phenomenology* or there is, in Thomas Nagel's
> influential terminology (1979), *something it is like* to perceive. And given
> that there is *something* it is like to perceive, we can ask *what it is like* to
> perceive: what, specifically, it is like to see a pink elephant, to be tickled,
> or to smell coffee. Yet as philosophers such as Nagel and Frank Jackson
> (1982) have argued, there is an important sense in which scientific theo-
> ries of perception do not really address the issues surrounding perceptual
> consciousness. One key role for the philosopher of perception, then, will
> be to theorize about perception in a way that gives due weight to its status
> as a conscious experience. This can also give us a consideration that we
> can use when it comes to assessing philosophical theories of perception:
> how accurately can it capture *what it is like* to have visual experiences?

> *Epistemology*: Another key feature of perceptual experiences that is not a
> primary consideration for those studying perception scientifically is that
> perception is *the* primary source of our knowledge of the world in which
> we live. Again, then, another key consideration for the philosopher of
> perception will be to develop a theory that both informs, and is informed
> by, epistemological considerations. A further consideration for a theory
> of perception, then, will be how well it can make sense of perception's
> role as a source of empirical knowledge.

To put it metaphorically, these considerations suggest that an adequate
philosophical theory of perception has (at least) two different *hats* to wear—
an epistemological hat and a phenomenological hat. As we shall see as we
work through different philosophical theories of perception, developing a
theory that can adequately wear both of these hats has proved a difficult task.
To oversimplify somewhat, what we find is that the better the phenomenological hat fits a theory, the more awkward the epistemological hat looks, and
vice versa.

What is more, these are not the only important considerations to bear
in mind when it comes to evaluating a theory of perception. For one thing,
philosophical theorizing must also be informed by scientific findings—a
philosophical theory that wears both of these hats adequately yet is inconsistent with scientific findings will not be of much value. We will come
back to the interaction between philosophy and the empirical sciences in
Chapter 8. In addition, there are also other philosophical considerations to
take into account, such as the fact that any theory of perception will claim
that certain things exist. Any theory can hence also be assessed in part by
querying whether or not these ontological commitments are metaphysically
acceptable (given the alternatives available). Moreover, as we shall see, certain

philosophical theories of perception incorporate metaphysical commitments about the world itself; if there are reasons to think that these commitments are mistaken, this will constitute a problem with that theory of perception.

As we proceed, we will evaluate each philosophical theory of perception in part by asking how well it wears the two hats, but we shall also bring these other considerations to bear where appropriate.

Three key principles

To enable us to provide some structure to the presentation of the philosophical theories and, in particular, to see critical ways in which different philosophical theories of perception are similar to, and different from, one another, I shall classify theories according to which of *three key principles* they endorse and which they reject. An interesting feature of these principles is that whilst they are all, broadly speaking, recommended by our own first-person understanding of what it is to be a perceiver, most theories of perception end up rejecting one or more of them.

The Common Factor Principle

The first of our principles begins from the observation that different experiences can be more or less *correct* or *successful*. Tradition distinguishes three cases:

Fully successful cases of perception—cases in which an object is seen and seen correctly or "as it is"—will be termed *perception* or, sometimes, *veridical perception*.[2] When it comes to the associated verb, if we find a subject "seeing" or "perceiving", it should be understood that we are dealing with a case of successful perception.

In contrast, *illusion* refers to cases in which an object is seen but seen incorrectly or "as it is not." So, for example, illusions includes cases in which a round object is seen to be oval, a blue object is seen to be green, or a tall object is seen to be short. Unfortunately, as there is no aesthetically acceptable verb form, when it is required, we will have to talk about subjects being under an illusion, or suffering from an illusion.

Finally, the term *hallucination* refers to cases in which it seems to the subject as though something is seen but where in fact nothing is seen. Classic examples include Macbeth's hallucination of a dagger and (arguably) Hamlet's hallucination of his father. Thankfully we have an acceptable verb form here: to hallucinate.

If we need a term that refers to an experience *regardless* of which of these three categories it fits into, we will use the term *visual experience*. Where you find this term it should be read as a generic term that includes perceptions, illusions, and hallucinations.

Now, the core of any philosophical theory of perception is an account of the nature of the mental state or event that occurs when we perceive. With this in mind, consider the following three (indistinguishable) situations: a subject is seeing an elephant that has been painted pink; a subject is under the illusion that the very same elephant, unpainted, is pink (perhaps because of new, experimental lighting at the zoo); a subject is hallucinating (or maybe dreaming) that they are at the zoo looking at a pink elephant. The Common Factor Principle says that in such indistinguishable or indiscriminable cases of perception, illusion, and hallucination the mental state or event that occurs is the same, regardless of which of these categories the visual experience falls into.

In order to be clear, let me say a little more about the idea that perceptions, illusions, and hallucinations have a "mental state or event" in common. The reason we need to say more is because, on one level at least, these three experiences are clearly different—they are a perception, illusion, and hallucination in turn! Given this, what does it mean to say that the mental state or event in these three cases is the same?

Let me explain by way of an analogy. Consider:

> two different sorts of burn, exactly alike in the type of physical injury they involve (call it type *B*), but differing with respect to what causes the injury; there are sunburns, in which *B* is caused by exposure to the sun, and scorches, in which *B* is caused by proximity to a source of heat.
>
> (Child 1994: 145)

In such a case, although there is a sense in which sunburns and scorches are different injuries, they nonetheless have an underlying "physical injury" in common—a burn of type *B*. Likewise, the Common Factor Principle states that although there is a sense in which indistinguishable perceptions, illusions, and hallucinations are different experiences, they nonetheless have a "mental state or event" in common: the latter claim about experiences being understood as analogous to the former claim about injuries. I will mark this by saying that, according to the Common Factor Principle, indistinguishable cases of perception, illusion, and hallucination have an "underlying" mental state or event in common.

With this clarification in mind, we can formulate the Common Factor Principle as follows:

(C) Phenomenologically indiscriminable perceptions, hallucinations, and illusions have an underlying mental state in common.

Why might we think that this principle is intuitively plausible? One important consideration is the fact that, *ex hypothesi*, subjects are completely unable to distinguish between the experience they have when they perceive, when they hallucinate, and when they suffer from an illusion. If we think that our introspective capacities must be able to turn up a difference between two mental states or events if there is a difference there to be turned up, then the fact that we cannot discover a difference between perceptions, illusions, and hallucinations would show that there *are no* differences between them. Even if we do not hold such a strong view of introspection, the fact that the experiences in these different situations can be indiscriminable could at least be seen as evidence, albeit defeasible evidence, that the subject's underlying mental state or event is the same across these situations.

A second reason, connected to and reinforcing this consideration, turns on evidence from psychology and neuroscience. We know from studying a range of phenomena that our ability to have *veridical* experiences depends upon the right kinds of activity taking place in our brains. Furthermore, we also know that if this brain activity is altered in certain predictable ways, subjects can be made to have illusory experiences. We are also confident that brain activity alone can be sufficient for a subject to have a hallucination. These considerations suggest that the nature of the experience is somehow determined by the underlying brain activity. Given this, it can then seem plausible to suppose that, if the same kind of brain activity occurs in a non-standard situation, the subject will nonetheless undergo an experience of the same kind.

Finally, there is also an appeal to everyday talk about visual experiences. Consider a case in which we do not know whether or not we are *seeing* a pink elephant or *hallucinating* one. In such a case we might naturally say that we are having the experience of *seeming to see* a pink elephant, where this is understood as something that could occur in both a case of veridical perception *and* a case of hallucination.

The Phenomenal Principle

The second core principle that we shall use to focus our discussions is the Phenomenal Principle. This is explained and endorsed in a well-known passage by H.H. Price in which he contends that:

> When I see a tomato there is much that I can doubt. I can doubt whether it is a tomato I am seeing or a cleverly painted piece of wax. I can doubt whether there is any material thing there at all. Perhaps what I took for a tomato was really a reflection; perhaps I am even the victim of a hallucination. One thing however I cannot doubt: that there exists a red patch of a round and somewhat bulgy shape, standing out from a background of other color patches, and having a certain visual depth, and that this whole field of color is directly present to my consciousness.
>
> (Price 1932: 3)

The Phenomenal Principle is formulated more clearly by Robinson (who also gives the principle its name):

(P) If there sensibly appears to a subject to be something which possesses a particular sensible quality then there is something of which the subject is aware which does possess that quality.

(Robinson 1994: 32)

To clarify the terminology here, "sensibly appears" is used to indicate that we are dealing with conscious awareness: so to say that there sensibly appears to me to be something pink is to say that pinkness is phenomenally present to me or characterizes what it is like for me. The Phenomenal Principle then states that, in such a case, there must actually *be* something pink of which I am aware.

It is important to note that the Phenomenal Principle has the form of a conditional (an if–then statement) with a phenomenological antecedent and a metaphysical consequent. It tells us that, in order for things to be a certain way for us phenomenologically, then certain things must exist.

The main motivation for endorsing the Phenomenal Principle derives from our own introspective knowledge of what it is like for us to have conscious experiences. You can test the strength of this motivation for yourself by closing this book and looking at it. The force behind the Phenomenal Principle is simply this: in order for your experience to be the way it is, blackness, pinkness, and rectangularity have to actually *be there* for you to be aware of—there must be current instantiations of these properties to adequately explain what it is like for you to have this experience. If there were nothing bearing these properties for you to be aware of, the thought goes, then your experience *could not* be as it is. The Phenomenal Principle codifies this by saying that, whenever we have an instance of this kind of conscious awareness, then there must be some*thing*—some object—that the subject is aware of and that bears the properties that characterize what it is like for the subject.

Are there any other arguments in favor of the Phenomenal Principle? Possibly; as with the Common Factor Principle, it might also be argued to be an implicit commitment of our linguistic practices. Take, for example, the phenomenon of afterimages. If you stare at a bright light for a while, you will usually find that, when you close your eyes, you are aware of a bright spot in the center of your visual field that is roughly the same size and shape as the light you were staring at. When having such an experience, you might assent to the truth of the following statement: I am aware of a bright, circular patch. In assenting to the truth of such a statement, you appear to be committing yourself to the existence of a bright, circular patch that you are aware of. This patch would be the kind of object that the Phenomenal Principle insists must be involved in every visual experience. So the defender of the Phenomenal Principle might also argue that the language we use in talking about our experiences incorporates a tacit commitment to the Phenomenal Principle.

The Representational Principle

Our final principle, the Representational Principle, states that visual experiences are *intentional* or *representational*.

When theorists claim that a visual experience is *intentional*, they are attempting to draw our attention to a particular feature of such an experience: that it is *about* something in the world—something other than itself or "beyond itself." This raises the question of how visual experiences come to have this intriguing property. A common contemporary understanding of *how* visual experiences have the property of being "about" something is to see them as *representing* that the world is a certain way.[3]

To enable us to refer back to it, let us specify a formal statement of the Representational Principle as follows:

(R) All visual experiences are representational.

To explain the notion of representation in more familiar terms, consider a map of London and a postcard of St. Paul's Cathedral. Both the map and the postcard *tell us about* St. Paul's. In virtue of this, both of these objects can be said to *represent* St. Paul's or, simply, to be *representations*.

Following up on this analogy will also enable us to highlight some key features of what is involved in saying that a visual experience is representational.

First, note that, inasmuch as they are both representations of St. Paul's, there are two key differences between the map and the postcard.

On the one hand, there is a difference in *how* they represent the cathedral. The map represents it symbolically and linguistically, with a cross symbol next to the words, "St. Paul's." The postcard represents it pictorially, with a photographic image of the building. Partly due to these differences in *how* postcards and maps represent, there is also a difference in *what* these two objects tell us about the cathedral. Whilst the map tells us *where* the cathedral is, the postcard does not tell us this but rather tells us about other things, such as the shapes and colors of its signature dome and clock towers, as well as other things about its surroundings.

By focusing on *what* these different representations tell us about St. Paul's, we can introduce an important piece of terminology: the *content* of the representation. When we talk about a representation's content, we are talking about what the representation *tells us*—about the information it *conveys to us*—and maybe also, on some accounts, *how* this information is presented.[4]

Here are some examples of philosophers making the claim that visual experiences have content:

> A visual perceptual experience enjoyed by someone sitting at a desk may represent various writing implements and items of furniture as having particular spatial relations to one another and to the experiencer, and as themselves as having various qualities . . . The representational content

of a perceptual experience has to be given by a proposition, or set of propositions, which specifies the way the experience represents the world to be.

(Peacocke 1983: 5)

Perceptual experience represents a perceiver as in a particular environment, for example, as facing a tree with brown bark and green leaves fluttering in a slight breeze.

(Harman 1990: 34)

[P]erceptual states represent to the subject how her environment and body are. The content of perceptual experiences is how the world is represented to be.

(Martin 1994: 464)

A further important feature about the notion of representation is that, in virtue of having a content—in virtue of *telling us something*—a representation can *misinform* us: it can tell us that things are a certain way when they are not. As Crane puts it, "to say that a state has content is just to say that it represents the world as being a certain way. It thus has . . . a 'correctness condition'—the condition under which it represents the world correctly" (1992: 139). For example, a misprinted map of London might tell us that St. Paul's is on the South Bank of the river Thames; a joke postcard might depict Nelson's Column rising out of the top of its dome. In these cases, the map and the postcard are still representations, and they still have content—they still tell us something—it is just in these cases, they are *misrepresentations*: what they tell us is not true but false.

We must be aware that there is a fairly innocent spatial understanding of the term "content". For instance, the "contents" of my pocket are, at present, some coins, keys, a cellphone, and lint. But the fact that my pocket has contents, in this sense, doesn't mean that it has correctness conditions or that it is potentially true or false. So we need to be aware that, sometimes, when people talk about the "content of perception" it is used as a way of referring to what is *in* our experience or what is perceived. It is not (necessarily) an endorsement of the Representational Principle.

I said at the outset of this chapter that all of these principles are motivated, in part, by our first-person understanding of what is involved in being a perceiver. What aspects of that understanding motivate the Representational Principle?

First, when we consider what it is like for us to enjoy visual experiences, it seems clear that perception is world-directed in some important way. In particular, perception plays a critical role in enabling us to find out about and navigate our environment. How could it do this if it were not the case that it carried information about that environment? Endorsing the Representational Principle can be seen as an attempt to capture this key feature of perception.

Second, there is our talk about experiences. We often speak of people seeing *that* the sky is blue, the sea is green, and so on. This might be taken to indicate that our everyday talk includes a tacit commitment to visual experiences having world-involving contents as the Representational Principle suggests.

Third, there is the observation that much psychology also treats visual experiences as representational. To claim otherwise—to deny the Representational Principle—might be seen to be, in some sense, anti-science. (This will be discussed in more detail in Chapter 8.)

Conclusion

Despite the initial plausibility of these three principles, as we shall see, the majority of theories of perception end up rejecting one or more of them. In the next five chapters, we shall see how theories of perception can be characterized by means of which of these principles are accepted and which are rejected.

Questions

- How plausible do you find classifying visual experiences as either perceptual (veridical), hallucinatory, or illusory?
- Should we require a theory of perception to wear the epistemological hat, or should we work out a theory based on other criteria and *only then* start doing epistemology?
- At a first glance, which of the three key principles do you find plausible? Why? Which do you find implausible? Why?

Notes

1. As we all know, human beings have a number of different perceptual faculties, or *senses*. The familiar five are sight or vision, hearing or audition, taste or gustation, smell or olfaction, and touch or tactition. Although there is debate over precisely how *many* senses we have—cases can be made for other senses, such as nociception (perception of pain) and proprioception (perception of limb position)—these other possible senses will not figure in this book. What is more, the senses of hearing, taste, smell, and touch will only be discussed toward the end of the book, in Chapter 9. Instead, the majority of this book will follow philosophical tradition and focus on philosophical theories of *sight*, or visual perception.

2. Sometimes, the term "veridical" can be used to mean that an experience somehow matches the world, even if it is not thereby a case of seeing. This is the source of claims that there could be, for example, a "veridical hallucination" (Lewis 1980). In the present context, "veridical" is not being used in this way—when we talk about "veridical perception," we are discussing cases of successful seeing.

3. This is not to say that one couldn't make a case for a different interpretation of intentionality. The terminology itself derives from Brentano (1995), who characterizes intentionality in three ways: as involving "the intentional (or mental) inexistence of an object," "reference to a content," and "direction toward an object" (1995: 88). One could, therefore, contend that a theory of perception counts perceptual states as intentional so long as it can count them as being somehow directed toward an object. However, the contemporary use of intentionality is most closely connected with the "reference to a content" characterization and, hence, to the notion that visual experiences contrive to be about things in virtue of being representational. We shall therefore restrict our understanding of intentionality in this way.

4. The distinction between a representation and its content is often characterized in terms of a distinction between representational vehicles and representational content. The vehicle of representation is the thing that is doing the telling—in the cases just discussed, the picture on the postcard and the icons on the map are the vehicles as they are doing the telling. The content of the representation is what the vehicle is saying—that St. Paul's is on the north bank of the Thames and that it has a large domed vault.

2   Sense datum theories

Overview

Theories that appeal to sense data typically accept both the Phenomenal Principle and the Common Factor Principle. These principles, together with some other unexceptional premises, can be used to argue that in all visual experience, whether perceptual or otherwise, we sense non-physical objects, which nowadays are usually known as sense data.

Pure versions of sense datum theory also reject the Representational Principle. Some difficulties for this theory are discussed, including claims that it gets the phenomenology of visual experience wrong and that it cannot deliver a satisfactory epistemology.

In the light of this, we introduce and briefly discuss versions of the sense datum theory that *accept* the Representational Principle—sensory core theory and percept theory.

Some more metaphysical objections to mental objects (sense data) are then considered.

Common Factor Principle   ☑

Phenomenal Principle   ☑

Representational Principle   ☒ / ☑

The Phenomenal Principle and misleading experiences

Sense datum theories of perception typically begin from an acceptance of the Phenomenal Principle: that if there sensibly appears to a subject to be something which possesses a particular sensible quality then there is something of which the subject is aware which does possess that quality. Now, in the misleading cases of illusion and hallucination, the Phenomenal Principle has an interesting consequence.

Consider hallucination first as it is the simplest case. When a subject hallucinates, there sensibly appears to that subject to be something that possesses at least one sensible quality. Take an hallucination of a pink elephant, for example. In such a case, there sensibly appears to the subject to be something that possesses the quality of pinkness. If we accept the Phenomenal Principle, this entails that there *is* something of which the subject is aware that possesses the quality of pinkness. Yet, as this is a case of hallucination, there is no suitable pink thing in the world—the pink thing of which the subject is aware cannot, therefore, be a worldly entity.

In the case of illusion, the considerations are similar. Once again, there sensibly appears to the subject of illusion to be something that possesses a sensible quality. For instance, if the gray elephant looks pink to the subject, then there sensibly appears to the subject to be something that possesses the quality of pinkness. The Phenomenal Principle therefore insists that there *is* something of which the subject is aware which possesses the quality of pinkness. Yet, whilst there is an experienced object in this case—the elephant—that object does not instantiate the property of pinkness so cannot be the pink thing of which the subject is aware.

These arguments give us the first stages of what are known as the *argument from hallucination* and *argument from illusion* respectively. They move from an endorsement of the Phenomenal Principle, together with the plausible claim that hallucinations and illusions are cases in which there sensibly appears to the subject to be something that possesses a sensible quality, to the conclusion that the subject is aware of something that cannot be identified with an everyday worldly object. More formally, the arguments work as follows:

Premise 1: (P) If there sensibly appears to a subject to be something which possesses a particular sensible quality then there is something of which the subject is aware which does possess that quality.

Premise 2(h): In hallucination, there sensibly appears to a subject to be something which possesses a particular sensible quality when there is no suitable worldly object at all.

Premise 2(i): In illusion, there sensibly appears to a subject to be something which possesses a particular sensible quality when there is no suitable worldly object that possesses that quality.

Conclusion (h): In hallucination, the something of which the subject is aware is not an everyday worldly object.

Conclusion (i): In illusion, the something of which the subject is aware is not an everyday worldly object.

If the subject is not aware of an everyday worldly object, what *is* the subject aware of? Well, whatever it is, it is pink. And as (we can safely stipulate) there is nothing pink in the subject's brain, the object of awareness in these cases is typically taken to be nonphysical. Given that hallucinations seem to depend only on processes *internal* to the subject—processes in the brain, for example—the object of hallucinatory experience is also typically (although not exclusively) taken to be mind-dependent and "private" to its subject, in the sense that only the subject of the hallucination can be aware of that particular object. The typical contemporary answer to the question of what subjects are aware of in cases of illusion and hallucination is therefore that subjects are aware of mental objects known as *sense data* (singular: *sense datum*).

This gives us the positive conclusion of the first stage of the arguments from illusion and hallucination (which, for simplicity's sake, I will combine):

Conclusion (+): In hallucination and illusion, subjects are aware of sense data.

Sense data and the Common Factor Principle

The next stage of the arguments from hallucination and illusion turn on an endorsement of the Common Factor Principle:

(C) Phenomenologically indiscriminable perceptions, hallucinations, and illusions have an underlying mental state in common.

The "underlying mental state" in question is the state of being aware of sense data of certain kinds. Given the positive conclusion of the first stage of the arguments from hallucination and illusion:

Conclusion (+): In hallucination and illusion, subjects are aware of sense data.

The Common Factor Principle licenses the inference to the further conclusion that we are aware of sense data in cases of veridical perception too.

Why might the sense datum theorist be tempted by the Common Factor Principle? Well, we have already mentioned the kinds of reasons why this principle might seem appealing but in the present case the kinds of considerations that are appealed to by sense datum theorists include the indiscriminability of hallucination from veridical perception, the continuity between hallucination and veridical perception, and causal considerations.

Indiscriminability

As noted in the opening chapter, in the abnormal cases of illusion and hallucination, the experiences we have can be indiscriminable from those we have in (the relevant) perceptual scenario. As Price contends:

> Is it not incredible that two entities so similar in all these qualities should really be so utterly different: that the one should be a real constituent of a material object, wholly independent of the observer's mind and organism, while the other is merely the fleeting product of his cerebral processes?
>
> (1932: 31–32)

Price argues that the indiscriminability of perception and cases of hallucination and/or illusion give us reason to think that, if one is an awareness of sense data, then so must the other be. In response to this kind of consideration, Austin wonders: "If I am told that a lemon is generically different from a piece of soap, do I expect that no piece of soap could look like a lemon? Why should I?" (1962: 50).

Perception to illusion continuity

The second consideration turns on the thought that our visual experiences will change from perceptual to illusory quite regularly. As examples of this, A.D. Smith mentions "the common phenomenon of looking at an article of clothing under the artificial lighting of a shop and discovering its 'real' color in daylight" and "the way in which our awareness of the colors of objects changes as dawn gives way to the full light of morning, or as dusk descends" (2002: 27). The contention here is that transitions from visual experiences that qualify as perceptual to visual experiences that qualify as illusory are pervasive. Given this, it would seem implausible to hold that they involve distinct kinds of awareness—an awareness of sense data in the illusory cases and some other kind of awareness in the perceptual cases.

Causal considerations

In addition to these considerations, we also have strong reasons to think that, in the case of hallucination, brain activity of the right kind is all that is needed (if the first stage of the argument from hallucination is correct) to create a sense datum of which the subject is aware. What is more, the subject's being aware of this sense datum *suffices* for the subject to have an experience that is indiscriminable from a perception. Given this, if the same kind of brain activity were to occur during a perceptual episode, then it should also be sufficient to create a sense datum of which the subject is aware.[1] And, as before, the existence and awareness of this sense datum would suffice for the subject to have an experience that seemed perceptual. So, regardless of the ways in which perceptions, hallucinations, and illusions may differ, there is good reason to think that they share a common element—a common awareness of sense data.

The time lag argument

The standard arguments from illusion and hallucination both attempt to prove something of a deceptive case and then extend that conclusion to perceptual cases too. The time lag argument does not involve two stages. Instead, it simply operates with the Phenomenal Principle together with the following premise:

> 2(t): In time lag cases, there sensibly appears to a subject to be something which possesses a particular sensible quality when the only suitable worldly object either no longer exists or has changed its qualities.

What makes this argument different from the others is that it attempts to include *all* cases—veridical and nonveridical—as time lag cases. An extra generalizing stage of the argument is not required.

The defense of this premise turns on two related considerations: first, that where distant objects are concerned, light from those objects takes a finite time to reach us; second, that the light from any object needs to affect us in order for us to perceive that object.

For instance, the distance to some stars is so large that, by the time the light from those stars reach Earth (and our eyes), the stars themselves have ceased to exist. Yet when the light reaches our eyes we have a visual experience of a star. This makes it a time lag case—a case in which there sensibly appears to a subject to be something that possesses a particular sensible quality when the only suitable worldly object no longer exists. Given the Phenomenal Principle, this entails that there must be something of which the subject is aware that possesses whatever qualities the "star" appears to have. As the star itself no longer exists, this provides another reason to think that the thing of which the subject is aware is a proxy star—a sense datum.

An alternative way of running the time lag argument is by considering the fact that light from the sun takes approximately eight minutes to reach us (Russell 1948: 204). When this light affects our sensory organs, say at time *t*, we do not have an experience of the sun as it is at *t*, but rather as it was at *t - 8 minutes*. This makes it a time lag case—a case in which there sensibly appears to a subject to be something that possesses a particular sensible quality when the only suitable worldly object has changed its qualities (cases of coincidental similarity aside). Given the Phenomenal Principle, this entails that there must be something of which the subject is aware that possesses whatever qualities the "sun" appears to have. As the sun itself has changed its qualities, this something must be a sun proxy—a sense datum.

Finally, the time lag argument can achieve full generality when we note that, in every case of visual experience, it will take a finite amount of time for light from the object to reach our eyes and be processed by our visual systems (Russell 1927: 155). Although in most cases the time lag here will be so miniscule the object will not have had time to cease to exist or to change its properties, we can contemplate the *possibility* that it might have done. And when we do, we see that we would have had the experience that we have regardless. The conclusion the argument aims to establish is, therefore, that *all* cases of visual experience are in fact time lag cases and hence that, in *all* cases of visual experience, we are aware of sense data.

Sense datum theory formalized

The sense datum theory proposes to analyze visual experiences (where, recall, this is neutral as to whether a case is perceptual, hallucinatory, or illusory) as follows.

> A subject S has a visual experience as of a property F if and only if S senses an F sense datum, D.

This analysis, as it stands, only suffices for a subject to have an experience *as of* a particular property. For this episode to constitute a *successful* perceiving of that property, or to constitute a perceiving of a particular object, O, then further other conditions must be met. These conditions will be discussed in Chapter 7.

Given that the sense datum theory analyzes perception as involving a particular *act* (of sensing) directed at an existent *object* (a sense datum), it is often known as an *act-object theory*.

To clarify this theory, we need to say something about both what sense data are and what the relation of sensing is.

As to the nature of sense data, they are typically defined as nonphysical objects of awareness, which are logically private to a single subject. In addition to this, the classical picture of sense data also insists that they "actually possess standard sensible qualities, for example, shape, color, loudness, 'feel' of various sorts [but] *possess no intrinsic intentionality*" (Robinson 1994: 2, my emphasis). This latter claim insists that, whilst it might be the case that when we have a given visual experience we take the sense data to be "of the world" as a matter of habit or custom, they are not "of the world" in their intrinsic nature. In their intrinsic nature, sense data possess "only sensible qualities which do not refer beyond themselves" (Robinson 1994: 2). So, although the standard sense datum theory endorses both the Phenomenal Principle and the Common Factor Principle, it does not endorse the Representational Principle. We will consider why this is shortly.

When it comes to the relationship of "sensing," a natural way to understand the notion is in a pseudo-perceptual way: as kind of like *seeing* sense data. If this is how we are to understand the notion then, as Gilbert Ryle points out (1990: 204–205), we would be left with a troublesome regress. If sensing D were a matter of perceiving D and D were perceived in virtue of sensing D^{*}' (as the sense datum theory of perception suggests), then we have simply ended up where we began. So the relationship of sensing needs to be understood in a nonperceptual way. Having said this, however, further analyses of this relationship have not been forthcoming. The relationship of sensing is typically left fundamental and unanalyzed. This is not necessarily a problem, though—as Wittgenstein says, "explanations come to an end somewhere" (1953: §1).

This gives us the sense datum theorist's take on the ontological structure of perception. What about the phenomenological side? In order to discuss this adequately, let me take a moment to introduce some important theoretical terminology.

Philosophical theories of the conscious aspects of mental states and events often utilize the notion of *phenomenal character*. To provide a theory of the conscious aspects of an experience is, then, to provide a theory of that experience's phenomenal character. The problem is that people disagree as to what phenomenal character is. On one influential reading, the defining feature of phenomenal character is that it is a property *of an experience*. Thus, Byrne suggests, we should begin by stipulating that "the phenomenal character of an experience e is a *property*, specifically a *property of e*: that property that types e according to what it's like to undergo e" (2002: 9). Yet there are theorists who agree that experiences have phenomenal characters but reject the claim that they are properties of those experiences. This is because those theorists take the defining feature of phenomenal character to be *what it is that we are aware of when we perceive/introspect*, and they argue that there is no reason to suppose that, in such cases, we become aware of properties *of experiences* (e.g. Tye 2000).

For this reason, I find it helps to keep things clear if we distinguish between *phenomenal* character and *presentational* character. The former, phenomenal character, is understood according to Byrne's definition—as the property *of an experience* that types that experience by what it is like to undergo it. The latter, presentational character, is understood as whatever it is that we become aware of when we perceive or introspect. As we shall see as we proceed, this distinction enables us to accommodate anything that anybody might wish to claim by *denying* that phenomenal characters are properties of experiences by treating whatever they say about phenomenal character as a claim about presentational character and then identifying an appropriate phenomenal character to fit.

To see how this works, consider what the sense datum theorist would say we are directly aware of when we perceive. On this theory, we are directly aware of sense data and their sensible qualities. So, the presentational character of an experience, according to the sense datum theory, will be constituted by the sensible properties of the sense data that the subject is aware of.

Although these sensible qualities are properties of sense data, and sense data are constituents of an experience, it would be a fallacy of composition to assume that these properties are thereby properties of the experience itself.[2] So these properties should not be identified with the *phenomenal* character of a sense datum experience. Yet there is an associated property that such an experience would have that would type it by what it is like to undergo it: it is the property the experience has of *being a sensing of sense datum (or collection of sense data) D*. The sense datum theorist can therefore identify this property with the phenomenal character of the experience.

Sense datum theory and the two hats

The phenomenological hat

As we have seen, the sense datum theory is motivated primarily by phenomenological considerations. In particular, it is motivated by the thought that you cannot do justice to what it is like to have an experience unless that experience actually involves an awareness of objects that bear the properties that characterize what it is like for us. However, it has been argued that the austere nature of sense data—as objects that only possess sensible qualities— makes it difficult for the theory to adequately capture the phenomenology of "real" experiences. This is Strawson:

> Suppose a non-philosophical observer gazing idly through a window. To him we address the request, "Give us a description of your current visual experience" [. . .] Uncautioned as to exactly what we want, he might reply in such terms as these: "I see the red light of the setting sun filtering through the black and thickly clustered branches of the elms; I see the dappled deer grazing in groups on the vivid green grass . . ." and so on.
>
> (1979: 43)

However, if the considerations presented in the arguments for sense data are accepted, it is possible that the subject might have an experience of this very kind even if there were no elms, no deer, no grass, etc. So we ask our observer to explain what his experience is like *without committing himself to the existence of the (purportedly) perceived objects*. If the sense datum theory is correct, then this ought to be possible by describing the sensible properties possessed by the immediate objects of his experience. As Strawson points out, however, a sensible subject "does not start talking about lights and colors, patches and patterns. For he sees that to do so would be to falsify the character of the experience he actually enjoyed" (1979: 43). Although the subject *could* attempt to exhaustively describe this in terms of patches of color, this would, according to Strawson, *falsify* the character of his experience—it would fail to adequately capture what it is like to have that experience.

A more specific phenomenological problem area for sense datum theory has concerned the experience of *depth*. The premise for this objection is that depth is a phenomenological feature of our visual experiences—that depth is, strictly speaking, a sensible quality. If this premise is accepted, then it seems that the sense datum theorist has three choices: either to claim that depth is a further *sui generis* sensible property that sense data can possess (a response Robinson [1994: 206] describes as "*ad hoc* and bogus"); to accept that the sense datum theory fails; or to accept that sense data are in fact three-dimensional and are literally at a distance from the perceiver (Jackson 1977: 102). Other sense datum theorists (such as Robinson 1994: 206–207) prefer to reject the premise, endorsing Berkeley's famous claim that "*distance* of itself . . . cannot be seen. For *distance* being a line directed end-wise to the eye, it projects only one point in the fund of the eye. Which point remains invariably the same, whether the distance be longer or shorter" (1910: 13). This response treats our awareness of depth as not, strictly speaking, part of the phenomenal nature of the visual experience at all but rather as a result of the cognitive states that naturally accompany the experience.

The epistemological hat

As we might expect from the fact that the sense datum theory is motivated primarily by phenomenological considerations, it has been criticized for being unable to adequately wear the epistemological hat.

Typically, the sense datum theorist will claim that we perceive external objects "in virtue of" the sensing of sense data. A realist version of sense datum theory, which endorses the mind-independence of the material world, is therefore typically known as *indirect realism*. "Indirect" because the "direct" or immediate objects of experience are sense data; material objects are the objects of experience only "indirectly."

This picture has led to the objection that, in claiming that we are only ever directly aware of sense data, and only *through* them aware of the external world, we "raise a veil" that separates us from the external world. Jonathan Bennett therefore calls this the "veil of perception doctrine" (1971: 69).

We need to be careful here. Some of the appeal of this objection is sensationalist, playing on the image of some kind of cognitive "ray" being aimed at the world by our minds but being thwarted by sense data that "get in the way." But most realist sense datum theorists would not deny that external objects *can be* objects of perceptual awareness, they would just hold that this awareness is *mediated* by sense data. As Dancy puts it, sense datum theory "does not have the consequence that external objects are unobservable; it purports simply to tell us something about what it is to observe them" (1985: 165).

To see how this might work, consider the relationship between seeing objects and seeing their surfaces. Jackson (1977) and Moore (1942) both argue that we do not directly "see" material objects but merely their facing surfaces. We then see the objects in virtue of seeing their surfaces. On the face of it, this is a reasonable claim. If we then view the relationship between sense data and objects on this model, it is no longer obvious that it involves a veil of perception. Nobody thinks that objects' surfaces "hide" the objects themselves from us—rather they "facilitate" or "mediate" this awareness. This is exactly the way that sense datum theorists view the relationship between our awareness of sense data and our awareness of (the facing surfaces of) objects (see Jackson 1994).

Even if the sense datum theorist can adequately rebut the objection that the theory precludes the awareness of external objects, a key epistemological question remains: how does perception, so understood, enable us to acquire knowledge of the external world?

Traditionally, sense datum theories of perception have been associated with *foundationalist* theories of epistemology. Foundationalism begins from the observation that many of our empirical beliefs are justified by the relationships they stand in to other beliefs. For instance, my belief that <London has a higher population than New Zealand> is justified by my beliefs that <the population of London is 7.5 million> and <the population of New Zealand is 4 million>, together with some background mathematical beliefs. However, my belief that London is more populous is only *conditionally* justified; it is only justified if my beliefs about the relevant populations are justified. So what justifies me in *these* beliefs? Well, the thought goes, other beliefs, such as beliefs about the results of recent censuses, and so on.

However, this suggests the threat of a worrisome regress. If *every* belief is only justified if *another* belief is justified, and if that belief is only justified if a yet *further* belief is justified, then it looks as though we will never be in a position to say that any of our beliefs actually is (unconditionally) justified.

To avoid this, the foundationalist claims that all of our empirical beliefs ultimately depend for their justification on certain *foundational* beliefs— beliefs that are justified in a special *unconditional* way.

What are these foundational beliefs? Well, as Lewis put it, "empiricists generally are agreed that nonperceptual synthetic knowledge rests finally on knowledge which is perceptual, and so find the root problem in the nature of perception" (1952: 170). The foundationalist's foundations are our beliefs about our own sensory experiences. Why these beliefs? Because, "When I perceive a door, I may be deceived by a cleverly painted pattern on the wall, but the presentation which greets my eye is an indubitable fact of my experience . . . The given element is this incorrigible presentational element; the criticizable and dubitable element is the element of interpretation" (Lewis 1952: 170).

The similarity between this claim and Price's phenomenological defense of the Phenomenal Principle is striking. According to Lewis, what marks out beliefs about our own experiences is that, whilst there is much that can be doubted, there is a core belief which is indubitable or incorrigible.[3] This explains why these beliefs are justified and hence apt to serve as our epistemological foundations.

According to traditional foundationalist versions of sense datum theory, then, our beliefs about the external world are inferred from and *justified* by beliefs about our own experiences.

Over the years, many philosophers have argued that such a claim renders sense datum theory fundamentally unable to deliver a satisfactory epistemology. The worry is highlighted by the very arguments that aim to show that sense data are necessary. As the second stage of the arguments from illusion and hallucination makes clear, the sense data that we are aware of in a case of perception are exactly the same as those we would have been aware of in an indiscriminable case of illusion or hallucination.

Given this, we can see that the sense datum theory is committed to the idea that an experience of a particular kind could occur in a nonveridical context. This has the consequence that we cannot move deductively from a belief about an experience to a belief about the world. Given the possibility of hallucinations, our having an experience of a certain kind does not *entail* anything about the world whatsoever. Induction is likewise problematic. An inductive justification would claim that we are justified in assuming that experiences of certain kinds are reliable indicators of the world's being a certain way because we have previously established the regularity of these two events coming together. Yet in the present case this is a nonstarter as we have no independent access to the world on which to establish that a certain kind of experience is correlated with the world's being a certain way.

At this point, purist sense datum theorists may turn to *abduction*; to suggesting that our belief that sense data correlate with the external world is justified as it is the best available explanation of certain evidence. In this context, the "evidence" is that experience is highly organized and predictable, both across senses and across time. The "best available explanation" of this evidence is then held to be that the experiences are reliably correlated with a highly organized and predictable external reality.

To see how this might work, imagine a scientist observing (what we now know to be) alpha particle tracks in a cloud chamber. At first, let us suppose, the scientist just sees the tracks. After careful experimentation, she realizes that the presence of tracks are reliably correlated with the presence of certain materials in the chamber. She therefore hypothesizes that these materials all emit a certain particle, which she calls an alpha particle. After a period of using the hypothesis, she becomes so familiar with the hypothesis that she starts to think and talk directly about alpha particles, bypassing the tracks in both thought and language. Indeed, she may even get to a point where she no longer really "sees" the tracks, in that she no longer perceptually attends to the tracks at all. Instead, she attends directly to the alpha particles (we might say, "sees" the alpha particles) *in virtue of* her more basic kind of awareness of the tracks. This is, I take it, pretty much how the abductive approach sees the role of sense data in visual experience.

However, some theorists—including some sense datum theorists—have worried that treating our belief in the external world as a "theory" formulated to explain the "evidence" is implausible. For example, Price contends that "we do not invent [the theory that there is an external world]. We have already on other grounds formed a conception of the physical world" (1932: 89). Likewise, Armstrong says that "surely we are not prepared to degrade bodies into hypotheses? We want to say that our assurance of the existence of the physical world is far stronger than any assurance we could obtain by indirectly confirming a theory" (1961: 30). Moreover, Price goes on to suggest that it is not the "best explanation" anyway—he claims there are a "thousand and one" other hypotheses, most of which are "much simpler" (1932: 89).[4]

Ryle suggests the epistemological problems with sense datum theory run even deeper than that of justifying our empirical beliefs. He wonders how, given the commitments of the sense datum view, we could get to a point where we had concepts of mind-independent entities to feature in the contents of these beliefs. He illustrates this concern with the following analogy.

> There is immured in a windowless cell a prisoner, who has lived there in solitary confinement since birth. All that comes to him from the outside wall is flickers of light thrown upon his cell-walls and tappings heard through the stones; yet from these observed flashes and tappings he becomes, or seems to become, apprised of unobserved football-matches, flower-gardens, and eclipses of the sun. How then does he learn the ciphers in which his signals are arranged, or even find out that there are such things as ciphers? How can he interpret the messages which he somehow deciphers, given that the vocabularies of those messages are the vocabularies of football and astronomy and not those of flickers and tappings?
>
> (Ryle 1990: 212)

The worry, suggests Ryle, is not how we *justify* our belief that our experiences refer to external reality but rather how we could ever have *come by* that belief in the first place.

Some theorists, who (a) take the arguments in favor of sense data to be strong, whilst (b) feel the force of the epistemological considerations just listed, yet (c) want to allow for us to have knowledge of the external world, have taken these considerations to show that we should endorse a metaphysical thesis known as Idealism. According to Idealism, the external world is not mind-independent after all, but mind-dependent. This enables "the physical world to come within the reach of direct perceptual awareness by taking it to be something which is logically created by facts about human sensory experience" (Foster 2000: 1). As Idealism is not a theory of perception, however, but rather a metaphysical theory about the nature of reality, I shall not discuss it further here.

Sense datum theory and the Representational Principle

As we have seen, the purest sense datum theorists do not also accept the principle that visual experiences are representational. Their austere view is that, although we naturally *take* our experiences to be of a world, this is a purely cognitive, rather than perceptual, matter—a matter of the way we *interpret* those experiences rather than a feature of the experiences themselves. Some theorists, however, have suggested that the difficulties classical sense datum theory faces show this to be a mistake.

Take the question of how we can move from experiences to beliefs about the world. As, on the sense datum theory, experiences themselves are not representational, we saw that empirical knowledge would have to be the result of some kind of *inference* from experiences to world. And, as we saw, an adequate account of how these inferences get started is not easy to come by. Indeed, the best account of this seems to involve treating our conviction that there is a stable, mind-independent external world as some kind of deeply held hypothesis—deeply held because it best explains why we have the sense experiences that we do.

Moreover, it is questionable whether treating the world-involving aspects of experience as purely cognitive *effects* of visual experiences, rather than perceptual phenomena themselves, provides a phenomenologically apt picture of what actually happens when we have visual experiences. As Price says, "we simply jump straight from the awareness of A to the thought of B, without any preliminary wondering or considering of evidence, indeed without any rational process whatever" (1932: 140–141).

To avoid this, it may be appealing to endorse the Representational Principle in addition to the Phenomenal Principle and the Common Factor Principle. The thought would be that, if visual experiences *also* have a representational component, then they would tell us about the world as part of their very nature. In this case, we would not need to develop and endorse a theory about the world—a visual experience would, in a sense, wear the world on its sleeve.

The sensory core theory

One way in which we might augment classical sense datum theory with the Representational Principle is if we take visual experiences to be comprised of *both* a phenomenal component, involving the direct awareness of sense data, *and* an additional representational component, which tells us about the world.

Such a modification of the classical sense datum theory would therefore hold that classical sense datum theorists, as understood above, were half right. They were right, the thought goes, in seeing that an awareness of mental objects is required to accommodate the Phenomenal Principle. They were also right in treating the sense data themselves as not being representational.

Where they went wrong, however, was in thinking that full-fledged visual experience was *nothing more than* an act of sensing sense data of various kinds. According to this line of thought, where the sense datum theorists took themselves to have given a full account of visual experience, they had in fact given only an account of the "sensory core" of visual experience.

Price is a notable advocate of this kind of theory.[5] In discussing the case of someone hallucinating a pink rat, he says that the correct analysis of the situation is that the man is both "acquainted with a pink sense datum" and "takes for granted the existence of a rat" (1932: 147). These two states of mind "arise together . . . all in one moment. The two modes of 'presence to the mind', utterly different though they are, can only be distinguished by subsequent analysis" (1932: 141).

On a two-component sense datum theory, normal visual experience involves a subject both (i) sensing or being acquainted with sense data and (ii) "taking for granted" that an appropriate material object exists. To give a full account of visual experience, then, the notion of something's being "taken for granted" must be further explained. In discussing this, Price makes it clear that "what is taken for granted is . . . *that* so and so is the case—that a material thing exists here and now, that it has a surface of such and such a sort, that it is grass, etc.—in short, what is taken for granted is a *set of propositions*" (1932: 166).

The second component, then—the nonsensory component—is a representational component. It involves the subject's representing the world to be a certain way—the way specified by the relevant "set of propositions"—and taking it for granted that the world is as represented.

The sensory core theory therefore proposes to analyze the neutral category of visual experience as follows:

A subject S has a visual experience as of a property F if and only if:

- S senses an F sense datum, D, *and*
- represents that Fness is instantiated (and takes this for granted).

Like the sense datum theory proper, the sensory core theory will also hold that the presentational character of the experience will be given by the sensible properties of D and the phenomenal character of the experience will thereby be its property of *being a sensing of D*.

Percept theory

Earlier, we noted that the classical sense datum theory has been criticized over whether its focus on "lights and colors, patches and patterns" can adequately capture the rich phenomenology of visual experiences. The sensory core approach has an answer to this objection: "to allow that purely cognitive features can alter experience" (Robinson 1994: 206). "If this line of thought is acceptable," he says, "then we could describe depth [for example] as experiential, but not bed-rock phenomenal. It is experiential because it is not like the judgment of [a] radar operator, but enters more intimately into the experience itself. On the other hand, it is not truly phenomenal, because, for Berkeleian reasons, it is not given qualitatively in experience" (Robinson 1994: 207).

However, this attempt to accommodate the fact that more properties seem to be experientially salient than the classical sense datum theory would predict has been criticized by Firth as being phenomenologically flawed.

> The phenomenological fact is simply that in perception we are *conscious*, in one sense of the word, of physical objects, without at the same time being conscious, in another sense of the word, of the entities which have traditionally been called "sense data". Perception, in short, is not a twofold state; and since we *are* conscious of physical objects we cannot possibly be conscious of sense data in the distinctive manner required by the Sense datum theory.
>
> (1965: 223)

Essentially, Firth's contention is that properties such as hardness and coldness are properties that belong to perception—that can literally be *sensed*—whereas the sense datum theory claims that only properties of sense data can be sensed, all else being supplied by the associated cognitive features.

Moreover, Firth suggests, the willingness to countenance depth as an additionally phenomenologically present property "represents a first step toward the recognition that in perception we are conscious of *many* qualities and relations which do not differ in their phenomenological status from those few which have traditionally been attributed to sense data" (1965: 220–221). To account for this, he goes on to develop an alternative way of adding the Representational Principle to classical sense datum theory, which he calls the percept theory.

What distinguishes the percept theory from the sensory core theory is the denial of the idea that our perceptual awareness of "sensible qualities" such as color and shape proceeds by way of sensing sense data, and that our perceptual awareness of other qualities, such as depth (perhaps), clumsiness, reptilianness, and felineness, proceeds by way of a *distinct* process of interpretation. According to Firth, we are conscious of all of these different qualities *in the same way*.

If Firth is right, then two possibilities present themselves: either we are aware of *all* of these qualities in the kind of way that the classical sense datum theorist takes us to be aware of shapes and colors, *or* we are aware of these qualities in some other way.

The first option would require that we are aware of properties such as clumsiness, reptilianness, and felineness by being aware of objects that *actually possess* those properties. However, as Robinson points out, mental objects cannot literally *be* clumsy, reptilian or feline (1994: 29). This leaves us with the second option: if we can be aware of these properties by being aware of sense data, and if our awareness of all qualities proceeds in the same way, then this is *not* by way of being aware of something that actually possesses those qualities.

Instead, Firth's view seems to be that we are aware of all qualities in a *different* way. He suggests instead that, while the mental object does not actually *have* these properties, it *represents itself* as having them. Sense data are not *really* clumsy or reptilian or feline, they just *represent themselves* as being clumsy, reptilian or feline. As mental objects also represent themselves as being mind-independent, Firth calls them "ostensible physical objects" (1965: 222).[6]

So the percept theory offers the following analysis of visual experience.

A subject *S* has a visual experience as of a property *F* if and only if:

- *S* senses a sense datum, *D, which*
- represents that *F*ness is instantiated.

In sum, the percept theory claims that there are mental objects in visual experience, which, unlike sense data classically conceived, have both sensible *and* representational properties. In normal experience, however, we are not aware of their intrinsic sensible properties *at all*. All our attention is directed at the world, by way of being aware of what these mental objects *represent*.

Firth does allow that, when we engage in the process of perceptual reduction—when we focus on what we "really see" in perception—we can become aware of the properties actually possessed by sense data. However, he denies that this shows that we were aware of sense data all along: rather, in his view, perceptual reduction "has the effect of replacing a state of perceptual consciousness [of an ostensible physical object] by a state in which we are aware of sense data" (Firth 1949/1965: 237).

To clarify the relationship between these three theories—classical sense datum theory, sensory core theory and percept theory—let us reflect on a familiar example. Consider a subject perceiving a circular coin that is tilted on its side. Although there is a sense in which the coin presents an elliptical face to the perceiver—its silhouette would be elliptical, for example—subjects may not notice this, taking the coin to be circular. Our three theories will provide importantly different accounts of such an experience.

The classical sense datum theorist would hold that the subject of this experience would be consciously aware of ellipticality in virtue of sensing an elliptical sense datum. The fact that she does not notice this ellipticality is due to her familiarity with such cases meaning that, on the basis of this experience, she interprets the coin to be circular. When focusing on the phenomenology, however, the subject is consciously aware of ellipticality.

According to the sensory core theorist, the subject is consciously aware of ellipticality in one sense (by sensing an elliptical sense datum) whilst being consciously aware of circularity in another (because the subject represents the coin as being circular and takes it for granted that this representation is correct).

Finally, on the percept theory, the subject is consciously aware of circularity alone. This is because, despite actually being elliptical, the mental object represents itself as circular, and it is the way it represents itself as being, rather than the way it is, that determines the subject's phenomenology. The subject can, however, become aware of the ellipiticality of the mental object by engaging in a process of perceptual reduction.

Sensory core theory, percept theory, and the two hats

The epistemological hat

Both sensory core theory and percept theory aim to avoid some of the epistemological problems of pure sense datum theory by introducing a representational component. This component is supposed to be the foundation of our empirical beliefs.

However, as sensory core theorists allow that we are aware of *both* the properties that the sense datum possesses (in a sensory way) *and* the properties that are represented (in a more cognitive way), they face a dilemma. Either they allow that the representational component is somehow based (in an epistemically relevant way) upon the sensory component, or hold that it is distinct.

If they take the former option, and hold that the representational component is based upon the sensory component, then this seems to fail to yield a significant epistemological advance over the pure version of sense datum theory. If they take the latter option, then they need to either allow that the interpretative component arises *simultaneously but independently* of the phenomenal component, or that this component is caused by or automatically prompted by the phenomenal component in some nonepistemically relevant way. Whichever way they go, this not only leaves the sensory core view owing some kind of story of how and why the sensing and the taking for granted are always (or at least usually) "appropriate" to one another, it also seems to conflict with the intuition that, when we form a belief about the world on the basis of perception, we do so because of the way things *seem* (phenomenologically) to us.

The percept theory, of course, takes the latter option. Yet it doesn't face the same set of objections as it holds, in essence, that in normal perception, the phenomenal component *just is* the representational component. According to the percept theory, when we form the belief that an object is blue on the basis of perception, we do so because our experience *represents* the object as blue.[7]

Whilst this gives the percept theory a putative *epistemological* advantage over the other theories that posit mental objects, it comes at the cost of a putative *phenomenological* disadvantage.

The phenomenological hat

As we have seen, the percept theorist holds that the properties we are aware of in everyday perception—the constituents of presentational character—are in fact properties that can (usually) only be had by mind-independent objects: properties such as clumsiness, reptilianness, and felineness. So the properties that we are aware of when we perceive, according to the percept theory, will *not* be the sensible properties of the sense datum *D*, but rather of the properties that *D represents* to be instantiated. Because of this, the phenomenal character of the experience will no longer be its property of *being a sensing of something that is F*, but rather its property of being a sensing of *something that represents Fness*.

With this made clear, we can actually see that percept theory embodies a *rejection* of the Phenomenal Principle. That principle, recall, says that:

> (P) If there sensibly appears to a subject to be something which possesses a particular sensible quality then there is something of which the subject is aware which does possess that quality.

As we have seen, the percept theorist claims that there are more sensible qualities—qualities that things can sensibly appear to possess—than the sense datum theorist can allow. The percept theorist will certainly accept that there are many cases in which the antecedent of the Phenomenal Principle is met without the consequent thereby being true. To see this, take a particular case in which there sensibly appears to a subject to be something which possesses the (now) sensible quality of clumsiness. The percept theorist does *not* agree that, in such a case, there is something of which the subject is aware which *actually* possesses that property. Rather the claim is that there is something of which the subject is aware which *represents itself as* possessing that property. So the percept theory *does not* endorse the Phenomenal Principle, even though it retains the commitment to mental objects.

Yet recall that a significant motivation for the Phenomenal Principle was that, in order for your experience to be the way it is, the properties that you are sensibly aware of have to actually *be there*. That the only way for your experience to be as it is is for there to be current instantiations of these properties that you are consciously connected to. The percept theory cannot agree with this.

One further phenomenological point that is worth mentioning is that a central argument for percept theory turns on the phenomenological claim that we cannot actually distinguish a sensory component and an interpretative component in experience. This claim seems to be contradicted by the fact that many philosophers have taken themselves to have distinguished such a thing. Indeed, Lewis describes the distinction between the purely sensory and the interpretative components as "one of the oldest and most universal of philosophic insights" (1929: 38).

Metaphysical objections to mental objects

To conclude this chapter, let us consider some objections to the feature that classical sense datum theories, sensory core theories and percept theories have in common: the postulation of private mental objects.

In the present philosophical environment, the very fact that sense data are held to be nonphysical would be reason enough for them to be viewed with deep suspicion. But not only are they nonphysical; they are also existent in a very strange kind of way. Barnes (1965: 143–152) asks a number of pertinent questions, including the following. Does a particular sense datum persist while I blink or is it replaced by a new one? Do sense data change in size as I move closer or further away, or are they constantly replaced by new smaller or larger sense data? If one sense datum moves across a visual field, does the whole package of sense data (the visual field) change, or do the different component sense data change their relative positions? If sense data really exist, the thought goes, these questions must have answers.

Whilst it is of course open for sense datum theorists simply to stipulate answers to these queries, Barnes worries about the fact that there seems to be no ground for choosing one answer over another. "It may be said that to answer these questions is not important," he accepts. "I am inclined to agree that it is not; but the only reason I can see for this is that, [sense data] being wholly fictitious entities, we can attribute to them what qualities we please" (1965: 150). The thought here is that the fact that these metaphysical questions do not admit to any principled investigation suggests that the metaphysical realm in question does not really exist.

Another metaphysical worry is brought to light in an objection that, according to Chisholm (1942: 368), is originally due to Gilbert Ryle: the "Problem of the Speckled Hen". When you perceive a speckled hen, you are likely to see that it has a large number of speckles without being able to see precisely how many speckles it has. Whilst the hen, as an existing object, has to have a determinate number of speckles (given the metaphysical principle that to be is to be determinate), our *perception* of the hen is indeterminate as to its speckledness.

The difficulty that this indeterminacy creates is that, as sense data are what we are immediately aware of in perception, and as our awareness is indeterminate, it seems to imply that the sense data will have to be indeterminate in nature. This can be argued to contravene the metaphysical principle cited above.

In response to this objection, sense datum theorists might stipulate that sensing something does not entail being aware of every feature of that thing (Robinson 1994: 193). Yet this doesn't quite seem to solve the problem. It is one thing to allow that we might fail to notice some feature of a sense datum but quite another to claim that a sense datum could have features that we are unable to become aware of. It seems that the speckled hen could be just such a case. Even if I try to count the hen's speckles, I may be unable to. If the sense datum is determinate as to its number of speckles, this must therefore be a feature of the sense datum that I am unable to become aware of. As Armstrong says, this "has the paradoxical consequence that objects specially postulated to do phenomenological justice to perception are now credited with characteristics that lie quite outside perceptual awareness" (1968: 220–221).

Questions

- How compelling are the arguments in favor of sense data? Where are their weaknesses?
- Which of these theories gives the better account of the phenomenology of visual experiences? Why?
- How compelling are the metaphysical objections to mental objects? Should they make us avoid such objects in our theories of perception?

Notes

1. Even if the brain activity is not exactly the same in the case of perception, we can be sure that there will be brain activity of some kind. And if brain activity of some kinds can suffice for the existence and awareness of a sense datum (as in the case of hallucination), there is at least a strong case that brain activity of other kinds (in perception) would likewise suffice.
2. Fallacies of composition occur when a property of a constituent of O is assumed to thereby be a property of O. For example, it is clearly a fallacy to assume that, as atoms have the property of being invisible to the naked eye, anything that is composed of atoms will also have the property of being invisible.
3. To say that something is indubitable is to say that it cannot be doubted. To say that something is incorrigible is to say that it cannot be corrected. However, I'm not sure that either of these two notions is quite what the foundationalist is looking for. To see why, note that there are two

reasons why it may be impossible to doubt something, or impossible for something to be corrected. In the first case, either because it could be false, but we're not cognitively equipped to doubt it, or because it simply couldn't be false (it is infallible). In the second case, either because it could be false, but you are in a far better position than me to know whether it is true or false (so although you might get it wrong, you're guaranteed to be in a better position than me), or because it simply couldn't be false (it is infallible). For the purposes of epistemology, it looks to be the second sense of indubitability and/or incorrigibility that is relevant, which suggests that the really important notion is that infallibility—of being unable to be false.

4. As an example he mentions the hypothesis that God causes all of our experiences. As to whether this hypothesis, or any other, is simpler than the external world hypothesis, I leave the reader to decide.

5. It is also associated with Thomas Reid, who says that "sensation, taken by itself, implies neither the conception nor belief of any external object. It supposes a sentient being, and a certain manner in which that being is affected; but it supposes no more. Perception [here being used in a more specialist sense] implies an immediate conviction and belief of something external—something different both from the mind that perceives and from the act of perception. Things so different in their nature ought to be distinguished; but, by our constitution, they are always united. Every different perception is conjoined with a sensation that is proper to it" (2002: XVI).

6. There may be some dispute over whether a percept represents itself as being, say, reptilian, or whether it represents a physical object as being reptilian. Yet Firth is concerned to distinguish ostensible physical objects (sense data) from physical objects strictly speaking. Given this, it would be unclear to what extent an ostensible physical object would be ostensibly physical unless it presented itself as being something it is not—i.e. physical. For this reason I think the reflexive representational content makes best sense of Firth's claims.

7. Of course, if the percept theorist holds that mental objects represent themselves as being clumsy, or reptilian, or feline (as Firth seems to suggest), this does yield an epistemological objection. Why should the fact that a mental object tells us that it is, say, feline, justify us in believing that something in the world is feline?

Further reading

Three books, all entitled *Perception*, dominate the further reading for sense datum theory. Price's *Perception* (1932) is an early defense of mental objects in the guise of the sensory core theory, Jackson's *Perception* (1977) defends sense datum theory and addresses the epistemological objection to sense datum theories (Chapter 6), and Robinson's *Perception* (1994) is, in my view, the classic contemporary defense of sense data. Although Robinson eventually (and tentatively) favours an antirealist version of the theory, the majority of the book is an argument for the claim that perception involves sense data and takes no stand on the metaphysical question.

In addition to these books, R.J. Swartz (ed.), *Perceiving, Sensing and Knowing* (1965) contains some useful papers, including Firth's "Sense Data and the Percept Theory," in which the percept theory is defended, and Barnes's "The Myth of Sense Data," which is the *locus classicus* of the metaphysical objection to mental objects.

3 Adverbial theories

Overview

Adverbial theories retain the Common Factor Principle but reject the Phenomenal Principle and the Representational Principle. Adverbialists reject the need to appeal to the *objects* of acts of sensing to explain what it is like for the subject, appealing instead to *ways* of sensing.

The formulation of adverbialism is discussed in detail, as is its connection to qualia theory from the philosophy of mind, and objections to adverbialism are then discussed.

Common Factor Principle ☑

Phenomenal Principle ☒

Representational Principle ☒

Imagine that we see a red triangle. According to the sense datum theory, to see a red triangle is, in part, to sense a red, triangular sense datum. As we have seen, the mental entity that this commits us to has been argued to be problematic, both epistemologically and metaphysically.

These concerns have led some to think that there must be something wrong with the Phenomenal Principle, given that it is this principle (albeit together with the Common Factor Principle) that is the origin of the commitment to mental objects. This principle, recall, claims that:

(P) If there sensibly appears to a subject to be something which possesses a particular sensible quality then there is something of which the subject is aware which does possess that quality.

Barnes argues that this principle is based on a fallacy. "That something appears pink to me is not a valid reason for concluding either that that thing is pink or that there is some other thing which is pink" (1965: 153). As Robinson also notes when discussing the arguments in favor of mental objects, our language is stocked with idioms, such as "seems," "appears," and "looks," which we can confidently use to assert, for instance, that a nonpink elephant *seems* pink (1994: 40).

This kind of objection can be augmented by showing how statements that appear to commit us to the existence of certain objects can be reinterpreted so as to avoid such commitments. A highly influential approach to this project, which in turn generated an alternative theory of perception, focuses on the possibility of providing adverbial translations of such sentences.

To explain: note that many familiar sentences of English relate a subject to an adjectivally modified object. Thus:

1   Lucy had a heavy bag.

2   John wore a broad hat.

For each of these sentences, the subject (John/Lucy) bears a certain relationship (having/wearing) to a certain object (a heavy bag/a broad hat).

If sentences 1 and 2 are *true* then we appear to be committed to the existence of those objects—if it is *true* that Lucy has a heavy bag, then the heavy bag that Lucy has must exist.

However, the following sentences have a similar surface structure.

3   Dave gave an energetic performance.

4   John wore a broad smile.

Sentences 3 and 4 also seem to relate subjects to objects in the very same way. Given this, we might think that, if sentences such as 3 and 4 are true, then we must also be committed to the existence of certain strange objects—performances and smiles—which can both be adjectivally modified and to which we can bear relationships of giving and wearing.

However, we don't have to see things in this way. Although 3 and 4 have the *subject : verb : adjective : noun* form, they can both be translated into a *subject : verb : adverb* form whilst retaining their sense.

This translation has three stages. First, we map across the subject. Then we convert the noun from the original sentence into a verb (thus, in the case of 3 and 4, "performance" becomes "performed" and "smile" becomes "smiled"). Finally, we convert the adjective that modifies the noun into an adverb that modifies the verb, thus "energetic" translates as "energetically" and "broad" as "broadly". For 3 and 4, this yields the following translated sentences:

3_{trans} Dave performed energetically.

4_{trans} John smiled broadly.

What is notable here is that 3_{trans} and 4_{trans} both make sense and intuitively mean the same as the pre-translated versions, 3 and 4.

Now let us try this with 1 and 2. Once the three-stage translation process is completed, we get the following sentences:

1_{trans} Lucy bagged heavily.

2_{trans} John hatted broadly.

Unlike the previous case, 1_{trans} and 2_{trans} are not sensible sentences of English and therefore could not mean the same as sentences 1 and 2.

The moral of the story is that, whilst some sentences that have the *subject : verb : adjective : noun* surface form can be translated into *subject : verb : adverb* form without losing their sense or changing their meaning, others, such as 1 and 2, cannot.

Where we *cannot* perform these translations, the thought goes, we *really are* ontologically committed to the existence of the objects referred to in true versions of those sentences.

However, where we *can* perform the translations, then even true sentences do not *really* commit us to the existence of their objects, they are just loose ways of talking. In the case of sentences such as 3 and 4, what we are really committed to are not objects such as performances and smiles which can be adjectivally modified but, rather, events of performing and smiling which can be modified adverbially.

In this light, consider the kind of sentence that, it was suggested, carries an implicit commitment to the existence of mental objects.

5   Paul had a pink sense datum.

6   Julie had a triangular afterimage.

Then take these statements and push them through the translation to get:

5_{trans} Paul sensed pinkly

6_{trans} Julie afterimaged (=sensed) triangularly

Opponents of mental objects then contend that 5_{trans} and 6_{trans} mean the same as the original sentences. This is then argued to show that, contrary to first impressions, 5 and 6 do not commit us to the existence of problematic mental objects after all. Instead, like 3 and 4, they only commit us to subjects sensing in certain ways.

Adverbialism

These considerations have been taken to show the way to an alternative theory of perception that does not posit mental objects. An *adverbial* theory of perception contends that visual experiences are not episodes of sensing sense data but are rather episodes of sensing *in particular ways*.

Adverbialism, as a theory of perception, is easy to misunderstand. There is something in the translation argument above that can make the theory look like a verbal dodge, not a substantive theory of perception at all. As Cornman, himself a defender of adverbialism, says, "merely devising an artificial terminology in which the problems [faced by sense data] do not arise neither solves nor dissolves the problems" (1971: 188). But, as we shall see, adverbial theories of perception offer much more than an artificial terminology.

In getting away from the sense of artificiality, an important thing to note is that, although the adverbs that are appealed to in these particular translations are nonstandard, the underlying idea is actually quite familiar. Imagine that, instead of seeing a red triangle, you see a tree through heat haze. In such a case, we do not see a blurry tree—the tree doesn't become blurry—rather we see the tree *blurrily*. The object we see doesn't change; the *way* we see the object changes.

In many ways, this observation is the core of an adverbial theory of perception. For example, when I *see* a red object, according to the adverbialist, I don't sense a red mental entity but rather sense the *material* entity in a particular *way*: *redly*. As Ducasse, one of the original adverbialists, put it: "To sense blue is then to sense *bluely* [. . .] Sensing blue, that is to say, is a species of sensing—a specific variety of the sort of activity generically called 'sensing'" (1942: 232–233).

Now adverbialists agree with sense datum theorists in endorsing the Common Factor Principle, which claims that:

(C) Phenomenologically indiscriminable veridical perceptions, hallucinations and illusions have an underlying mental state in common.

If a subject sees a stick half-immersed in water, according to the adverbialist, the subject doesn't sense a bent stick but rather senses a straight stick *bently*. Or, to stay with the present example, if I see a white object under red light, and thereby suffer from the illusion that I see something red, I once again sense redly, but in this case, a *white* object is sensed redly.

A hallucination of a red object will also involve my sensing redly, it is just that, in this case, *nothing* is thereby sensed. I still sense in a certain way—redly—but no *object* is thereby sensed.

According to adverbialism, then, *what it is like* for me is a matter not of the *object* sensed (as there may not even be an object) but rather of the *way* I sense.

For this reason, adverbialism embodies a *rejection* of the Phenomenal Principle. That principle says that:

> (P) If there sensibly appears to a subject to be something that possesses a particular sensible quality then there is something of which the subject is aware which does possess that quality.

In both the illusory and hallucinatory cases just described, we have seen that there can sensibly appear to a subject to be something that possesses the sensible quality of redness *without* its being the case that there *is* something of which the subject is aware that possesses that quality. In the case of the bent stick illusion, the only object of which the subject is aware is straight, not bent, and in the case of a hallucination of something red, there is *no* object of which the subject is aware at all.

Instead, in both of these cases, its *sensibly appearing* to the subject as though something is bent or red is accounted for, not by *what* the subject senses, but rather by the *way* the subject senses: in these cases, the subject senses *bently* or *redly*. In all of the different cases—veridical, hallucinatory, or illusory—the subject is simply in a distinctive kind of experiential state.

So the adverbialist proposes to analyze visual experiences as follows.

> A subject S has a visual experience as of a property F, if and only if S senses F-ly.

As with the sense datum theory, this is an analysis of the *neutral* category of visual experience. For such an episode of sensing to qualify as a *perception* of *F*ness, other criteria will need to be met. This is the subject of Chapter 7.

Adverbialism and metaphysics

Take an adverbial statement, such as "Jones senses redly." At a first pass, there are two ways in which we might analyze this.

The first is to analyze such a statement as committing us to the existence of an event whose particular *nature* as an event is described by the adverbial modifiers. This analysis reads "Jones senses" as committing us to the existence of an event of sensing of which Jones is the subject, and "redly" as ascribing the property of being *redly* (whatever that may be) to the event.[1]

The second option is to treat "Jones senses redly" as a subject–predicate statement. According to this analysis, "Jones" refers to the subject and "senses redly" is a predicate, which functions to ascribe the property to the subject, Jones, of *sensing redly*.

Of course, each analysis carries different metaphysical commitments, so an argument for one analysis over the other might contain metaphysical considerations.[2] For present purposes, however, I don't want to detour into these arguments; instead, let us focus on broader metaphysical issues.

By some of its defenders at least, adverbialism was conceived of as a theory of perception that not only avoided the commitment to mental objects but that more generally avoided the commitment to any kind of *dualistic* metaphysics. Instead, adverbialism was intended to be consistent with a monist materialistic metaphysics. However, more recently, adverbialism has been closely linked with *qualia theory* from the philosophy of mind (Crane 2000), a theory which has itself been argued to be committed to a form of dualism (e.g. Chalmers 1996). Let us therefore take a moment to explore this.

Consider, once again, the sense datum statement, "Jones senses a red sense datum." As we have seen, this statement ascribes a sensible quality—phenomenal or sensible redness—to a mental object, and states that Jones stands in the sensing relation to this object. In this way, the sense datum theory offers an explanation of why it is *like this* for Jones—Jones experiences red because he is aware of a sense datum that instantiates phenomenal redness.

Given this, a natural reading of the adverbial equivalent, "Jones senses redly" takes it to both identify a sensory event and ascribe a property to that event; a property which is marked by "redly." If we follow this similarity through, the most natural interpretation would take this property to also be a phenomenal or qualititative property: a property that explains why it is *like this* for Jones. On this natural reading of adverbialism, then, the adverbialist, just like the qualia theorist, "holds the qualities sensed in experience to be modifications of experience itself" (Crane 2000: 177).

As you can see from Crane's quote, qualia theorists hold that the qualities sensed in experience—in our terms, the constituents of the experience's *presentational character*—are properties of the experience: *qualia*.[3] Moreover, it is these properties that type the experience by what it is like to undergo it. So, on a qualia theory, both the phenomenal character and the presentational character coincide.

However, at least one advocate of the events analysis of adverbialism, James Cornman, denies that terms such as "redly" do "function to ascribe this kind of qualitative property to an event." Instead, he suggests, they "function to specify more precisely a particular event" (1971: 271). As he is reported to have said elsewhere, "'redly' does not ascribe any non-sortal property to some event, nor does it ascribe any property which constitutes the manner in which the event occurred. . . . Instead, 'redly' serves only to *internally classify* John's sensing" (Elugardo 1982: 36).

To this extent, Cornman agrees with adverbialists, such as Tye, who prefer to analyze adverbial statements as subject–predicate statements. Tye contends that "the predicate 'is a sensing-redly' . . . really means 'is a sensing with the red qualitative character' where 'red' is a concealed description with a comparative normal cause connotation" (1984: 204–205).

In essence, both Cornman and Tye argue that, rather than treat terms such as "redly" and "red qualitative character" as ascribing special irreducible phenomenal properties to either subjects or events, we should treat them as "topic neutral" (Smart 1959). That is to say, these terms should be understood in such a way that "a Greek peasant's reports about his sensations can be neutral between a dualistic metaphysics and [a] materialistic metaphysics" (Smart 1959: 150). To this end, Smart suggests that when we say that a sensing has the "red qualitative character" or is a "sensing redly", we merely mean something like the following: the sensing is a sensing of the kind that normally occurs when we are visually presented with objects (lights, etc.) that are red, where "red" has its normal meaning.

In this way, the adverbialist could allow that experiences have what we have been calling *phenomenal characters*—properties that type the experiences by what it is like to undergo them. For instance, the property of a perception of a red object that types it by what it is like to undergo it is, according to this type of adverbialism, its property of *being a sensing redly*, which, of course, unpacks as its property of being a sensing of the kind that normally occurs when we are visually presented with objects (lights, etc.) that are red.[4]

The motivation for this interpretation of adverbial statements is to avoid attributing any properties to the sensory event that preclude a materialistic identification of the sensory event with a brain event. A brain event, it is argued, can be a sensing of the kind that normally occurs when we are visually presented with a red object. In this way, some adverbialists hoped to offer an alternative to sense datum theory that was consistent with a monist materialistic metaphysics.

Nevertheless, it is important to note that, even if there are interpretations of adverbialism that are not committed to the existence of qualia, adverbialism does serve to highlight the possibility of something that is central to qualia theory—the possibility of developing a theory of the visual experience that is not relational or does not have the act–object form.

The many property problem

Let us now turn to some objections to adverbialism. Thus far, we have been discussing simple adverbial statements of the form "Jones senses redly." Yet, as Jackson points out:

> Our statements about afterimages are not just to the effect that an image is red, or square, or whatever; they are also to the effect that an image is red *and* square *and* . . . [The problem for] the adverbial theory turns on this point that an afterimage has many properties, and will be referred to as the many property problem.
>
> (Jackson 1975: 129)

Let us imagine, then, that we are looking to provide an adverbial analysis of the following statement: Jones is experiencing a red, square afterimage (Jones is sensing a sense datum which is both red and square). How should we analyze this?

Sensing F-ly and G-ly

The most obvious response would simply be to say that to sense a red, square sense datum is to sense redly *and* squarely. This would give us the following conjunctive principle of analysis:

"X senses an F, G, etc. sense datum" is to be analyzed as "X senses F-ly *and* G-ly *and* etc."

So, "Jones is experiencing a red, square afterimage" would be analyzed as "Jones is sensing redly *and* squarely."

This analysis has the advantage of explaining the entailment from "I have a red, square afterimage" to "I have a red afterimage" and "I have a square afterimage." It faces the following problem.

There is an important difference between the following two total afterimage experiences:

7 Simultaneously having a red, square afterimage *and* a green, round afterimage.

8 Simultaneously having a red, round afterimage *and* a green, square afterimage.

According to the conjunctive principle of analysis, the adverbial translation of these would be:

7_{trans} Sensing redly *and* squarely *and* greenly *and* roundly.

8_{trans} Sensing redly *and* roundly *and* greenly *and* squarely.

But these are equivalent. Hence the conjunctive formulation doesn't seem able to account for the differences between these total experiences.

If you're not sure about this, consider the following sentences and their putative analyses:

9 Jones has a red, round afterimage and a green, square afterimage.

9_{trans} Jones senses redly and roundly and greenly and squarely.

10 Jones has a red, square afterimage.

10_{trans} Jones senses redly and squarely.

Whilst 9_{trans} entails 10_{trans}, 9 does not entail 10. The fact that the entailments go awry suggests that the translations are not in fact equivalent.

Sensing F-ly G-ly

An alternative response to the many property problem is suggested by the ambiguity of the following:

11   Dave sang impressively loudly.

There is an interpretation of this which reads as conjunctive (Dave sang impressively and he did so loudly)—both adverbs modify the verb.

However, an alternative interpretation reads impressively as modifying not the verb but the adverb (it was the volume of Dave's singing which was impressive rather than the singing itself).

The thought would be that our principle of analysis would not have to be conjunctive (where both adverbs modify the verb) but, instead, accumulative, where each additional adverb modifies the previous one. Thus:

"X senses an F, G, etc. sense datum" is to be analyzed as "X senses F-ly G-ly etc."

So, when we say that Jones had a red, square afterimage, we should analyze this as follows:

Jones sensed redly squarely.

Rather than take both adverbs as modifying "sensed" (i.e. as being modes or ways of sensing), we take one adverb to modify the verb and the other to modify the first adverb.

This leads to the first problem—how are we going to nonarbitrarily decide which adverb modifies the verb and which modifies the first adverb? There seems to be no principled reason to answer this question in a particular way.

Even if we do, we run into another problem. Let us say that we decide that squarely modifies sensing and redly modifies squarely. Now "redly" means something *different* in "Jones sensed redly" and "Jones sensed redly squarely," whilst "red" means the *same* in "Jones had a red afterimage" and "Jones had a red, square afterimage." This suggests once more that the analyses are not equivalent.

Another way of seeing this is to look at the entailments. "Jones had a red, square afterimage" *entails that* Jones had a red afterimage. But "Jones sensed redly squarely," *does not entail that* Jones sensed redly. To see this, note that (on the accumulative analysis) "Dave sang impressively loudly" does not entail that Dave sang impressively—his singing might have been impressively loud but otherwise unexceptional.

Sensing FG-ly

The final way Jackson suggests we might try and solve the many property problem is as follows:

> "X senses an F, G, etc. sense datum" is to be analyzed as "X senses FG(etc.)ly."

Where FG-ly names a *simple* (fundamental) mode of sensing, *not* a complex, derivative mode of sensing which is built up out of semantically significant components.

So, the claim that "Jones has a red, square afterimage" should instead be analyzed as "Jones sensed red-square-ly."

In response to this, Jackson objects that:

> On this view, someone who remarks on the common feature in having a red, square afterimage and having a red, round afterimage [must be interpreted as] making a plain mistake—the first is sensing red-square-ly, the second sensing red-round-ly, which are different, and that's that. But far from being a plain mistake, this remark looks like an evident truth.
> (Jackson 1975: 133)

A further problem is that afterimages can also have other properties—fuzziness and sharpness for example. But if I have a red, square, fuzzy afterimage, then this must be analyzed as sensing red-square-fuzzy-ly—so sensing red-square-ly isn't, as it happens, basic.

Jackson suggests that if the basic level of adverbial analysis has n components (i.e. is sensing F_1-F_2- . . . . -F_n-ly), he will be able to point out another component at level $n+1$ so the adverbialist "cannot ever give even a single example of a basic mode of sensing, and thus cannot ever complete even one of his adverbial analyses" (Jackson 1975: 133).

Sensing of-an-F-G-ly

However, Tye (1975) follows Sellars (1975) in complaining that Jackson has missed the point. According to Tye and Sellars, the correct interpretation of the view is arrived at by the following grammatical transformations.

12   John has a sensation of a red square, becomes

13   John has an of-a-red-square sensation.

Note that the phrase "of-a-red-square" in 13 is functioning as an adjective modifying the noun "sensation". We then do our adverbial transformation to get:

14   John senses of-a-red-square-ly, or, as it is sometimes put,

15   John senses in an of-a-red-square manner.

Tye goes on to suggest that, on this approach, "manners of sensing are conceived of as resembling and differing from one another in ways systematically analogous to the ways in which their 'corresponding' physical objects, i.e. their normal causes, resemble and differ from one another" (1975: 139). Thus, "red" and "square" in "an of-a-red-square manner" have a sense which is "*derivative from* and *analogous to*" (Tye 1975: 140) their sense when applied to normal physical objects. Thus the relationships which seem to hold between sensings can be accounted for as parasitic on the relationships that hold between physical objects—it is the resemblances between red, round and red, square *objects* which explain the resemblances between red, round and red, square *sensings*. This analysis is therefore claimed to rebut Jackson's concern that we will never have a basic mode of sensing by providing a sense in which sensing in "an of-a-red-square manner" *does* include "red" and "square" as components.[5]

The complement objection

A further objection concerns the fact that, where we have a particular *object*, both one property and its complement (i.e. its opposite) cannot simultaneously be instantiated by this object. For example, one particular object cannot simultaneously have the properties of both redness and not-redness (say, blueness)—or be hot and cold, or big and small, etc.

The same seems to apply for actions. "[I]t is not possible for a person at a given time to V both F-ly and non-F-ly. I can sing badly easily enough, but I cannot sing both well and badly at the same time; I can run quickly, but not both quickly and slowly; . . . and so on and so forth" (Jackson 1977: 69).

However, where sensing is concerned, it seems that we clearly *can* sense both F-ly and non-F-ly at the same time—"I may have a red and a green afterimage at the same time" (Jackson 1977: 69).

How can we explain this? Well, Jackson suggests that the only plausible reply is to say that, "though one cannot V both F-ly and non-F-ly at a given time, one can V F-ly with respect to A and non-F-ly with respect to B. For instance I can, during a concerto, listen happily to the strings and unhappily to the piano" (Jackson 1977: 69).

Of course, whilst we may be able to understand this in the case of perception (I am sensing whitely with respect to the cue ball and redly with respect to the object ball), how might we make sense of this where hallucinations are concerned when there are no appropriate physical things to be sensing F-ly with respect *to*? If such objects are required to solve this problem, it "is hard to see what [they] could be other than the mental objects of the act-object [i.e. sense datum] theory" (Jackson 1977: 69).

Tye suggests that this problem can be avoided by allowing that there are many *different* sensings going on at the same time. This response raises a worry over whether it is possible for the same person to be the subject of two simultaneous visual sensings, but Tye suggests that this is no more outlandish than a subject being on the end of two simultaneous punches or stabbings. "After all," he says, "having a visual sensation . . . is something which happens to one, given the appropriate stimuli (rather than something one consciously does)" (1984: 207).[6]

Adverbialism and the two hats

The phenomenological hat

Inasmuch as adverbialism is initially presented as a response to the sense datum theory, we might think that it suffers from the same problems when it comes to getting the phenomenology right. For example, if sense datum talk of lights and colors, patterns and patches cannot capture what it is like for a subject, then it would appear that neither could talk about sensing light-ly, color-ly, pattern-ly, and patch-ly.

This objection would miss the point of the appeal to the adverbial transformations. The reason adverbialists highlight the availability of these transformations is as a means to show that whatever can be said in terms of sense data can also be said *without* committing ourselves to such things. Unlike the sense datum theorist, the adverbialist does not have to be committed to the claim that the phenomenology of *any* experience can be captured so simply.

To consider what the adverbialist might have to say about the phenomenology of a more complex experience, consider what Tye's approach would have to say about Strawson's example (from Chapter 2) of seeing the red light of the setting sun filtering through the black and thickly clustered branches of the elms, seeing the dappled deer grazing in groups on the vivid green grass, and so on.

Tye's translations would take this report and transform it into the following:

14$_{Strawson}$ Subject S senses of-the-red-light-of-the-setting-sun-filtering-through-the-black-and-thickly-clustered-branches-of-the-elms-and-the-dappled-deer-grazing-in-groups-on-the-vivid-green-grass-ly, or, as it is sometimes put,

15_{Strawson} Subject S senses in an of-the-red-light-of-the-setting-sun-fil-tering-through-the-black-and-thickly-clustered-branches-of-the-elms-and-the-dappled-deer-grazing-in-groups-on-the-vivid-green-grass manner.

This seems to be a pretty accurate report of what it is like for subject S to have this experience and, note, a report that can be true regardless of whether or not the subject is perceiving or hallucinating.

However, when considering the success of this kind of move, we must bear in mind that, unless a qualia interpretation is offered (see below), these statements are supposed to be understood in a topic-neutral way. In other words, they should be understood as claiming that the subject senses in the kind of way that is normally caused by the red light of the setting sun filtering through the black and thickly clustered branches of the elms and the dappled deer grazing in groups on the vivid green grass. Once this is clarified, we might wonder whether this approach actually offers an *explanation* of why this state has the phenomenology it does or whether it simply takes this for granted.

In particular, recall that the sense datum theorist would insist that, to do justice to the phenomenology of this experience—which, given the acceptance of the Common Factor Principle, could of course occur in the *absence* of red light, vivid green grass, and the like—we must explain how it is that we are consciously aware of redness and vivid greenness. In response to this, the sense datum theorist, by way of the Phenomenal Principle, contends that it is because we are aware of objects that instantiate these properties. What can the adverbialist offer in place of this explanation? Given that the kind of sensing that is normally caused by the red light of the setting sun (etc.) could occur in its absence, what explains the sensible appearance of redness and vivid greenness? It seems that the adverbialist (at least, the adverbialist who is not also a qualia theorist) has no explanation to offer. Instead, they seem to have to hold that it is just a brute fact about the kind of sensing that is caused by the red light of the setting sun (etc.) that it has the phenomenology it does.

If the adverbialist *does* offer a qualia interpretation of adverbialism, then it will of course face objections that qualia theories face. For instance, they face the objections that visual experiences are *transparent* or *diaphanous*. The qualia theorist claims that, when we introspect, we are aware of properties *of our experiences*, yet the claim that visual experiences are transparent suggests otherwise. To claim that an experience is transparent is to claim that, when one introspects that experience, one does not discover any properties of the experience itself, only properties of the objects of experience. As Harman puts it:

When you see a tree, you do not experience any features as intrinsic features of your experience. Look at a tree and try and turn your attention to intrinsic features of your experience. I predict that the only features there to turn your attention to will be features of the presented tree, including relational features of the tree "from here."

(Harman 1990: 39)

This is supposed to be a phenomenological observation. It tells us that, when we introspect our visual experiences, all we find are the features of the worldly objects. If this is correct, it stands as a phenomenological problem for theories that claim that we are aware of properties of *experiences* when we introspect.

In addition to these concerns, Butchvarov argues that either form of adverbialism "is incapable of doing justice to the most obvious and indeed essential phenomenological fact about perceptual consciousness . . . namely, its intentionality, its object-directedness" (1980: 272). To explain this, he draws attention to the fact that, according to adverbialism, even a successful case of perception "is a case of consciousness in virtue of the state of sensing it involves" (Butchvarov 1980: 273). Yet, he goes on to point out, that state of sensing itself is, on the adverbialist theory, not object-directed in and of itself. This means, he suggests, that "what makes [the sensory state] object-directed is not what makes it a case of consciousness, [which] conflict[s] with the spirit, if not the letter, of the thesis of the intentionality of perception" (Butchvarov 1980: 273).

The epistemological hat

On the face of it, adverbialism looks to have one up on the sense datum theory, epistemically speaking. This is because it doesn't have intermediate objects of awareness to "get in the way" of real, external objects.

As we saw, the sense datum theory claims that, when we have veridical experiences of objects in the world, we are aware of these objects indirectly, *in virtue of* being aware of *different* objects: sense data.

The adverbialist, on the other hand, does not have to make such a claim. According to adverbialism, when we experience objects in the world, we are aware of *those very objects*, by sensing in a particular way. So adverbialism can allow that we are aware of material objects *directly*, and hence demand the title of *direct* realism.

This claim has been challenged. Following on from the phenomenological objection outlined above, Butchvarov argues that the mere fact that object "x is causally related to S's sensing in a certain way can no more reasonably be described as S's being conscious of x than the fact that the presence of carbon monoxide in the air is causally related to S's having a headache can be described as S's being conscious of carbon monoxide" (1980: 273). In other words, Butchvarov argues that S's sensing in a particular way, even in the best possible cases in which this is appropriately caused by an object, cannot ever amount to being *conscious of* that object. This casts doubt on whether adverbialism can really be said to be a theory that enables "direct" awareness of the external world.

In addition to this concern, adverbialism is not obviously in any better a position than sense datum theory when it comes to the epistemological question of how our empirical beliefs are justified.

A pure adverbialist theory, just like the pure sense datum theory, rejects the Representational Principle. That is, a pure adverbialist theory insists that there is *nothing more* to a particular visual experience than sensing in the right kind of way. As was the case with the classical sense datum theory, it is difficult to see how having such an experience—an experience that could occur without the world playing ball—could put us in a position to *know* anything about the world. If we stick with a foundationalist epistemology, then the question of how we *move* from a justified belief about our own sensory states to a belief about the world crops up for the adverbialist, just as it did for the sense datum theorist.

As was the case with the sense datum theory, one could also develop variants of adverbialism by also endorsing the Representational Principle. I leave this as an exercise for the reader.

Questions

- Can the adverbialist accommodate what it is like to have a rich visual experience of the kind we normally enjoy when looking at a complex scene?
- What kinds of "mixed" theories of perception could be created by adding the Representational Principle to adverbialism? Think back to the sensory core theory and percept theory for suggestions.
- Is the adverbialist any better placed than the sense datum theorist when it comes to wearing the epistemological hat? Would a mixed theory do a better job?

Notes

1. The familiar Davidsonian analysis of events (1980) would go further and hold that both "being a sensing" and "being had by Jones" are also predicated of a bare event particular. Yet there are other metaphysical analyses of events, which our discussions need not go into, so for present purposes let us stick with the simplest way of understanding this analysis.
2. Tye (1984) contends that the subject–predicate analysis is to be preferred to the event analysis as, he argues, the event analysis faces similar metaphysical problems to those faced by the sense datum theorist. For

instance, Tye wonders what the event analysis might say about a situation in which "I see a tiger in the distance and it appears to me to have numerous stripes (though no definite number). How many sensings do I undergo? One for each apparent stripe? But, as far as I am aware, there is no definite number of apparent stripes" (1984: 208–209). However, it seems that there is a reply available to the event adverbialist—to say that I am sensing in an indefinite-number-of-stripes manner.

3. "Qualia" is a plural and is pronounced *kwar-lee-ah*; the singular is "quale" (*kwar-lay*).

4. What is the *presentational* character of an experience according to this version of adverbialism? This is a tricky question. Earlier, we suggested that the adverbialist could claim that, in perception, we sense the (external) property *red* redly, in illusion, we sense *white* redly, and in hallucination, *nothing* is sensed redly. Perhaps we could identify *what* is sensed with the presentational character? This would provide an adequate result in the perceptual case—the presentational character would include the external property of redness—but would have a very odd consequence in the case of illusion: it would entail that, when we misperceive something white as red, we are directly aware of *whiteness*. This just seems wrong. Perhaps, then, we ought to (given the endorsement of the Common Factor Principle) extrapolate from the minimal case of hallucination and hold that, strictly speaking, an adverbial experience of sensing redly *lacks* presentational character. This also seems strange.

5. What is the impact of these considerations when we turn our attention away from the translations themselves to the positive adverbial theories? As Tye's remarks indicate, those who interpret the adverbial terms topic-neutrally are likely to think these condsiderations miss the point—even complex terms such as of-a-red-square-beside-a-green-triangle merely point us toward the normal cause of such episodes of sensing. These considerations do, however, raise more issues for a qualia interpretation of adverbialism as they pose the question of how, once an experience has been broken down into its many constituent qualia, the red quale gets put back together with the square quale and the green quale with the triangular quale, rather than the other way round.

6. It is worth noting at this point that the claim that sensing is passive is highly controversial. For instance, Alva Noë's *Action in Perception* is an extensive argument for the basic idea that "perceiving is a way of acting. Perception is not something that happens to us, or in us. It is something we do" (Noë 2005: 1).

Further reading

Most of the critical material in this chapter is presented in Frank Jackson's 1975 paper, "On the Adverbial Analysis of Visual Experience" published in the journal *Metaphilosophy*. This paper is followed by responses by Michael

Tye ("The Adverbial Theory: A Defence of Sellars against Jackson") and Wilfrid Sellars ("The Adverbial Theory of the Objects of Sensation").

Tye's 1984 paper, "The Adverbial Approach to Visual Experience," published in *The Philosophical Review*, contains useful discussions of the subject-predicate and event analyses of adverbial statements.

Panayot Butchvarov's 1980 paper, "Adverbial Theories of Consciousness," contains a number of phenomenological objections to adverbialism.

Tim Crane discusses the connections between adverbialism and qualia theory in his 2000 paper, "The Origins of Qualia."

Wilfrid Sellars's classic 1956 essay, "Empiricism and the Philosophy of Mind" is a complex, detailed attempt to build an adequate epistemology alongside a rejection of sense datum theories. (As we have seen, Sellars endorsed an adverbial theory of perception, although adverbialism itself is not discussed in this essay.) Paul Coates's 2007 book, *The Metaphysics of Perception*, defends a Sellars-inspired adverbialist theory of perception.

Adverbialism is also defended in more recent papers by Uriah Kriegel ("Intentional Inexistence and Phenomenal Intentionality" and "The Dispensability of [Merely] Intentional Objects") and Alan Thomas ("An Adverbial Theory of Consciousness").

4 Belief acquisition theories

Overview

Belief acquisition theories (also known as doxastic theories) argue that visual experience is no more than the acquisition of belief. This claim is explained and discussed before some critical considerations are raised.

These include the objections that the perception can take place in the *absence* of beliefs being acquired, that the theory fails to allow that animals and children can be perceivers, that it cannot explain our ability to acquire new concepts, and that it is refuted by a phenomenon known as blindsight.

Common Factor Principle	☑
Phenomenal Principle	☒
Representational Principle	☑

An alternative approach to both sense datum and adverbialist theories focuses on the fact that, when it comes to perceptual experience, what is *important*, from an evolutionary standpoint, is the nature of the information about the world it provides us with. As Armstrong puts it, "It is clear that the biological function of perception is to give the organism information about the current state of its own body and its physical environment, information that will assist the organism in the conduct of life" (1968: 209).

In other words, the very reason we have perceptual systems is to enable us to gain knowledge about the environment in which we have to live and prosper (ignoring, for the present, perception of the organism's bodily states).[1]

According to a highly influential philosophical theory of *knowledge*, at least part of what it is to know *that x* is to believe *that x* and for *x* to be the case (i.e. to be true).[2]

> This is a most important clue to the *nature* of perception. It leads us to the view that perception is nothing but the acquiring of true or false beliefs concerning the current state of the organism's body and environment. . . . Veridical perception is the acquiring of true beliefs, sensory illusion the acquiring of false beliefs.
>
> (Armstrong 1968: 209)

As is indicated by this quote, the belief acquisition theorist *accepts* the Common Factor Principle (in earlier work, Armstrong calls the parallel between veridical and nonveridical cases "the parallel on which the Argument from Illusion rightly insists" [1961: 83]). Given this, the belief acquisition theorist holds that phenomenologically indiscriminable visual experiences have an underlying mental state in common.

An interesting question is whether or not the belief acquisition theorist accepts or rejects the Representational Principle. In one sense, the event of perceiving is the event of acquiring beliefs, and that *event* does not possess intentionality. However, the things that are acquired *do* possess intentionality. So there is a very clear sense in which perception *can be* said to be intentional on a belief acquisition theory. It is just that, as Armstrong puts it "the intentionality of perception reduces to the intentionality of the beliefs acquired" (1968: 211).

What about the Phenomenal Principle? That principle states that:

> (P) If there sensibly appears to a subject to be something which possesses a particular sensible quality then there is something of which the subject is aware which does possess that quality.

If we accept that the antecedent of the Phenomenal Principle can be met in both good and bad cases[3]—that is, accept that in cases of illusion and hallucination there sensibly appears to be something that possesses a particular sensible quality—then the claim that perception is *nothing but* the acquisition of beliefs seems to entail a *rejection* of the Phenomenal Principle. Hallucinations would be cases in which there sensibly appears to be something that possesses a particular sensible quality when in fact there is not. In such cases, the sense datum theorist's putative "non-physical object of immediate apprehension is simply a ghost generated by my belief that I am seeing something" (Armstrong 1961: 84).

Perception as the acquisition of beliefs

Given Armstrong's claim that perception and illusion (and, by extension, hallucination) involve the acquisition of beliefs, together with the claim that the same mental state occurs in indiscriminable cases of perception and hallucination, we can provide a first pass analysis of the belief acquisition theory's claim about the neutral category of visual experience as follows:

A subject S has a visual experience as of a property F if and only if S acquires the belief that something is F.[4]

As is indicated in the quote from Armstrong above, if this belief is *true* then the subject will thereby be said to *see* that something is F; if it is false, the subject will be under an illusion (or hallucinating).

In addressing this theory, it is important to be clear that the key theoretical claim is not that perception is believing but rather that it is the *acquiring* of belief. Normally, to say that a subject has a certain belief doesn't entail that there is any *occurrent* mental event—anything going on in the subject's mind *at that time*. We continue to believe certain things (e.g., that dogs are mammals) even when we are not actually thinking that thought—for example, when thinking about something else, or when asleep. But perceiving something *is* an occurrent mental phenomenon. So it is important to be aware that this analysis does not hold that perception is believing (which may be a nonconscious, dispositional state), but that perception is the *acquiring of beliefs*. The acquiring of a particular belief is something that happens *at a particular time* and hence is plausibly an occurrent mental phenomenon.

However, even with this clarification made, the theory still faces an obvious problem (which is why I said that the above analysis is "first pass"). Suppose you have your eyes closed and I *tell you* that the cat is on the mat. You trust me and thus acquire the *belief* that the cat is on the mat, but you do not *see* the cat on the mat. This indicates that the simple claim that perception is the acquisition of belief needs augmenting.

Armstrong himself doesn't say much at this point. He toys with the idea of adding "*by means of the senses*" to the analysis above, yet, of course, this will not solve the problem. When I tell you that the cat is on the mat, you acquire this by means of the senses—you *hear me* tell you—but again this doesn't mean that you *see* a cat on a mat.

Pitcher (1971), however, discusses this problem more deeply. He initially attempts to distinguish the episodes of belief acquisition that constitute perception from those that do not by saying that the relevant beliefs are those that are acquired through the use of *the relevant sensory organ*. He goes on to note, however, that one could form the belief that an object was cold, or hard, or sharp, by touching it with one's eyes, so this belief would be acquired by using my eyes, yet I don't *see* that the object is cold, hard, or sharp.

He therefore considers changing this, for the case of visual perception, to using our eyes *in the standard visual way*. This would rule out using my eyes to *feel* a property as a nonstandard use of eyes. Yet imagine a case in which I am trapped in a clear-walled but soundproof room and somebody holds up a sign to tell me that the cat is on the mat. This belief is acquired through using my eyes in the standard visual way, but my acquiring this belief doesn't entail that I see whatever it is I learn.

In response to this, Pitcher (1971) further elaborates his analysis by placing conditions on the *kinds* of acquired beliefs which might constitute perception. He goes on to stipulate that the beliefs acquired must be *perceptual* beliefs where, by a perceptual belief, Pitcher means a belief (or more strictly, a set of beliefs) whose overall richness corresponds exactly to the richness of all the propositions which specify how things *look* to the subject.

Belief acquisition theory and the two hats

The epistemological hat

As we noted at the beginning of the chapter, belief acquisition theory is designed so as to be able to adequately wear the epistemological hat. There are two key features of the position that are intended to make it epistemically preferable.

The first advantage is that, as we have done away with mental objects as direct objects of perception, we could now be argued to have no veil of perception separating us from the world (as we saw, however, the same could also be said of adverbialism). As we saw in Chapter 2, however, the force of this "objection" to sense datum theory is somewhat sensational.

Another potential advantage this theory has, at least over foundationalist versions of sense datum theory and adverbialism, is that the beliefs we acquire in perception are *already* about the world. So there is no question of how we might justifiably *move* from our experiences, or beliefs about our experiences, to beliefs about the world. Yet, of course, if we assume that our empirical beliefs are justified and that these beliefs are either identical to, or justified by, some of the beliefs we acquire when we perceive, then there still remains the question of how the beliefs we acquire through perception are justified.

Epistemology provides us with a number of theories of justification that could play this role. For instance, a belief acquisition theorist could endorse a coherentist theory of justification. Unlike the foundationalist we met in Chapter 2, the coherentist denies that our empirical beliefs depend for their justification on foundational beliefs that are justified in a special *unconditional* way. Instead, the coherentist holds that *all* beliefs are justified in the same way: by the relationship they stand in to other beliefs. In more detail, a coherentist belief acquisition theorist would hold that a belief we acquire when we perceive will be justified so long as (1) it coheres with or stands in suitable inferential relationships with the other members of the belief set of which it is now a part, and (2) the belief set itself is coherent.

Armstrong himself, however, appeals to an importantly different theory of justification, which he calls the "thermometer" view:

> Suppose that "p" is true and A believes that p, but his belief is not supported by any reasons. [... What justifies such a belief?] My suggestion is that there must be a *law-like connection* between the state of affairs

Bap [A believes that p] and the state of affairs that makes "p" true such that, given Bap, it must be the case that p.

(Armstrong 1973: 166)

The thermometer analogy functions as follows. So long as a thermometer is working properly, there is a law-like connection between the temperature of the environment and the reading on the thermometer. Likewise, so long as our belief-forming mechanisms (our perceptual mechanisms) are working correctly, then there will be a law-like connection between aspects of the external environment and our beliefs about those aspects. "When a true belief unsupported by reasons stands to the situation truly believed as a thermometer stands to the actual temperature, then we have non-inferential knowledge" (Armstrong 1973: 166).

On Armstrong's view, if there is a law-like connection between our beliefs and the environment, then our beliefs will be justified.

You might be wondering at this point how we could *know* whether or not our beliefs stand in this relation, but, according to Armstrong, we do not need to *know* this, it just needs to be the case (in other words, it is a metaphysical condition, not an epistemological one).

Indeed, it is this feature that makes the thermometer view so different from both foundationalist and coherentist theories of justification—it does not require that the subject *be aware* that their beliefs stand in a law-like relation to the facts. Instead, it allows that beliefs can be justified by factors that are not "cognitively accessible" to a subject. For this reason, such a theory is known as an *externalist* theory of justification (as opposed to *internalist* theories, such as foundationalism and coherentism). According to an externalist theory, the factor that justifies a subject in holding a belief need not function as the *reason* for which the subject holds the belief—the subject may hold the belief for other (internally accessible) reasons or they may simply be caused to have that belief as on a belief acquisition theory of perception—but they will nonetheless be justified in holding that belief.

Critics of the view may yet dispute the claim that endorsing the belief acquisition view constitutes a significant epistemological advance over the other theories we have considered. If the belief acquisition theorist endorses coherentism, for example, then all the epistemological work is being done by the relationship that the acquired beliefs stand in to our other beliefs. Alternatively, if the belief acquisition theorist endorses an externalist theory of justification, as Armstrong does, then again, all the epistemological work is being done by the claim that certain beliefs can be justified by things outside our ken.

There seems no reason that a sense datum theorist or adverbialist could not endorse either of these views. This would potentially give such theories all the purported epistemological advantages of belief acquisition theory. If these theorists *don't* endorse such theories of justification, it is because they want to hold onto the idea that, somehow, our empirical beliefs are justified by the sensory aspects of our perceptual experiences. Yet, of course, this is just the feature of perceptual experiences that belief acquisition theorists seem to overlook, as we shall now discuss.

The phenomenological hat

The most intuitively difficult aspect of the belief acquisition theory is in its account of *what it is like* to have a visual experience. You may note that I haven't yet said anything about what the phenomenal character or presentational character of an experience is according to the belief acquisition theory. This is, I confess, because I'm not sure that it applies. The belief acquisition theorist identifies visual experiences with episodes of acquiring beliefs, and I suspect that this theorist would deny that the episode of acquiring beliefs *has* a phenomenal character. I may be wrong about this, however.

Despite this, the question of why there should be something it is like to undergo an experience on the belief acquisition theory can still be posed. Yet there are features of the theory that can be called upon to explain this. First of all, at least on Pitcher's version of the theory, when we perceive, we don't strictly speaking acquire *a* belief but, rather, a body of rich and detailed beliefs. The richness and detail of our experience is reflected in the richness and detail of the beliefs we acquire.

In addition to this, we not only acquire beliefs about the world; we also acquire beliefs about *our experiences*. When I perceive a cat, I not only acquire the belief that <there is a cat on the mat>, I also acquire the belief that <*I see that* there is a cat on the mat>. Now imagine that *you* believe that you see a cat on a mat. What would you say if I asked you *what it is like* for you? Well, you would probably say that it is like seeing a cat on a mat.

It is not clear that this quite scratches the itch. Perhaps *you* would say that "merely" believing that you see a cat on the mat would be like *actually* seeing a cat on the mat. But isn't this because there is *already* something it is like to *actually* see a cat on the mat? It is not clear that the simple appeal to beliefs that one sees something can explain this all on its own.

Another way of pressing the point is by appeal to the idea of a philosophical *zombie* (Chalmers 1996). Zombies are beings exactly like us in all physical respects but which lack conscious experiences. In this context, the concern is this. If all there is to having visual experiences is acquiring beliefs, couldn't a creature acquire beliefs in the way envisaged by the belief acquisition theorist *without* being conscious? In other words, wouldn't a *zombie* have visual experiences as understood by the belief acquisition theory?

Perception without belief acquisition

These phenomenological concerns express what seems to me to be the underlying intuitive objection to belief acquisition theories: that they leave something out.

One way in which the theory can seem to leave something out is that it seems there are occasions in which we *experience* something to be a certain way *without* believing it to be that way. If experiences are *nothing more than* the acquisition of beliefs, then there doesn't appear to be room for this kind of disconnect.

Examples of this include such things as optical illusions. Take the famous Müller–Lyer illusion in Figure 3.1.

The left line looks longer than the right line, but because we know the illusion, we don't end up *believing* that the left line is longer than the right line. If anything, we may even end up believing that both lines are the same length. Despite this, we still have an experience as of one line's being longer than the other. Doesn't this show that we need to distinguish between the visual experience of the lines and the beliefs we form *on the basis of this experience* and hence cannot assimilate the former to the latter?

Both Armstrong and Pitcher consider this and respond in the same kind of way. Pitcher's response is the most detailed, so I will outline this.

Pitcher distinguishes between three types of case (which are not supposed to exhaust the options but provide three points on a spectrum).

1 *First Cases*: the normal or standard cases where the subject does believe things are as they look.
2 *Middle Cases*: "although it looks to Q as though there is an x at u, nevertheless Q, for some reason or other, is not quite sure that there is, in fact, any such x at u" (Pitcher 1971: 91). As an example of this, imagine that, when the sun is out, you might be unsure whether or not you see water on the road in front of you. In such a situation you withhold judgment as to whether the world is as it appears to be.
3 *Last Cases*: "although it looks to Q as though there is an x at u, Q nevertheless does not [acquire] the perceptual belief that there is an x at u—on the contrary, he acquires the firm belief that there is not an x at u."

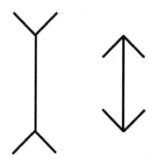

Figure 3.1

Examples of last cases include seeing a bent stick in water or an optical illusion such as the Müller–Lyer illusion. Even though the stick *seems* bent or the lines *look* different lengths, we do not believe that they are.

The general way in which Pitcher and Armstrong deal with these problem cases is as follows. First cases are as normal. We just straightforwardly acquire the belief that there is an *x* at *u*. In middle cases, however, whilst the same processes are at work, we don't immediately believe that there is an *x* at *u* (as we do in first cases) because things being this way conflicts with some of our other beliefs. Nevertheless, in these cases we still acquire a strong *inclination* to believe that there is an *x* at *u*.

Similarly, in last cases, the same processes are at work once more, but, as the subject is familiar with his senses deceiving him in such contexts, the inclination to believe that there is an *x* at *u* is completely suppressed. Even if the subject is so familiar with the illusion that she not only doesn't believe that there is an *x* at *u*, but actually believes the opposite—that there is *not* an *x* at *u*—we can still say that there is a "suppressed inclination to believe" at work here because if the subject *had not* known about this kind of illusion, she *would have* believed that there was an *x* at *u*.

If, by "inclination to believe", the belief acquisition theorist is really talking about an inclination, then having an inclination to believe is *not* believing, just as my having an inclination to go to the gym is not the same as my *actually* going to the gym (more's the pity). Given this, it is difficult to see why being *inclined* to believe that I see a cat on the mat should suffice for me to have a visual experience *as of* a cat on the mat.

> Armstrong, it is true, thinks that, underlying this abstract fact, there is something in the brain which provides the concrete vehicle of this potentiality—some neural process or structure which, given the whole functional organization of the brain, would suffice to put the subject into the relevant belief-state if the inhibiting beliefs (themselves neurally realized) were absent. But even if such a neural item exists, its presence does not help to meet the difficulty. For since its intrinsic properties are exclusively physical, and since its only psychological significance is in terms of its *potential* to yield or form a certain type of belief, this item would still not furnish the subject with an experience, or provide anything else that was accessible to introspection.
>
> (Foster 2000: 107)

At different points, however, Armstrong defines an inclination to believe in different ways. In *Perception and the Physical World*, for example, he defines it as "a thought held back from being a belief by other, contradictory, beliefs" (1961: 86). This definition raises the possibility that an "inclination to believe" in fact names a particular kind of mental state—*like* a thought or belief but, because of the presence of contradictory beliefs, with a restricted functional role—rather than a disposition to form a belief.

It has also been argued that, by denying the existence of a visual experience that is distinct from our beliefs, the belief acquisition theory entails that we only *see* what we *notice*, where to notice something is to form a belief about it. This is then claimed to be refuted by the fact that we *can* actually see more than we notice. For instance, Fred Dretske (1969) argues that when we read a page of text, we don't form beliefs about every single letter although (to explain our ability to read) we must nevertheless *see* every single letter. If this were correct, it would once more point to a level of seeing which preceded our conceptualizations of it in belief. However, we should be careful of reading too much into the term "belief". If we are merely talking about a minimal level of discrimination and identification, then we *do* discriminate (most of) the letters. We can see this if we note that, were we to misidentify a letter we would probably misread the word and the sentence wouldn't make fence (Goldman 1976: 151).

Perception, belief, and our conceptual capacities

The belief acquisition theory has also been argued to have the unwelcome consequence that conceptually unsophisticated creatures, such as infants and animals, cannot enjoy perceptual experiences. Consider the following argument:

1	(Premiss)	Infants and animals have visual experiences.
2	(Statement of theory)	Visual experiences are just the acquisition of beliefs.
3	(Premiss)	Having beliefs involves having concepts.
4	(Premiss)	Infants and animals *don't* have concepts.
5	(from 2, 3 and 4)	Infants and animals don't have visual experiences.

Clearly 1 and 5 are contradictory, so something has to give somewhere.

Some philosophers would reject premise 1. Pitcher himself seems to say some things which suggest he would take this line. For example, he says that a requirement:

> for a perceiver, Q, to be capable of [acquiring] the (perceptual) belief that there is an x at u, is that Q have the concept of an x. Thus I take it that a one year old child cannot [acquire] the (perceptual) belief that there is a digital computer before him, since he does not have that concept. If this is right . . . it follows that it cannot look to a one year old child as though there is a digital computer before him. And I think this consequence is in fact true.

> (Pitcher 1971: 94)

But Pitcher could be saying that, as the child lacks this concept, he couldn't have *this very experience*, but of course, this leaves it open that the child might have a *different* experience when looking at the computer. This interpretation doesn't entail a rejection of 1.

If we would prefer to hold on to 1, that seems to leave us with having to reject either 3 or 4 to hold on to the belief acquisition theory of perception.

Daniel Dennett has defended a theory of belief that could be argued to be consistent with a rejection of 3. Dennett contends that, to have beliefs, one must be "a system whose behavior is reliably and voluminously predictable via the intentional strategy" (1981: 59), where this strategy involves treating the system whose behavior is to be predicted as a rational agent, then figuring out what beliefs and desires this agent ought to have, given its place in the world and its purpose, and then predicting that it will act to satisfy its desires in the light of its beliefs (1981: 61). If this strategy works, then, on Dennett's view, the system is a true believer. This strategy would provide a way in which we could allow subjects to have beliefs without assuming that they have concepts (or, at the very least, a way in which we could make the question of whether a subject has beliefs *prior* to the question of whether a subject possesses concepts).

Armstrong himself takes the other option and rejects 4. To do this, he draws a distinction between mediate and immediate forms of perception in terms of inferential and noninferential beliefs. The noninferential beliefs are those we form about the "visual properties" (Armstrong 1968: 234) of objects. As Armstrong says, this is a fairly small group and includes those characteristically visual properties such as shape, color, size, etc.

> [W]e see immediately that there is a thing having certain visual properties before us, and . . . this, by an automatic and instantaneous inference, produces the further belief that there is a cat's head or a sheet of paper before us. It is only the visual properties of things that can be immediately perceived by the eyes.
>
> (Armstrong 1968: 235)

If concepts of the visual properties are the basic concepts which go to make up our immediate experiences, then so long as infants had *those* basic concepts, they could have an *immediate* experience which was identical to an adult's. What would differ would be the *inferred* beliefs drawn automatically on the basis of this experience (due to the differences in conceptual sophistication).

Does an infant have such basic concepts? When discussing what it takes to have a concept, Armstrong suggests that:

> [If a] child reaches out for blue blocks, but never reaches out for green blocks . . . is not its behavior a manifestation of a true belief, acquired by

means of its eyes, that there is a difference in color between the blue and the green blocks? And could it not be said to possess the *concepts* of blue and green . . . even if in a very primitive form?

(Armstrong 1968: 246)

Beliefs involve concepts. Acquiring the belief that a particular object is red involves possession of the concept of red. Possession of the concept entails a general capacity of the perceiver, in at least some set of circumstances, to differentiate between things that are red and things that are not red.

(Armstrong 1968: 339)

Although language is a *way* in which we can treat square things differently from nonsquare things, it is not the only way. General behavioral capacities provide another possibility: the ability to treat square things in a different way to nonsquare things could be said, at the very least, to constitute *some* kind of possession of the concept (even if it is not possessed in as rich a sense as it is by us language users).[5]

What is more, this level of concept possession would not only enable young children to have concepts (hence beliefs, hence visual experiences), it would also do the same for animals. For example, we could imagine Skinnerian operant conditioning which would train a pigeon to peck at squares and only squares (perhaps it received food when pecking a square and electric shocks when pecking any other shape). If such a behaviorally manifested discriminatory capacity is held to suffice for possession of the relevant concept, then the pigeon could be said to acquire beliefs about the squareness of things in its surroundings and hence to have visual experiences.

Acquiring new concepts

A related objection is raised by Dretske: "if a man cannot see an *x* because he is ignorant of *x*-ish things, how could such unfortunate people relieve their ignorance?" (1969: 37). There are two potential objections here.

The first is clarified by Goldman, who argues that, "if persons are born without empirical concepts, building them gradually from early perceptual experience, then perception cannot consist in the acquisition of beliefs from the beginning" (1976: 152).

In other words, there is a potentially vicious circle raised: if perception involves the acquisition of belief, and beliefs are composed of concepts, but perception is itself the source of concepts, then how do we first acquire the concepts we need to possess in order to have perceptual experiences?

The second objection is a little less straightforward. Imagine that we are trying to train our pigeon from above to distinguish squares from nonsquares (i.e. are trying to get the pigeon to learn the concept *square*)— doesn't the pigeon have to be able to perceive a difference between squares and nonsquares in order for this to be possible? How can this be if the pigeon doesn't already have the concepts?

More formally, the concern is this. Let us assume that perception is no more than the acquiring of sets of beliefs. How can we individuate visual experiences (i.e. determine which visual experiences are the same as one another and which are different)? Well, as there is *no more* to a visual experience than the acquisition of beliefs, then the obvious principle of individuation would be as follows:

> Two visual experiences are the same if the sets of acquired beliefs are the same.

But if the beliefs we can acquire are limited by the concepts we possess, then a problem concerning our ability to acquire *new* concepts arises. Suppose that we are trying to teach an infant who already possesses the general color concept *red* to distinguish between two specific *shades* of red: *pillar-box red* and *cherry red*. In other words, let us suppose that we are trying to teach the child the concepts of *pillar-box red* and *cherry red*. The obvious way to do this would be to show the child samples of *pillar-box red* and *cherry red*, and to tell them which one was which.

As we are supposing that the child doesn't yet have these concepts, then as both shades are shades of red, when the child acquires beliefs about the shades which contain a place for a color (i.e. the child acquires the belief <the object is x>), this place would be filled with the same generic concept (which we accept the child *does* possess): *red*.

But then the sets of beliefs the infant would acquire on looking at these shades would be the same, and, according to the principle of individuation that naturally follows from this theory, the infant's perceptual experiences would be the same. If the infant's experiences of these two shades are the same, how would it be possible for the child to use these experiences as a basis from which to *learn* to distinguish between the shades?

The problem is, in order for concept learning to get off the ground, we need infants to be able to perceptually distinguish between two shades *even if* they don't distinguish between the shades at the level of belief. As the theory of perception as belief acquisition says that the two levels are *the same*, the theory as it stands doesn't seem able to account for this.

One way of avoiding the worry about breaking into this circle would be to say that, where the basic visual properties are concerned, we have a large number of these concepts (indeed, as many concepts as there are basic visual properties) *innately*—present from birth. After all, *if* it is true that the infant can distinguish between the different colors, even if it has not yet *tied* this discriminatory capacity to any particular kind of external behavior, then there might be a sense in which the infant could be said to already have these concepts.

Blindsight

In addition to these philosophical objections, there are also some objections to the belief acquisition theory based on findings from empirical science.

For instance, there is a pathological phenomenon, well known among visual psychologists, called *blindsight*, which has had a great deal of influence on recent philosophy of perception. Blindsight subjects typically have damage to brain area V1—the primary visual cortex—which effectively "maps" the retinal input. Because of this, damage to a localized area of V1 will often result in a *scotoma*—a blind spot—in part of the visual field. As we would expect, if a stimulus is presented to a subject in their blind spot, the subject claims to be unable to see it. However, as Larry Weiskrantz and his colleagues discovered in the 1970s, if subjects are instructed to *guess* whether a stimulus is present in that area, or to guess its orientation or direction of motion, some subjects perform significantly better than chance. Indeed, some subjects can even perform better than chance when asked to guess, say, which of an X or an O is presented. This shows that, despite subjects lacking conscious experience of the area behind the blind spot, information from that area is nevertheless getting through to the subject in such a way that it can be retrieved in the right circumstances.

The problem this raises for the belief acquisition theory is that a blindsight subject can acquire beliefs, via his or her eyes, about the part of the environment that corresponds to the blind spot. This suggests, therefore, that acquiring beliefs, using the eyes, about the relevant part of the visual field does not, in fact, suffice for the subject to have a visual experience corresponding to that part of the visual field.

Questions

- Can we see more than we notice? Or, to actually *see* something do we need to be cognitively aware of it in some way?
- How plausible do you find the belief acquisition theorist's attempts to deal with the problems of conceptually unsophisticated perceivers?
- Is perception nothing more than the acquisition of beliefs?

Notes

1. As the prominence of epistemological considerations in these introductory sections might suggest, the belief acquisition theory of perception is far more focused on adequately wearing the epistemological hat than the phenomenological hat. As we shall see, however, this has left the theory open to serious objections.

2. "At least part of" because, even if true belief is *necessary* for knowledge, the highly influential theory does not think that it is *sufficient* as well, but rather that some kind of justification condition is also needed.

3. I express this as a conditional because Armstrong's claim that the "non-physical object of immediate apprehension is simply a ghost generated by my belief that I am seeing something" (1961: 84) *could* be read as *denying* that the antecedent of the Phenomenal Principle is met in bad cases. I do not discuss this here, however, as it is inconsistent with the assumed acceptance of the Common Factor Principle. This possibility will therefore be discussed in more detail in Chapter 6.

4. Pitcher (1971) raises a concern with the term "acquisition" inasmuch as it implies obtaining something which one did not previously have. As we can continue to perceive an unchanging scene (I see the cup on the table at t1, I still see it at t2, etc.) it would seem strange to say that we *acquire* the belief that the cup is on the table at t2 as we already believe that from perceiving it there at t1. To avoid this implication, Pitcher prefers to use the locution "causally receives" as we can keep causally receiving a belief even if we already have it. With this point made, however, I will stick with "acquire."

5. The idea that possession of certain concepts is a matter of having certain skills and abilities has been defended more recently. For instance, Gregory McCulloch argues that "our having the experience-informing concepts we do have is constituted [. . .] by our abilities to move around and engage with the things in our surroundings" (1995: 140), and, likewise, Alva Noë has argued that part of what it is to have certain concepts is to have a range of tacit expectations as to how the appearances of certain objects will change under movement (2005: 77) and insists that this kind of skill is "obviously the sort of skill that non-linguistic animals and infants can possess" (2004: 183–184).

Further reading

The belief acquisition theory is developed by David Armstrong in his books *Perception and the Physical World* (1961) and *A Materialist Theory of the Mind* (1968). Pitcher's closely related development of the theory can be found in his *A Theory of Perception* (1971) especially Chapter 2.

Alan Goldman's 1976 paper, "Appearing as Irreducible in Perception" is an excellent and readable critical discussion of the belief acquisition theory, and Fred Dretske's 1969 book, *Seeing and Knowing* (especially Chapter 1, Sections 1 and 2) contains detailed arguments for the claim that we need to make room for a more basic, nonepistemic level of perception in our theorizing.

5 Intentional theories

Overview

Intentional theories of perception accept the Representational Principle, and treat visual experiences as a kind of propositional attitude in which subjects take the attitude of perceiving toward an intentional content.

In this chapter, we discuss a variety of different kinds of intentionalist theory, including *representationalism*, which claims that the phenomenology of a visual experience is determined by its content. We then go on to discuss a number of important issues for intentionalists, focusing in particular on the nature of perceptual *content*.

Common Factor Principle	☑
Phenomenal Principle	☒
Representational Principle	☑

We have already discussed the Representational Principle, which claims that:

(R) All visual experiences are representational.

As noted in the previous chapter, beliefs are also representational—they tell us things about the world. And a standard philosophical treatment of belief analyzes belief as a *propositional attitude*.

On this view, beliefs involve a subject taking the relationship (attitude) of belief toward a content (proposition): if I believe *that* Paris is in France, then I take the attitude of belief toward the propositional content <Paris is in France>.

In the previous chapter, we looked at the view that attempted to *reduce* visual experience to the acquisition of belief. Although this theory has failed to acquire many adherents over the years, it has suggested an alternative theory of perception that has since become quite popular; an *intentional* theory of perception:

> I [take] as "intentionalist" . . . the theory which treats perception as a kind of propositional attitude, akin to belief.
>
> (Crane 1998: 233)

> An intentional theory of perception claims that visual experiences have an intentional content that represents the world as being some way. This is to see experiences as akin to propositional attitudes such as beliefs.
>
> (Martin 1994: 745)

Like the theory of perception as belief acquisition, these approaches see important similarities between perceptions and beliefs, but, unlike that theory, they do not attempt to simply *reduce* the former to the acquisition of the latter. Instead, intentionalist theories retain the distinction between the perceptual and conceptual components—they allow that visual experiences are something over and above beliefs and the acquisition of beliefs.

Yet the intentionalist does insist that visual experiences are importantly *analogous* to beliefs: that, like beliefs, visual experiences have *intentional* or *representational* contents that represent the world as being a certain way. Moreover, on the intentionalist view, the subject takes an attitude toward that content that is importantly like the attitude of belief in that it doesn't entail the truth of that content. As Byrne puts it, "perception constitutively involves a propositional attitude rather like the *non*-factive attitude of believing, *exing* (meant to suggest experiencing)" (2009: 437). So, rather than claim that, in perception, the subject *believes* that such-and-such is the case, the intentionalist view is that, in perception, subjects *ex* that such-and-such is the case.

Varieties of intentionalism

Intentionalists endorse the Representational Principle—they claim that all visual experiences are representational.

In addition to this, intentional theorists—at least those that we will be considering in this chapter—accept the Common Factor Principle. In the bad case of hallucination, the intentionalist will claim that the subject is having a visual experience with the same representational content as in the indiscriminable good case; it is just that in this case the content is false. And just as my believing that such-and-such is the case says something about how I take the world to be, whilst not entailing that the world *is* that way, my *exing* that such-and-such is the case also does not entail that the world is that way—I could be in the same intentional state whether perceiving or hallucinating.

This is the basic intentionalist thesis. There are, however, a number of ways in which this basic idea has been developed.

One key choice point concerns the relationship between phenomenology and the intentional components of experience. There are three main positions that are taken here, which I will call *strong phenomenology-first intentionalism*, *strong content-first intentionalism* and *weak intentionalism*.

What makes all three of these approaches variants of intentionalism is that they all endorse the Representational Principle:

(R) All visual experiences are representational.

However, as their names suggest, the first two positions also endorse a somewhat stronger claim, which I will call the Mirroring Thesis:

(M) Change in phenomenology ↔ Change in representational content.

In English, the Mirroring Thesis states that there will be a change in phenomenology, or what it is like to have an experience, if and only if there is a change in the experience's representational content.

As (M) is a biconditional, it is important to remember that it should be read both ways. We can call these LR (for reading from left to right) and RL (from right to left) in turn:

(M)LR: That any change in phenomenology necessitates a change in representational content; and

(M)RL: That any change in representational content necessitates a change in phenomenology.

Strong phenomenology-first intentionalism

As the name suggests, this version of intentionalism treats phenomenology as the basic notion. Typically, phenomenology-first intentionalists hold that visual experiences have representational content *in virtue of* their phenomenology. The underlying idea is that, if there is something it is like to have an experience, then that alone suffices for the experience to be the kind of thing that could be true or false. Take the experience you are having now—it seems plausible to suppose that, given only what it is like for you, your experience is *accurate* if and only if there is a book (or suitably book-like object) in front of you (Siewert 1998).

This is developed into an argument by Byrne (2001). He asks us to imagine an idealized subject enjoying two consecutive experiences—e and e^*—that differ in their phenomenology. The fact that there is a difference in phenomenology means that, if experience e changes to experience e^* at t, the subject (being ideal) will notice the change. As the subject notices that things have changed, it seems to follow that the way *things seem* to the subject has changed or, alternatively, that the way the world *is represented to be* has changed. We can express this by saying that experiences e and e^* represent the world to be different or, alternatively, have different contents.

This argument allows us to conclude that, if the phenomenology of an experience changes, then so will its content—the world will have to be slightly different in order for the experience to be accurate. This gives us the left–right reading of (M)—that any change in phenomenology will yield a change in representational content.

Of course, if experiences have content in virtue of their phenomenology, then it seems we can get the right–left reading too—if two experiences differ in what they represent, they must therefore present the world to be slightly different—in Byrne's terms, the way things seem to the subject must be different. This is just to say that they differ in their phenomenology. So phenomenology-first approaches typically endorse (M) in both directions.

As there is scope for a strong phenomenology-first intentionalist to endorse different theories of an experience's phenomenal character, it is difficult to offer a precise analysis of what is involved in a subject's having a visual experience as of a property F. The basic idea, however, is that subjects will have an experience *of property* F when they have an experience with a phenomenal character that delivers a content in which Fness features.

Now, given that the phenomenology-first approach gives explanatory priority to an experience's phenomenology, they allow us to explain what it is for an experience to have content by appealing to its phenomenology. But there is still a need to provide a theory of the phenomenal features of visual experiences. Phenomenology-first theorists typically endorse a qualia-based account of the kind touched on in Chapter 3, according to which experiences have certain intrinsic, nonrepresentational consciously accessible properties (qualia) that are responsible for the experience's phenomenology.[1] Although the qualia themselves are nonrepresentational, once we have an experience with certain qualia, the thought goes, we can "read off" a content from the phenomenology thus provided. This explains how the experience itself can be representational, even though the qualia themselves are not.

Strong content-first intentionalism

This version of intentionalism also endorses both (R) and (M) but, unlike phenomenology-first intentionalism, takes *content* as the most basic notion and attempts to explain what it is for a state to be conscious or to have phenomenology in terms of its having the right kind of content. There are two standard approaches here.

According to *higher order* versions of intentionalism, we have lots of first-order sensory representations (representations of the world produced by the senses), but these are not automatically conscious. They become conscious when the subject has the right kind of higher order state *about* that first-order state. Exactly how this is spelled out differs according to different theorists.

Lycan (1996) argues that the higher order state is analogous to a first-order visual experience. A first-order sensory representation *R* will be conscious when, and only when, an internal "scanner" is producing higher order representations *about R*. (This position is therefore known as a higher order perception [HOP] or higher order experience [HOE] theory.)

Rosenthal (1990), on the other hand, argues that the higher order state is a belief. On this view, a first-order sensory representation *R* will be conscious when, and only when, the subject has a higher order belief *about R*. (This position is therefore known as a higher order belief [HOB] or a higher order thought [HOT] theory.)

So, a higher order version of content-first intentionalism will propose the following analysis of visual experiences:

A subject *S* has a visual experience as of a property *F* if and only if:

- *S* is in a first-order state, *R*, that represents that *F* is instantiated; and
- *R* is scanned/the subject of a higher order belief.

The currently more popular form of intentionalism is a *first-order* form, which—confusingly—is often called *representationalism*.

Typically, first-order strong content-first intentionalists (from here: *representationalists*) do not hold that entertaining a certain content *suffices* for the presence of phenomenology. The standard approach is to hold that a first-order sensory representation *R* is conscious when, and only when, it (i) has the right kind of content *and* (ii) plays the right kind of functional role. Thus, Tye, for example, holds that sensory representations are conscious when they have PANIC (Poised, Abstract, Nonconceptual Intentional Content) (1995: §5.2). On this view, the "right kind" of content is content that is both *abstract* (does not refer to particular objects) and *nonconceptual* (does not require the subject to possess the concepts used to specify the content); the "right kind" of functional role is that the mental state be *poised*: poised to impact upon the subject's cognitive processes.

Representationalism therefore proposes the following analysis of visual experience:

A subject *S* has a visual experience as of a property *F* if and only if:

- *S* is in a first-order state *R* that represents that *F* is instantiated, which meets other further conditions.

As both the higher order and first-order variants of intentionalism attempt to explain consciousness in terms of content, they face the inverse problem to that faced by the phenomenology-first theorists. Recall that phenomenology-first theorists needed a theory of what it is for an experience to have phenomenology with which they then explain what it is for an experience to have content. Content-first theorists, on the other hand, need a theory of what it is for a state to have a certain kind of *content* in order to explain what it is for an experience to have *phenomenology*. This will be discussed in more detail below.

Weak intentionalism

Weak intentionalists endorse the Representational Principle (R) but reject (M). That is, although weak intentionalists agree that all visual experiences have representational content, they do not agree that any changes in phenomenology will necessarily be matched by changes in representational content (or vice versa). Given this, weak intentionalism is compatible with different claims about the nature of the perceptual state.

(M)LR claims that any change in phenomenology necessitates a change in representational content. In response to this, weak intentionalists have presented examples in which it is claimed that phenomenology can differ while representational content remains the same. For example, suppose we see a tree from 100 metres away. This experience would represent the tree to have a certain height, h. Now suppose we walk toward that tree. Weak intentionalists have claimed that our experience of this tree from 50 metres would still represent the tree to have height h—so would have the same content—yet would be clearly phenomenally distinct (adapted from Peacocke 1983).

Alternatively, look at the room you are in. This experience represents the layout of the room. Now close one eye. Due to using only one eye instead of two, this experience will be subtly phenomenally different. Yet, claim weak intentionalists, it will still represent the layout of the room to be the same (Peacocke 1983). Or, imagine looking at two red points of light against a black background and shifting attention from one light to the other. There is arguably a phenomenal difference between the experience of attending to one and attending to the other, but it is not clear whether there is a representational difference between the two experiences (Chalmers 2004).

A final case in which weak intentionalists claim that phenomenology can differ whilst representational content remains the same is based on a thought experiment known as the *inverted spectrum hypothesis*. Suppose the phenomenological color you see when you look at blue things is the same as the color I see when I look at yellow things. Now consider you and I looking at the blue sky. Intuitively our experiences differ in phenomenology but (arguably) have the same representational content.

(M)RL claims that any change in representational content necessitates a change in phenomenology. As an objection to this claim, Ned Block develops a clever variant of the inverted spectrum hypothesis. Suppose that you are taken (in your sleep) to a new planet—Inverted Earth—in which objects have the inverse of their colors here on Earth. However, to ensure you don't

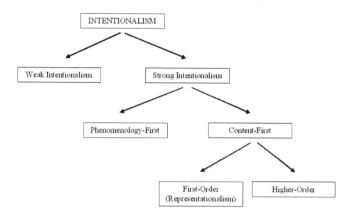

Figure 5.1

notice the difference, you are fitted with a pair of color-inverting lenses. So, when you wake up and see the yellow sky, you have an experience of blue, just as you did on Earth; likewise, when you see the red grass, you have an experience of green. Weak intentionalists have contended that, over time, the representational contents of your experiences will change to fit your new surroundings. Now the (blue) experience you have when you look at the sky will have the content <the sky is yellow>, whereas on Earth it had the content <the sky is blue>. If so, then we have a case in which experiences with the same phenomenology (experiences of a clear sky on Earth and Inverted Earth) differ in representational content (Block 1990).

Figure 5.1 gives a visual structure of the different theories of perception that fall under the general heading of intentionalism.

Theories of perceptual content

When it comes to discussions of intentionalism, deciding on which intentionalist theory of *perception* is only half the job: you also need to decide on a theory of *perceptual content*. A discussion of some of the key choice points for this follows.

The nature of contents

There are many different theories of propositions or contents. Here we will discuss three influential ones. On each of these theories, our linguistic specification of a content expresses a proposition that is identified with the content. The differences between the theories turn on their different conceptions of what propositions are.

- *Possible world contents:* According to the possible world theory of content, our linguistic specification of a content—that "the cat is black" for example—serves to cleave possible worlds in two: those in which the proposition is true and those in which it is false. Possible worlds theories of content identify content with that set of possible worlds in which the proposition is true.
- *Singular (Russellian/Millian) contents:* An alternative theory of content is the singular content theory. The linguistic specification of a content contains singular terms, predicates, connectives, and so on. On the singular content theory, the propositions actually have the referents of the singular terms and predicates as constituents. For instance, the proposition expressed by "the cat is black" is part-constituted by the cat itself and the property of blackness.
- *Fregean contents:* Rather than claiming that objects and properties are constituents of propositions, the Fregean holds that propositions are constituted by *modes of presentation* of objects and properties.

How should we choose between these alternatives? Well, one consideration turns on the fact that the representationalist theories that we are considering in this chapter endorse the Common Factor Principle. Suppose, then, that we were to claim that perceptual contents are *singular*. It would seem that two experiences of distinct yet qualitatively indiscriminable objects would therefore have different contents—as an experience of object *a* as black would have the content <*a* is black> whilst an experience of (qualitatively identical) object *b* as black would have the content <*b* is black>. As these contents are different, it would seem that the representationalist would have to accept that the phenomenal characters of these two experiences differ. With this in mind, Colin McGinn argues that:

> the content of experience is not to be specified by using any terms that refer to the object of experience, on pain of denying that distinct objects can seem precisely the same: so when we are describing the content of an experience, we should not make singular reference to the object of the experience.
>
> (McGinn 1982: 39)[2]

Another consideration that is relevant to the particular case of perception is that theories of content should, in some sense, be *true to the phenomenology*. This has also been the source of an argument in favor of Fregean theories over singular content theories. Consider color experience. Suppose we have a number of experiences of one and the same white surface. Naturally, on a singular content view, we would take all of these experiences to have contents that are part-constituted by the property of *whiteness*. Yet, the Fregean might argue, by suitable manipulation of hidden lights—a manipulation that takes place without the subject's knowledge—this surface could be made to *look* different colors at different times. A content that is constituted by the property itself cannot account for this, so instead (the argument goes), we need to see that the contents of our experiences of this surface are constituted by different *modes of presentation* of that surface property.

A natural response for the singular content theorist to make is to say that, in those cases in which the surface *does not* look white, we are therefore under an illusion—we are *misrepresenting* the color of the surface. Suppose that the lighting is arranged in such a way that the white surface looks pink. In such a case, the singular content theorist would *not* hold that the content of this experience is constituted by the property of whiteness. Not only would this be false to the phenomenology, it would also have the consequence that the experience qualified as veridical—because the surface *really is* white. Instead, the singular content theorist would claim that the content is part-constituted by the property of *pinkness*. This is both true to the phenomenology and to our intuitions that the subject's experience is misleading.

Internalism/externalism[3]

A further important question about the nature of perceptual contents concerns the question of whether the contents of a particular subject's visual experiences are fixed solely by features of the subject's brain, central nervous system and/or body, or whether the environment that the subject is in also plays a part.

> *Internalists* about perceptual content hold that once you have fixed the physically internal states of the subject you thereby fix the contents of their visual experiences. This has the consequence that any two physically identical subjects will be in states with identical contents, regardless of any differences in the physical or social environments in which they live.

> *Externalists* about perceptual content, on the other hand, hold that external relations are also partly responsible for fixing contents. According to externalists, therefore, physically identical subjects may have experiences with different contents.

Tyler Burge defends externalism in the case of perceptual content by considering a Twin Earth style argument (2007b).[4] He asks us to imagine two distinct entities—as small shadow (an O) and a similarly sized and shaped crack (a C). Although these objects are both very small and their discrimination does not carry any evolutionary advantages, it turns out that Os are very common in the environment whereas Cs are very rare.

Burge then asks us to imagine a subject, P, who has grown up being confronted with Os. He contends that "perceptual representations are formed and obtain their content through regular interactions with the environment. They represent what, in some complex sense of 'normally', they normally stem from and are applied to" (Burge 2007b: 203). Given this, the perceptual state that P enters when he encounters an O will be veridical—it will represent that an O is present. Now imagine that P, unbeknownst to him, encounters a C. According to Burge, our theory ought to treat this as a misrepresentation—P misrepresents a C as an O.

Now Burge asks us to imagine a counterfactual case. Suppose that the optical laws are different and that, in P's environment, there are no longer any visible Os. Suppose, however, that P's history is exactly as it was in the original environment, it is just that wherever P saw an O in the original case, in the counterfactual environment he saw a C. As the normal causes of P's perceptual states have changed, Burge contends that they will now be representing Cs, not Os.

Finally, suppose that, where P saw a C in the original environment, he also sees a C in the counterfactual environment. Given their identical histories, we need not suppose that there are any physical differences between P in the original environment and P in the counterfactual environment. Nor need we suppose that there are any differences between the light that impacts upon P in the two scenarios. Despite this, Burge insists that where P misrepresented the C as an O in the original environment, in the counterfactual environment, P *correctly* represents the C as a C. Despite all the physical similarities, there is a difference in their perceptual contents—the contents are determined, in part, by the nature of the environment.

In order to see how internalists might attempt to counter this argument, recall the claim, from our discussions of phenomenology-first versions of intentionalism, that there are certain truth-conditions that an experience possesses merely in virtue of the phenomenology that it has. If this claim is found compelling, then we might think that Burge's characterizations of the perceptual contents are too fine-grained—that P's experiences do not distinguish between Os and Cs. This is the kind of response taken by Gabriel Segal, who argues that P's experiences actually have a less precise content and merely represent the presence of a thin, dark mark that could be either a shadow or a crack (1989).

How we resolve this depends upon whether we place more importance on the causes or effects of our experiences in fixing on assignments of content. If we focus on the fact, as Burge does, that they are experiences of distinct entities, then this will seem to license the attribution of distinct contents. Alternatively, if we follow Segal and focus on the fact that things will seem the same to P and hence P will *behave* in the same way, regardless of whether or not the object is a crack or a shadow, then this can seem to license the attribution of a common content.

Conceptual/nonconceptual

When we discussed the theory of perception as belief acquisition, we saw that the theory faced objections concerning the apparent ability to perceive possessed by conceptually unsophisticated creatures such as infants and animals. In addition to this, it has been argued that perception provides us with far more information, and at a far greater level of detail, than we could possibly bring under concepts (Dretske 1981). In response to these concerns, a number of intentionalists (including representationalists) *reject* the claim that perceptual content, like belief content, has to be conceptual in nature. If we no longer insist that all forms of representational content must be conceptual, the door is then open to introduce a *nonconceptual* form of content. And this is just what many theorists do.

Essentially, the suggestion is that there are lots of mental states that represent the world around the subject to be a certain way. Sometimes, to be in one of these states requires that we have the concepts which are used to specify the content of the state. For instance, we can't *believe* that cheese is made with milk unless we have the concepts of *milk* and *cheese*. If this is the case, then we say that such a state has *conceptual content*.

The claim is that there are other mental states that represent the world to be a certain way (e.g., perceptions), which we can entertain *even though we don't have the concepts which are used to specify the content of the state*. Our experience of a Mark Rothko picture can still represent the presence of a very precise shade of yellow, even though we don't have a concept of that particular shade. So, many intentional theorists about perception hold not only that perception is an intentional state, but that it is a state with a special kind of *nonconceptual* content.

Laid out more formally, an argument for nonconceptual content might look something like this:

1 Visual experiences provide us with a lot of very rich detail.
2 This richness must be reflected in the experience's representational content.
3 To capture this richness, we need to specify this content using a fine-grained taxonomy of properties.
4 This taxonomy of properties outstrips our conceptual scheme.
5 Therefore (from a standard definition of nonconceptual content), the content of visual experience must be (at least partly) nonconceptual.

The argument begins from the intuition that, if we stop and take stock of the scene before our eyes, we become aware of just *how much* fine-grained information our experiences provide us with.[5] Given this, we need to capture this richness in an ascription of content. How should we go about this? The two most fully developed theories of nonconceptual content—Christopher Peacocke's Scenario Content (1992: §3.1) and Michael Tye's PANIC (1995: §5.2; 2000: §3.4)—begin the task of specifying a nonconceptual content in a similar fashion:

> [I]magine a large, transparent matrix placed over the visual field. Each cell in the matrix covers a tiny portion of the field; within each cell, there is an ordered sequence of symbols for various features of any surface at that location in the field (for example, distance away, orientation, determinate color, texture, etc.)
>
> (Tye 1995: 140).

> For each point [. . .] identified by its distance and direction from the origin [something like a point of view in the case of vision], we need to specify whether there is a surface there and, if so, what texture, hue, saturation, and brightness it has at that point.
>
> (Peacocke 1992: 63)

Both Tye and Peacocke begin the task of formulating an experience's nonconceptual content by mapping all the points in the perceiver's field of view, and then, for each point, cataloging the surface properties that the experience represents as being instantiated at that point.

In order to do this adequately, we will need to employ a fine-grained taxonomy of properties in order to capture the richness that seems to be available to us in perception. How fine-grained? Well, the characteristic understanding of the perceptual richness motivation seems to be that an adequate account of perceptual content ought to capture the richness of visual experience *to the limits of a subject's discriminatory capacities*.

Given that we can discriminate so many colors, when we try to characterize the detail available to us in experience, it seems that words, or, more accurately, the concepts we have available to describe the experience, must fail us. Even if we had command of every color name in the color dictionary—all 4,000 of them (Tye 1995: 139)—our conceptual capacities would still be woefully short when it comes to trying to capture the numerous shades of color we can discriminate in experience. So, any taxonomy of properties which is fine-grained enough to capture a subject's discriminatory capacities will (or maybe even must) radically outrun the conceptual capacities a subject has available for thinking about experiences.[6]

We move from here to the conclusion with a definition of nonconceptual content: "For any state with content, S, S has a nonconceptual content, P, if a subject X's being in S does not entail that X possesses the concepts that canonically characterise P" (Crane 1992: 143).

Given that nonconceptual content is *defined* as a content which does not require its bearer to possess the concepts required for its formulation, the conclusion that the type of content required to characterize the richness of visual experience is nonconceptual follows straightforwardly.

A further motivation behind the appeal to nonconceptual contents is that it also enables us to account for the perceptual similarities which appear to exist between animals and humans. As having an experience with a certain nonconceptual content does not require the subject to possess those concepts, it leaves it open for animals to have experiences with nonconceptual contents just like ours (with due note taken of the different levels of discriminatory prowess of different animals).

Importantly, the claim is not that a given state might have conceptual content (if we happen to have the concepts) or nonconceptual content (if we don't). Instead, what makes a state conceptual or nonconceptual is whether one's having the concepts is a *necessary condition* of one's being in that state. A given state might still be nonconceptual *even if we have the concepts used to specify the content*, so long as we could have been in that state had we not had the concepts.

How do experiences get their contents?

In this chapter, we have considered different intentionalist theories of *perception* as well as different theories of perceptual *content*. Before we move to seeing how well these theories wear our two hats, one further issue needs to be raised.

As we saw when we discussed the different intentionalist theories of perception, phenomenology-first versions of intentionalism hold that an experience's phenomenology dictates what its content is—that its content can be *read off* its phenomenology.

Content-first versions of intentionalism, of course, can't say this. These theories, recall, explain what it is for a state to have phenomenology by appealing to the content it has. So an account of what it is for a state to *have* a content of a certain kind is needed in order to thereby explain what it is for an experience to have phenomenology of a certain kind. This means that, to be complete, content-first theories must address the question of how experiences *get* their contents: In virtue of what does a given experience have the particular content it does?

Representationalists have typically endorsed some kind of reductive, naturalistic theory of content. This is because this approach offers to provide a two-stage naturalistic explanation of consciousness. The first stage involves the explanation of consciousness in terms of content or representation—this is the representationalist theory discussed above. Then, if we can provide a naturalistically acceptable account of what is involved in a state's having a particular content, we have thereby provided a naturalistically acceptable account of what is involved in a state's being conscious.

Although there are many naturalistic theories of content in the literature, including the "asymmetric dependence" theory of content (Fodor 1992), "success semantics" (Whyte 1990), "conceptual role semantics" (Harman 1987), and various hybrid accounts, representationalists have tended to endorse variants of a *teleosemantic* theory of content (see, e.g., Dretske 1995: 15; Tye 1995: 153; and Lycan 1996: 75).[7] Although there are a number of different variants, the core of teleosemantic theories is their focus, in attributing contents to mental states, on what the *biological function* of these states are.

Despite this, there is no reason why (at least so far as I can see) representationalism could not be combined with *any* of these theories of content, and, indeed, it would be an interesting question which of these theories fits best with representationalism. Given this, what are the key considerations for a representationalist when it comes to deciding which theory to endorse?

Given the nature of the representationalist claim, probably the most important consideration is that, as the representationalist insists that what it is like to have an experience is explained by its representational content, an adequate theory of content must ascribe contents to experience that are as rich and detailed as that experience's phenomenology. What is more, it must also be able to explain and predict the kinds of content–phenomenology *covariation* that are stipulated by the Mirroring Thesis. The Mirroring Thesis, recall, states that any change in phenomenology necessitates a change in representational content. With this in mind, consider two experiences, e and e^*, which differ in phenomenology. According to the Mirroring Thesis, these two experiences must, therefore, differ in content. But because the representationalist insists that *content* is the primary notion, the difference in content has to *explain* the difference in phenomenology, rather than the other way around. So an adequate theory of content must predict changes in representational content in all and only those situations in which what it is like to have the experience would change. How well the theories of content outlined above can explain these features is an important topic for further research.[8]

Representationalism and the two hats

As there are a number of different intentional theories of perception, I will focus the present discussions on the question of how well the most popular of these theories—representationalism—manages to wear our two hats.

The phenomenological hat

A leading motivation for representationalism has been that it can adequately capture the phenomenology of experience *without* requiring an appeal to either qualia or sense data in the bad cases.

In Chapter 3, the *transparency* objection to qualia theories was discussed. To claim that an experience is transparent, recall, is to claim that, when one introspects that experience, one does not discover any properties of the experience itself, only properties of the objects of experience.[9] This phenomenological claim has been used to argue not only *against* qualia theory but also *for* representationalism. Effectively, the defense of representationalism on the basis of transparency is that it is the last man standing. This defense goes like this (Tye 2000):

Transparency tells us that the properties we are aware of in experience appear to be properties of presented *objects*. There is, therefore, strong phenomenological evidence that the *presentational character* of a visual experience is constituted by properties of *objects*. To claim, therefore, that the properties we are aware of in perception are properties *of experiences*—as qualia theorists do—would be to convict visual experiences of massive error. This is claimed to be implausible.

If the presentational character of a particular experience is constituted by properties of objects, then perhaps it is constituted by the very properties of the mind-independent objects that we *see*. However, argues Tye, the possibility of indiscriminable hallucinations shows that this cannot be the case. In such cases, we can entertain a presentational character of this kind without there being any appropriate mind-independent objects.

Well then, if presentational character is not constituted by the properties of mind-*independent* objects, then perhaps it is constituted by properties of mind-*dependent* objects—sense data. However, Tye suggests that this claim is unacceptable for "a whole host of familiar reasons" (2000: 46).

Representationalists, however, have an answer. The properties that constitute presentational character are indeed properties of objects. But they are not necessarily properties that are *currently instantiated* by objects. Instead, they are properties that the experience *represents as being instantiated*. In this way, suggests the representationalist, the phenomenon of transparency can be accommodated without having to find objects to actually bear the relevant properties.

On this view, the presentational character of an experience is constituted by the everyday mind-independent properties. The *phenomenal* character of the experience—the property of the experience that types the experience by what it is like to undergo it—is the experience's property of *representing that these properties are instantiated* or, alternatively, the experience's property of *having thus-and-such a representational content*.[10]

The representationalist thus rejects the Phenomenal Principle. That principle claims that if there sensibly appears to a subject to be something that possesses a particular sensible quality then there is something of which the subject is aware which does possess that quality. According to the representationalist, there sensibly appearing to a subject to be something that possesses a particular property is a matter of the experience's *representing* that something possesses that property. For this to be the case, nothing *actually* need possess that property at all.

The qualia theorist might respond to transparency by trying to show that we can, in fact, be aware of properties of experiences in introspection. Tim Crane, for example, contends that when you remove your spectacles you become aware of blurriness without taking the *objects* to be blurry. This, Crane suggests, shows that we are aware of blurriness *as a property of our experience* (2003).

The representationalist, of course, must deny this. This means that we are owed an alternative explanation of what the experience of blurriness consists in. Tye's response is to actually *deny* that we are aware of blurriness at all. Instead, our experiences simply *fail* to represent the sharp boundaries that the objects, in fact, have. So it is not that, in such experiences, we are aware of something that is *not* a property of an object—blurriness—but rather that we *fail* to be aware of one of the properties that the objects have: the property of having a sharp outline (Tye 2003).

Perhaps the most significant objection to the content-first account of phenomenology—in both its higher order and first order (representationalist) guises—turns on the role played in the account by functionalist considerations.

As we have seen, first-order content-first theorists (representationalists) account for the phenomenology of an experience of *F*ness by appeal to the subject's being in a state that has a representational content in which *F*ness features.

Yet consider the following "*a priori* suspicion" (Kriegel 2002): If representation of property *F* *alone* suffices for the subject of this representation to be consciously aware of *F*ness, then property *F* *could not* be represented unconsciously. This seems implausible. Instead, the thought goes, there must be something *else* that distinguishes conscious representations of *F*ness from nonconscious representations of *F*ness.

And, indeed, this is borne out when we consider specific content-first theories. We have already seen that the higher order theorists require that a first-order representation, to be conscious, must be either scanned or the subject of a higher order belief. We also noted when we were discussing first-order theories that, to be conscious, a representational state *also* has to play the right kind of functional role.

This means that, in all of these cases, the subject's being in a state that represents *F*ness *cannot*, by itself, explain why *F*ness sensibly appears to the subject. This raises the question of why these additional considerations—playing the right functional role; being scanned by an internal scanner; being the subject of a higher order belief—have the ability to change a nonconscious state into a conscious state.

As a way of making this concern vivid, we might wonder why, given that *F*ness can be represented nonconsciously, an (in itself) *unconscious* representation *becomes conscious* just in virtue of playing a particular functional role? But why couldn't there be a case in which this representation plays this functional role *without* thereby making its subject conscious? If there could, then this suggests that the content-first theorist's account of why there is something it is like to enjoy a visual experience may be lacking.

The epistemological hat

According to conceptualist versions of intentionalism—versions that hold that the contents of visual experiences are *conceptual*—empirical beliefs arise simply from endorsing the contents of visual experiences. This allows for the possibility that, on such a view, empirical beliefs can be *rationally*, and not just causally, grounded by visual experiences.

Moreover, the regress problems do not arise for such a view—when we justify a belief by pointing to another belief, we can always ask what justifies that *further* belief. (It is in response to this challenge that Armstrong, as we saw, adopted an externalist conception of justification.) Here the situation is different. When we respond to the challenge, "Why do you believe that *p*?" with the answer, "Because I perceive that *p*," we are not pointing to another belief as justifying the initial belief but an *experience*. And the question of what justifies an *experience* sounds odd—experiences are not the sorts of things that can be justified: we just have them, that is all. As long as having an experience that represents that *p* is adequate justification for believing that *p*, which on the face of it it seems to be, we look to have an adequate epistemology.

This account of the justification of empirical beliefs has been challenged— it has been argued that, as we could have a visual experience in which we bear the *ex*ing attitude to the content *that p* when *p* was false (in the case of hallucination, say), having an experience in which we *ex* that *p* is *not* adequate justification for believing that *p*—but a more pressing concern is the fact that, as things stand, this approach is not available to the majority of intentionalists (at least, the majority of *strong* intentionalists) as they reject conceptualism in favor of nonconceptualism about perceptual contents.

Whilst this move does have the advantage of (purportedly) getting the phenomenology right, it comes at an epistemological cost: we can no longer simply talk about the experience's content being endorsed in belief.

To have access to this account of empirical justification, then, the non-conceptualist needs to say something about the relationship between the nonconceptual contents of visual experiences and the conceptual contents of beliefs, such that the former can be an epistemically suitable ground for the latter.

One response by nonconceptualists has been to say that belief contents and nonconceptual perceptual contents *do* stand in rational relations to one another. For example, if a nonconceptual content specifies a way of filling out space around the subject (as Peacocke's scenario contents, discussed above, do), then some beliefs *about* the layout of space will be inconsistent with this content, or entailed by it, or made probable by it, and so on (Heck 2000).

Another response has been to hold that visual experiences and beliefs have the same *whole* contents:

> when a perception that *p* causes a belief that *p*, the *whole* contents of
> these two states are of the same type—*p*. [... B]elief *conceptualises* the
> content of perception. So treating the transition from perception to
> belief in terms of whole contents allows us to explain how perceptions
> have contents that can be the contents of beliefs.
>
> (Crane 1992: 155)

Conceptualists, however, are unlikely to be swayed. Even if perceptual contents can stand in rational relations to the contents of beliefs, they will contend that visual experiences with nonconceptual contents cannot be genuine *reasons* for a subject—reasons that figure as such from the subject's point of view—unless they have conceptual content.

As Brewer argues, "even though being in [a state with nonconceptual content] may make it advisable, relative to a certain external end or need, for [a subject] to make the judgement or hold the belief in question, it cannot provide her own reason for doing so" (2005: 219).

Questions

- How plausible is the claim that what it is like to have an experience is just a matter of the experience's representational content?
- Can a nonconceptual content theorist provide an adequate account of the epistemological role of perception?
- Can any naturalistic theory of content successfully predict the kind of content variations required by the Mirroring Thesis?

Notes

1 Let me note, at this point, that there are other conceptions of qualia in the literature. There are also different *theories* of these properties (including theories that claim that they are physical properties and theories that claim they are nonphysical properties). The 1997 book *Explaining Consciousness: The Hard Problem*, edited by Jonathan Shear, gives a good overview of some of the proposed theories of qualia.

2. In light of this consideration, McGinn (1982) suggests we should limit the contents of experiences to merely *existential* contents. Others have argued that this isn't quite right: experience doesn't just tell us *that there is* a black and pink book there but that *a particular* book is black and pink. They have therefore tried to incorporate McGinn's insight in a singular content view by holding a version of a view in which indiscriminable experiences share some kind of content *schema*, which delivers a singular content in a particular context and determines the experience's phenomenal character. For instance, Burge (1991) develops a view on which visual experiences of a certain kind have a (non-truth-evaluable) *demonstrative* content of the form <That object is F>, which is shared by indiscriminable perceptions and hallucinations. Then, when the subject has an experience of this kind in a suitable environmental context—one which contains a suitable object (say, *o*)—the demonstrative picks out the relevant particular and, using this, creates a singular, truth-evaluable

content, $<o$ is $F>$. If the case is hallucinatory, however, this demonstrative fails and no singular content is created (see also Soteriou 2000). Tye (2009) develops a version in which hallucinations do have contents, but that they are *gappy*. Schellenberg (forthcoming) develops a Fregean version of the gappy content approach.

3. The terms "internalism" and "externalism" are used in many areas of philosophy, so we must be clear what we are being internalist/externalist *about*. In particular, in this context, internalism/externalism about perceptual *content* should be distinguished from internalism/externalism about *phenomenology* and internalism/externalism about *justification* (as discussed in the previous chapter). Internalism about phenomenology claims that internal physical duplicates will share phenomenology; externalism, that features external to the brain and body can determine phenomenology. Having said this, internalism about perceptual content is a natural partner of internalism about phenomenology—if we are internalist about phenomenology and if phenomenology fixes content, then content will also be fixed by the internal states of the subject. Likewise, externalism about phenomenology is often found with the content-first approach as a number of plausible naturalistic theories of content are externalist. This means that changes in environment can lead to changes in content. If it is also held that content fixes phenomenology, then changes in environment will also yield changes in phenomenology.

4. Classic presentations of Twin Earth arguments include Hilary Putnam's "The Meaning of 'Meaning'" (1975), which argues that natural kind terms get their meaning from the physical environment, and Burge's own (2007a) "Individualism and the Mental," which argues that some terms get their meaning from features of our social environment.

5. At this point, let me flag that this intuition has been challenged by recent empirical work on change blindness and inattentional blindness. These findings will be discussed in Chapter 8.

6. This claim has recently been challenged. John McDowell argues that, "in the throes of an experience of the kind that putatively transcends one's conceptual powers—an experience that *ex hypothesi* affords a suitable sample—one can give linguistic expression to a concept that is exactly as fine-grained as the experience, by uttering a phrase like 'that shade', in which the demonstrative exploits the presence of the sample" (1994: 56–57). In other words, although we cannot capture the rich detail of experience using concepts such as "red," "yellow," "burnt sienna," etc., we *can* conceptually capture this detail by using demonstrative concepts that pick out the very detail that is supposed to be problematic—we can think about it as *that shade*. Concerns have been expressed with this response. The conceptualist seems to need to argue that the perceiver must have this demonstrative concept in order to be able to have the experience. But isn't that upside down? Doesn't the perceiver have an experience with a certain feature and *thereby* come to be able to

demonstrate that feature? If this is so, then we need to be able to make sense of the idea that the experience can have this feature *prior* to the perceiver's deploying a demonstrative concept.

7. To provide a little more detail for those who are interested, I will briefly outline the approach taken by the representationalist Michael Tye, who combines a teleosemantic approach with a dash of causal covariation. Tye contends that, "experiences represent various features by causally correlating with, or tracking, those features under optimal conditions" (2000: 64). So, in order for mental state M to represent *F*, M must covary with *F*ness under optimal conditions. When are conditions optimal? "In the case of evolved creatures, [optimal] conditions for vision involve the various components of the visual system operating as they were designed to do in the sort of external environment in which they were designed to operate" (Tye 2000: 138). Thus, suppose that an organism evolved in environment E and that, in E, M reliably covaries with *F*. Now suppose that the organism's sensory mechanisms were selected for because they provided it with information about the environment in which it evolved (E). According to Tye's theory, M will therefore represent *F*.

8. Another important consideration, at least for content-first theorists, is that the metaphysical theory of content must tie up in an appropriate way with the chosen psychosemantic theory. This means that content-first theorists are likely to also be singular content theorists as it is difficult to see how a naturalistic theory of content could ascribe contents constituted by modes of presentation. Intentionalists who hold a Fregean theory are therefore far more likely to be phenomenology-first theorists. So, in many ways, the kind of argument considered above—which claimed that singular contents cannot be true to the phenomenology—is also an argument in favor of a phenomenology-first theory.

9. To the extent that the phenomenon of transparency constitutes an objection to qualia theories, it will of course constitute an objection to variants of intentionalism—perhaps weak intentionalism or strong phenomenology-first intentionalism—that posit qualia to account for the phenomenological features of visual experiences. Further concerns with appealing to qualia may include the fact that they have proved difficult to fit into the materialist/physicalist world of science (Levine 1983; Chalmers 1996).

10. Tye actually claims that, when we introspect, we are aware of "aspects of the *content* of the experience" (1992). If an experience represents that the Pacific Ocean is blue, say, we can say that *blueness* is a component of the content of the experience and it is this that we are aware of. Because of this, Tye then officially goes on to *identify* the experience's phenomenal character with its representational content (its PANIC). But we must remember that Tye is here using the term "phenomenal character" in the way we have been using the term "presentational character." As we are using the term, phenomenal characters are properties of *experiences*

and, even though experiences *have* contents, the contents they have are not *properties of* those experiences. Everything that Tye *wants* to say by identifying phenomenal character with PANIC, however, is captured in the presentation here.

Further reading

Mike Martin's "Perceptual Content" (1994) is an excellent introduction to intentionalism in the philosophy of perception. A somewhat more technical overview of the different approaches an intentionalist might take can be found in David Chalmers's 2004 paper "The Representational Character of Experience."

For the transparency motivation, see Gilbert Harman's "The Intrinsic Quality of Experience" (1990). For a defense of the Mirroring Thesis, see Alex Byrne's "Intentionalism Defended" (2001).

For higher order versions of intentionalism, see Bill Lycan, *Consciousness and Experience* (1996) and David Rosenthal, "A Theory of Consciousness" (1990). First-order versions of intentionalism (representationalism) can be found in Dretske's paper "Experience as Representation" (2003) and Michael Tye's books, *Ten Problems of Consciousness* (1995) and *Consciousness, Color and Content* (2000).

Susanna Siegel's entry in *The Stanford Encyclopedia of Philosophy*, "The Contents of Perception" (http://plato.stanford.edu/entries/perception-contents) is an excellent survey of the various issues hereabouts. Specific discussions of whether perceptual contents are internalist or externalist can be found in Gabriel Segal, "Defence of a Reasonable Individualism" (1991), Martin Davies, "Individualism and Perceptual Content" (1991), and Tyler Burge's "Cartesian Error and the Objectivity of Perception" (2007b).

A good introduction to the issues surrounding nonconceptual contents is Tim Crane's 1992 paper, "The Nonconceptual Content of Experience". Richard Heck's (2000) paper, "Nonconceptual Content and the 'Space of Reasons'" pays specific attention to the epistemological role of experiences with nonconceptual contents.

A good place to start thinking about naturalistic theories of content is Barry Loewer's essay "A Guide to Naturalizing Semantics" (1997).

6   Disjunctive theories

Overview

Disjunctive theories of perception reject the Common Factor Principle. They argue instead that indiscriminable experiences can nonetheless be experiences of different kinds. Different versions of disjunctivism are discussed.

The focus of the remainder of the chapter is on disjunctivism about phenomenology and its employment in the defense of a philosophical theory of perception known as naive realism or relationalism. Issues discussed include what theories the disjunctivist can provide of bad case experiences of hallucination and where illusion fits into the picture.

Common Factor Principle   ⊠

Phenomenal Principle   ?

Representational Principle   ?

As the principles above indicate, the distinctive feature of disjunctive theories of perception lie in their rejection of the Common Factor Principle. Disjunctivists claim that the mental states involved in a good case experience of perception and a bad case experience of hallucination *are different*, even in those cases in which the two experiences are indiscriminable for their subject.

Why "disjunctivism"? We can see the answer to this question when we consider the disjunctivist's analysis of the neutral category of visual experiences. Putting illusions to one side for a moment (we will come back to them shortly), the disjunctivist proposes to analyze visual experiences as follows:

A subject S has a visual experience as of a property F if and only if:

- either S perceives an F,
- or S has a hallucination of an F.

To see how this is supposed to work, consider the following example (due to Child 1994: 145). Suppose that there are only two ways of producing a "likeness" of subject S—by either drawing S or photographing S. The resultant objects—the photograph of S and the drawing of S—both qualify as *likenesses of S*. Whilst there is something common to both photographs of S and drawings of S inasmuch as they both qualify as *likenesses of S*, this is not because they have some common property *in virtue of which* they are both likenesses of S. Instead, the right way of understanding the category "likeness of S" is as *disjunctive*: something is a likeness of S if and only if it is *either* a drawing of S *or* a photograph of S. Indeed, we can present an analysis of the category of "likenesses" that parallels the analysis of the category of visual experience as follows:

An object O is a likeness of S if and only if:

- either O is a drawing of S,
- or O is a photograph of S.

For the disjunctivist, the category of visual experiences (of F) is like the category of likenesses (of S): it is fundamentally *disjunctive*.

There is obviously more for the disjunctivist to say about what is involved in both of the two core cases. *What is it* to have a perception of an F? *What is it* to have a hallucination of an F? In principle, these questions could be answered in any way: one could offer, say, an adverbialist account of what it is to have a perception alongside a sense datum account of the hallucinatory case. In practice, however, disjunctivism has typically been used in the service of a *naive realist* or *relationalist* theory of perception. Such a theory would therefore encompass an endorsement of the Phenomenal Principle, at least for cases of perception. This will be discussed below.

Interestingly, unlike every other theory we have considered, the disjunctive nature of the disjunctivist's claim means that there is no need to come up with *extra* conditions by which a visual experience can qualify as a case of perception. Instead, if a disjunctive analysis of visual experience is correct, then a visual experience is a case of perception if and only if it is not hallucinatory.

This way of understanding the neutral category of visual experience enables the disjunctivist to offer an interesting reinterpretation of *seems* statements. Recall that, in the opening chapter, we discussed a motivation for the Common Factor Principle that turned on the fact that, if we did not know whether we were *seeing* or *hallucinating* a pink elephant, we might naturally say that we were having the experience of *seeming to see* a pink elephant. On the face of it, such a statement can appear to commit us to a good case/bad case common factor: something that could occur in *both* a case of perception *and* a case of hallucination.

However, the disjunctivist will follow J.M. Hinton (1967, 1973) and argue that a statement such as, "I seem to see a pink elephant" is just "a more compact way of saying" something like this: "*Either* I see a pink elephant, *or* I am having a hallucination of a pink elephant." Once this translation of the seems statement has been provided, there is no longer any pressure to think that the truth of "I seem to see a pink elephant" commits us to the presence of a good case/bad case common factor.

Instead, where the statement, "*Either* I see a pink elephant, *or* I am having a hallucination of a pink elephant" is concerned, there are *two* different ways in which this disjunctive sentence can be made true—either by its being true that I *actually do* see a pink elephant, or by its being true that I don't see a pink elephant, but that it is for me *as if* I did. As Don Locke puts the point: "'This is a woman, or a man dressed as a woman' does not assert the presence of a woman/transvestite-neutral entity . . . its truth depends simply on the presence of either a woman or a transvestite, as the case may be" (1975: 467).

The core disjunctive claim is therefore that:

> We should understand statements about how things appear to a perceiver to be equivalent to a disjunction that either one is perceiving such and such or one is suffering a . . . hallucination; and that such statements are not to be viewed as introducing a report of a distinctive mental event or state common to these various disjoint situations.
>
> (Martin 2004: 37)

So, disjunctive theories hold that perceptions and hallucinations of a particular kind *do not* have an underlying mental state in common.

The causal objection

This claim—that perceptions and hallucinations are *different* mental states—has been argued to conflict with the causal facts about perception. It seems clear that, in order for perception to take place, the perceived object must causally affect the subject's sense organs and thereby affect the subject's brain.

This can be developed into an argument against disjunctivism as follows:

1 It is possible for intermediate stages of this causal chain to be activated in a nonstandard manner (say, by direct stimulation of the retina, optic nerve or visual cortex).
2 If the intermediate stages of the causal chain were to be activated in a nonstandard manner, this would not alter the latter stages of the causal

chain. So long as the earlier stages were accurately replicated, the latter stages would be the same.

3   If the latter stages of the causal chain were the same, then the same kind of experience would result. But this is just to say that the same kind of experience can be caused in both good cases and bad cases, contra disjunctivism.

There are reasons to be dubious of the soundness of this argument. Consider the following example. There is a "causal chain" for the production of legitimate banknotes, which begins with (I guess) an order from a competent authority and concludes with notes being printed out on a certain kind of machine. Suppose, then, that forgers manage to reproduce the machine that prints legitimate banknotes. In this way, we can say that the forgers "activate the intermediate stages of the causal chain in a nonstandard manner." Even though the latter stages of the causal chain are the same—those involving the functioning of the machine itself—the banknotes the forgers print on it will still be counterfeit. The "same kind of banknote" will not result, even though the immediate "cause" of the forgeries is the same as the immediate "cause" of genuine currency.

For a more philosophical reason to resist the causal argument, consider Hilary Putnam's Twin Earth argument (1975). Putnam asks us to imagine Twin Earth, a planet identical to Earth in every way save for the fact that the stuff which fills the lakes and rivers and falls out of the sky is not H_2O but an indiscriminable yet chemically *distinct* substance called XYZ (which the Twin Earth inhabitants nevertheless call "water"). On Earth, there is a subject called Oscar, and he also has a molecule for molecule replica on Twin Earth (who, despite being called "Oscar" by all who know him, we shall call Twin Oscar).[1]

Putnam's contention is that when Oscar believes that <the glass is full of water>, his belief will be made true if the glass contains H_2O; Twin Oscar's equivalent belief, on the other hand, will be true if the glass contains XYZ. As these beliefs have different truth conditions, they are thereby different *beliefs*. So, despite Oscar and Twin Oscar's physical and functional identity, Putnam suggests that they will have different beliefs.

It seems, therefore, that we can make sense of the possibility of two different mental states having equivalent proximal causes. If so, then the disjunctivist can resist the causal objection and allow that perceptions and hallucinations are distinct mental states, *even in situations where they have the same proximal causes.*

What exactly does the claim that perceptions and hallucinations are distinct mental states amount to? The thing is, *any* theory of perception is going to allow that there is a sense in which perceptions and hallucinations are different mental states—one is perceptual and one is hallucinatory after all. The claim that perception and hallucination do not have a mental state in common must be saying something more than the truistic claim that one is a perception and the other a hallucination. This raises the following question: Just how are perceptions and hallucinations different according to disjunctivism? There are a number of different possible answers to this, each of which yields a distinct form of disjunctivism. These are discussed below.

Epistemological disjunctivism

One possible answer to this question is to say that perceptions and hallucinations differ in their status as *perceptual evidence*. In other words, the epistemological disjunctivist denies that a subject's perceptual evidence is the same across indiscriminable cases of perception and hallucination.

Paul Snowdon draws attention to the possibility of epistemological disjunctivism when he suggests that we might "divide cases where it is true that it appears to the subject as if P into two sorts; one is where the subject is in a position to know that P . . . and others where the subject is in a position to know merely that it appears to be P" (2005: 140).

However, as Snowdon points out, it could be claimed that "a single basic sort of (inner) experience [has] quite different epistemological significance in different cases, depending, say, on the context and on facts about causation" (2005: 140). If so, then epistemological disjunctivism could allow that perceptions and hallucinations *do* have an underlying mental state in common. It would not, therefore, qualify as a type of disjunctivism as we are using the term.

If, however, the epistemological disjunctivist *denies* that perception and hallucination share a single basic inner experience, then the question remains: What is the nature of this difference?

Disjunctivism about metaphysics

Disjunctivism about metaphysics states that two mental states qualify as distinct so long as they have different *constituents*.[2]

This enables the disjunctivist to hold that perceived objects are actually *constituents* of the subject's perceptual experience. "No experience like this, no experience of fundamentally the same kind, could have occurred had no appropriate candidate for awareness existed" (Martin 2004: 39).

One concern about metaphysical disjunctivism is that it can look like it is only terminologically different from theories that *accept* the Common Factor Principle (call them common factor theories). After all, any theory is going to accept that there is a difference between perceptions and hallucinations in that, in the former case, but not the latter, something is *seen*.

Given this, it seems as though metaphysical disjunctivists and common factor theorists could agree on everything except what matters for sameness and difference of mental state. Whereas common factor theorists insist that the indiscriminability of perception and hallucination mean that they are experiences of the same underlying kind, metaphysical disjunctivists insist that the presence or absence of a seen object means that they are experiences of *distinct* kinds. If this were the case then, from the point of view of our interest in theories of perception, metaphysical disjunctivism doesn't look to be of significant interest.[3]

This is not to say, however, that metaphysical disjunctivists *have* to agree with common-factor theorists about everything. The metaphysical disjunctivist may insist that perceptions and hallucinations not only have different constituents but also differ in some *other* crucial way. For example, they may also contend that the two types of experience have different intentional contents or different phenomenal characters. These two possibilities are considered below.

Disjunctivism about content

Disjunctivism about content states that two mental states qualify as distinct so long as they have different *contents*.

If we want to endorse the Representational Principle, then we will accept that visual experiences have *contents*. Yet, suppose we preferred the singular conception of content. As the previous chapter focused on variants of intentionalism that accepted the Common Factor Principle, we quickly concluded that such a position was untenable and hence that perceptual content could not be singular for objects.

However, it is consistent for someone who endorses the Representational Principle to *reject* the Common Factor Principle. This leaves logical space for disjunctive variants of intentionalism, which claim that perception, hallucination, and illusion *differ* in their assignments of content to indiscriminable experiences. This in turn leaves open the possibility of assigning *singular* contents in cases of successful perception.

The question we now need to ask is this: should we *want* to claim that perceptions have singular contents?

Motivations

One argument in favor of this claim is that it enables our theory of perception to adequately accommodate the phenomenon of *particularity*: that our experiences appear to be of unique, individual objects.

This is, at base, an appeal to intuition. Look at the book in front of you. The intuitive appeal to particularity is that your visual experience tells you that it is *that very book* that is in front of you, not merely that *there is a book of a certain kind* in front of you. An appeal to singular contents—contents that are part-constituted by that very object—would be well placed to capture this.

Soteriou (2000) augments this appeal with an argument. He asks us to consider a subject wearing displacing glasses that shift the apparent location of objects rightwards, such that objects to the left of the subject look directly in front, objects directly in front of the subject look off to the right, and so on. Now imagine we have a red ball (A) placed to the subject's *left* such that the action of the displacing glasses makes it look as though there is a red ball *in front* of the subject. As things stand, the content of this experience is false. Yet we can make it true by adding a further, indiscriminable red ball (B), directly in front of the subject. Now there *is* a red ball in front of the subject, just as the experience represents there to be.[4]

Given this, it looks as though the content comes out true. Intuitively, however, there is something wrong with this experience. One way of trying to accommodate this would be to include a self-referential component into the content of the experience, such that the experience not only represents that <there is a red ball in front of me>, but also that <the red ball that appears to be in front of me is actually causing this experience> (Searle 1983). Given that the second, self-referential component of the content is not true—it is B that is in front of me, but A that is causing the experience of a red ball's appearing to be in front of me—this approach would count the experience as nonveridical. However, this approach has been criticized for getting the phenomenology wrong. The attribution of content to a visual experience is supposed to explain how things *seem* to us, and it is just not the case that it seems to us as though there is a causal relation between the object and our experience.

If this approach fails, then in order to account for the fact that the experience of the red ball fails to be a case of perception, Soteriou suggests that we should see the content of this experience as *singular*, not abstract. So, rather than the content of the experience being <there is a red ball in front of me>, which is true, it should be <A is a red ball and in front of me>, which is false as it is actually *B* in front of me. Thus, the thought goes, we should accept that perceptual contents are singular.

As noted in the previous chapter, a concern with this claim is that it entails that experiences of distinct but indiscriminable objects will differ in content. An experience of red ball A will have the content <A is a red ball and is in front of me> whilst an experience of indiscriminable red ball B will represent that <B is a red ball and is in front of me>. If the attribution of content to an experience is indeed intended to capture how things seem to the subject, then this would imply that how things seem to the subject of these two experiences would be different, which conflicts with the assumption that they are indiscriminable.

Soteriou replies that this objection can be overcome so long as we remember that, in this context, "indiscriminable" means *qualitatively* indiscriminable—indiscriminable in terms of qualities or properties. As the experiences will represent both A and B to instantiate exactly the same properties (given their assumed indiscriminability), then we should expect the experiences to seem the same to their subject.

Content disjunctivism and phenomenology

One question that arises here is that, given that the contents of indiscriminable perceptions and hallucinations can be different, how should we explain the fact of their indiscriminability? This is the most significant question facing disjunctive theories of all stripes.

One possibility for disjunctivists about content is to simply *detach* questions about perceptual *contents* from questions about perceptual *phenomenology*. This would enable us to say that perceptions and hallucinations *share* phenomenology despite differing in content. Essentially, this response treats *phenomenology* as a factor common to perception and hallucination, even if it denies that they have a *mental state* in common.[5] One might wonder, given this, whether disjunctivism ought, therefore, to be defined in such a way that such a position is ruled out as being disjunctivist. Alternatively, one might bite the bullet and insist that perception and hallucination could be indiscriminable *despite* not sharing phenomenal character. Such a position would therefore be a version of disjunctivism about phenomenology, to which we shall now turn.

Disjunctivism about phenomenology

Disjunctivism about phenomenology states that two mental states qualify as distinct so long as they have different *phenomenal character*. According to this variant of disjunctivism, perceptions and hallucinations *do not share* phenomenal character.

The return of the causal argument

This claim, however, can seem to fall to a more plausible version of the causal argument. This argument contends not that the same proximal conditions will create the same kind of *experience* but rather that the same proximal conditions will create a mental state with the same *phenomenology*. This is Horgan and Tienson's presentation of this argument:

> Distal environmental causes generate experiential effects only by generating more immediate links in the causal chains between themselves and experience, viz., physical stimulations in the body's sensory receptors ... These states and processes causally generate experiential effects only by generating still more immediate links in the causal chains between themselves and experience—viz., afferent neural impulses, resulting from transduction at the sites of the sensory receptors on the body. Your mental intercourse with the world is mediated by sensory and motor transducers at the periphery of your central nervous system. Your conscious experience would be phenomenally just the same even

if the transducer-external causes and effects of your brain's afferent and efferent neural activity were radically different from what they are.

(Horgan and Tienson 2002: 526–527)

The contention here is that even if there are reasons to think that changes in a subject's environment might affect *aspects* of the nature of a mental state (perhaps because it could make a "seeing of water" experience into a "seeing of twin water" experience), the "conscious [aspects of the] experience would be phenomenally just the same."

If this argument succeeds, then disjunctivism about phenomenology would be false, even if the other versions of disjunctivism could be rescued. Yet the passage just cited doesn't *argue* for the claim that "your conscious experience would be phenomenally just the same even if the . . . external causes and effects . . . were radically different." Rather, it just assumes it. So it would be open for the disjunctivist about phenomenology to simply deny this claim. Having said this, Robinson does claim that "if it were not the case that perceptual processes, however stimulated, were sufficient to generate experience, it would be a mystery why [perception-like] hallucinations should occur" (1994: 152), but the legitimacy of this motivation has been challenged (Fish 2009).

Modesty

Even if the causal argument can be overcome, disjunctivism about phenomenology can still seem strange: perceptions and hallucinations are accepted to be indiscriminable. Doesn't this just entail that they have the same phenomenal character?

Clearly a disjunctivist about phenomenology cannot accept this claim: indiscriminability cannot entail sameness of phenomenal character. However, this does put the onus on this kind of disjunctivist to explain and defend the contention that experiences with different phenomenal character can be indiscriminable.

Mike Martin argues that to simply *assume* that the indiscriminability of two experiences has to be accounted for by their sharing phenomenal character is to attribute to subjects unreasonably immodest epistemic powers. Consider a perception of an F and a perfectly indiscriminable hallucination of such. In virtue of what do both count as visual experiences as of an F? A modest answer to this question is that this is enough: something is a visual experience of an F just in case it is indiscriminable from a perception of an F. If indiscriminability is assumed to be a matter of sameness of phenomenal character, however, then "when I come to recognize the possibility of perfect hallucination just like my current perception, what I do is both recognize the presence of [the phenomenal character] . . . in virtue of which this event is . . . an experience [of an F], and also recognize that an event's possessing these characteristics is independent of whether the event is a perception or not" (Martin 2004: 47).

What about the possibility of "a situation in which [phenomenal character is different or] absent but in which a subject would be unable to discriminate through reflection this situation from one in which [an *F*] was really being seen" (Martin 2004: 49)? The modest conception of what is required for an event to qualify as visual experience would allow us to count such an event as an experience (as) of an *F* simply in virtue of this failure to discriminate. The alternative conception, however, could not count this as a visual experience as a/an *F*. In order to rule out the possibility of such scenarios, the defender of the idea that indiscriminability entails sameness of phenomenal character will have to assume that a careful subject simply cannot fail to recognize the presence and nature of phenomenal character when it is present, or the absence of phenomenal character when it is absent. This approach therefore has to "attribute to responsible subjects potential infallibility about the course of their experiences" (Martin 2004: 51).

This opens up the logical space for two experiences that do not share phenomenal character to be indiscriminable. So, disjunctivism about phenomenology is not ruled out *a priori*. But this doesn't give us a positive reason to endorse the thesis. Why would anybody want to endorse disjunctivism about phenomenology?

Naive realism

Typically, the motivation for endorsing disjunctivism about phenomenology is to defend a philosophical theory of the good cases of *perception* known as *naive realism* or *relationalism*.

According to the naive realist, in the good cases of perception, external objects and their properties "shape the contours of the subject's conscious experience" (Martin 2004: 64). Likewise, John Campbell outlines his relationalist view of perception by suggesting that, on this view, the "phenomenal character of your experience, as you look around the room, is constituted by the actual layout of the room itself: which particular objects are there, their intrinsic properties, such as color and shape, and how they are arranged in relation to one another and to you" (2002: 116).

A useful way of understanding this claim is to see the naive realist as endorsing the Phenomenal Principle, at least for the limited case of perception. Thus the naive realist holds that, whenever we have a case of conscious perception, there is something that the subject is aware of and that bears the properties that characterize what it is like for the subject. Unlike the sense datum theory, however, as naive realists endorse disjunctivism and thereby reject the Common Factor Principle, they are thereby enabled to say that these objects of awareness are actually the mind independent objects that inhabit the world.

Typically, naive realists also *reject* the Representational Principle on the grounds that perceptions do not *r*epresent things, they simply *present* them as being as they are. There is therefore no question of experiences being incorrect, as the Representational Principle would require. As Austin puts it, "our senses are dumb—though Descartes and others speak of the 'testimony of the senses', our senses do not tell us anything, true or false" (1962: 11; see also Travis 2004).

We can capture the naive realist's claim that the external world shapes the contours of the subject's conscious experiences by employing our terminology of presentational character. At a first pass, the suggestion is that the presentational character of a perception is actually *constituted* by the piece of mind independent reality that is being looked at. Such a view of presentational character enables the naive realist to claim that external reality is *literally* experientially present. To the extent that presentational character is constituted by external properties, the naive realist's take on presentational character is actually quite similar to the intentionalist's.

What about the *phenomenal* character of a perception? What does the naive realist have to say about the nature of the property of the *experience* that types it by what it is like to undergo it? Here naive realists depart from representationalists and instead go along with the sense datum theorists! Naive realists hold that the phenomenal character of a perception is its property of *being a sensing of* the elements of the presentational character.[6]

This claim does raise the question of what is involved in a subject's *sensing* or *being acquainted with* external reality. This is a critical part of a naive realist position, but without further explanation it can seem to be almost magical. Probably the most well developed answer to this question is presented by Alva Noë who develops an intriguing theory of perception, according to which "perceptual experience [is] an active form of engagement with the environment" (2001: 50). Noë rejects representationalism, arguing that we are not consciously aware of what the brain represents, and claims instead that we are rather consciously aware of what is *made available* by the various processes going on in the brain and body. How are parts of the world made available? By our having the ability to access the world using what he calls *sensorimotor skills*, where to possess a sensorimotor skill of a certain kind is to have a tacit understanding of how sensory stimuli change as a result of active movement. To use an example of Noë's, we have access to—we *see*—the (whole) cat even though part of it is occluded behind a picket fence because we implicitly know that, were we to move our bodies in *this* particular way, some bits of the cat would come into view whilst others would become occluded by the fence, and so on.[7]

In developing this suggestion, Noë claims that "you visually experience parts of the tomato that, strictly speaking, you do not see, because you understand, implicitly, that your sensory relation to those parts is mediated by familiar patterns of sensorimotor dependence" (2005: 77). Yet the appeal in this passage to the idea that some things *can be* seen "strictly speaking" is in fact a ladder that can be kicked away. To explain: Noë insists that we can still visually experience the back of a tomato even if we don't see it "strictly speaking," and our ability to experience the back of the tomato is claimed to rest upon our possession and exploitation of sensorimotor knowledge. Whilst this discussion makes its point by playing with the idea that we *do* see the front of the tomato "strictly speaking," in fact this is not the case. This is the key point: *nothing* is ever given to consciousness in its totality, so *nothing* is ever seen "strictly speaking"; instead, *everything* that we see is seen in virtue of our possessing and employing sensorimotor skills. As Noë insists that it is worldly objects and properties (including aspects and appearances) that are seen, then if this reading is correct, he can usefully be seen as endorsing naive realism, broadly speaking, together with a detailed, action-based theory of what it is to stand in the acquaintance relation to external reality.[8]

Now we see the crux of naive realism about perception, we can see why naive realists have to endorse disjunctivism about phenomenology: on this view of phenomenal character, it is clear that a hallucination *could not* share phenomenal character with a perception, even in cases in which the two experiences are indiscriminable for their subject. What can the naive realist who is disjunctivist about phenomenology say about the phenomenal character of indiscriminable *hallucinations*?

Disjunctive theories of hallucination

Positive disjunctivism

The positive disjunctivist insists that there is a positive story to tell about the phenomenal character of the hallucinatory state. For example, one might claim that hallucination involves the awareness of nonphysical objects—sense data—that are indiscriminable from physical objects. Such a claim is suggested by Austin's observation, mentioned in Chapter 2, that "generically different" objects such as lemons and bars of soap can, nevertheless, look exactly the same (1962: 50).[9]

A more sophisticated version of positive disjunctivism is presented by Mark Johnston (2004).[10] Johnston contends that, when we have a successful case of perception, we are aware of an instantiated *sensible profile*: "a complex, partly qualitative and partly relational property, which exhausts the *way* the particular scene before your eyes is" (2004: 134). Importantly, the sensible profile that we are aware of, says Johnston, is a *type* not a token; had we stood before an array of different particulars instantiating the same sensible profile, what we are aware of—the sensible profile—would have been the same. Then, when you have a hallucination that is indiscriminable from this experience, "you are simply aware of the partly qualitative, partly relational profile. [...] When the visual system misfires, as in hallucination, it presents uninstantiated complexes of sensible qualities and relations" (2004: 135).

On Johnston's view, there are, then, clear similarities between good cases and bad cases—in particular, in both cases the subject is aware of the same sensible profile. Yet there are important differences too. "When we see," says Johnston, "we are aware of *instantiations of* sensible profiles" (2004: 135; emphasis added). "When we hallucinate, on the other hand, we are *only* aware of the *structured qualitative parts* of such sensible profiles. Any case of hallucination is thus a case of 'direct' visual awareness of *less than* one would be 'directly' aware of in the case of seeing" (Johnston 2004: 137). The objects of hallucination are instead "proper parts" of the objects of seeing (Johnston 2004: 140).

The difficulty faced by positive views is that they flirt with what is known as the *screening-off problem* (Martin 2004). The screening off problem begins from the plausible claim that all that is needed for a hallucination to take place is the right kind of activity in the subject's brain.

To see the worry, take a simple, Austin-inspired sense datum theory of hallucination first. It seems reasonable to suppose that a certain pattern of neural activity must suffice for a subject to be aware of sense data in the bad case of hallucination. If this is so, what about the neural activity that occurs in the good case of perception? If this also suffices for the subject to be aware of sense data, and if—as is suggested—this awareness explains why the subject takes him or herself to be perceiving a real-world object, then this awareness of sense data would seem to "screen off" the supposed object-involving phenomenal character of the perception itself from explaining why the subject's experience is as it is.

If, however, it is claimed that the neural activity does *not* suffice for awareness of sense data in the good case of perception, then we might wonder why:

> if the mechanism or brain state is a sufficient causal condition for the production of an image, or otherwise characterised subjective sense-content, when the [objects] are not there, why is it not so sufficient when they are present? Does the brain state mysteriously know how it is being produced . . . or does the [object], when present, inhibit the production of an image by some sort of action at a distance?
>
> (Robinson 1994: 153–154)

It is less clear how Johnston's view fares here. At one point, he asks:

> Why isn't awareness of a sensible profile a common act of awareness as between seeing and hallucination? It may be held to be . . . But it does seem that once we adopt the act/object treatment of visual experience it is more natural to individuate an act of awareness occurring at a time in terms of an object that includes all that one is aware of in the relevant time.
>
> (Johnston 2004: 171)

As the perceiver is aware of more than the hallucinator (in that the perceiver is aware of the particulars that instantiate the sensible profile whilst the hallucinator is aware of the sensible profile alone), Johnston's suggestion seems to be that when we account for the perceiver's awareness of the particulars we thereby account for the perceiver's awareness of the sensible profile. There is then no *need* to introduce an additional awareness of an (uninstantiated) sensible profile.

It is not clear that this suffices to ward off the screening off problem. After all, if neural activity does suffice for awareness of an uninstantiated sensible profile in the bad cases, it should suffice in the good cases too. And this is the case whether or not we *need* to appeal to this to explain the fact that the subject is aware of a sensible profile at all. So Johnston's view may also be threatened by the screening off worry.

Negative disjunctivism

Given that a positive account of hallucination faces the screening off problem, some disjunctivists offer a *negative* account of hallucination instead. At the end of the previous section, we asked what account can the disjunctivist give of the phenomenal character of hallucination. The negative disjunctivist says that all we can say about indiscriminable hallucinations is that they are not veridical perceptions but are indiscriminable from them. In other words, the phenomenal character of a *hallucination*—the property of the hallucination that types it by what it is like to undergo it—is its property of *being indiscriminable from a veridical perception of a certain kind.*

If hallucinations are not indiscriminable from perceptions in virtue of having some property that renders them indiscriminable, how should we understand indiscriminability in this context?

This is a critical question for negative disjunctivists. Martin suggests that a hallucination of an *F* "is such that it is not possible to know through reflection that it is not one of the . . . perceptions [of an *F*]" (2006: 364). We can therefore define indiscriminability as follows:

> *x* is indiscriminable from a perception of an *F* if and only if *x* is such that it is not possible to know through reflection that it is not a perception of an *F*.

An important feature of this notion of indiscriminability is that it enables the negative disjunctivist to avoid the screening off problem. The key feature of the picture that enables this turns on the claim that indiscriminability properties have "inherited or dependent explanatory potential" and that such cases therefore "offer us exceptions to the general model of common properties screening off special ones" (Martin 2004: 70).

To explain the notion of a property having "inherited or dependent explanatory potential," consider the property of being an unattended bag in an airport, which causes a security alert. Sometimes objects with this property are harmless, but sometimes they contain a bomb. Now ask: does the property common to harmless and nonharmless objects—that of being an unattended bag in an airport—explain why there is a security alert in such a way that the special property of being a bomb in an airport is screened off from being explanatory? Not at all. Instead, the only reason the *common* property of being an unattended bag in an airport has the explanatory role it does is because, sometimes, this property is correlated with the *special* property of being a bomb in an airport. In such a case, we can say that the explanatory potential of the common property of being an unattended bag in an airport is "inherited from" or "dependent upon" the explanatory potential of the special property of being a bomb in an airport.

The negative disjunctivist exploits this by arguing that the key property of being indiscriminable from a perception of a certain kind—a property common to both perceptions and their indiscriminable hallucinations—has just this kind of inherited or dependent explanatory potential.

> Why did James shriek like that? He was in a situation indiscriminable from the veridical perception of a spider. Given James's fear of spiders, when confronted with one he is liable so to react; and with no detectable difference between this situation and such a perception, it must seem to him as if a spider is there, so he reacts in the same way.
>
> (Martin 2004: 68)

In order to explain why James shrieks when he hallucinates a spider, we not only have to say that his experience has the property of being indiscriminable from a perception of a spider but *also* that a perception of a spider constitutes, for James, a reason for shrieking. So the property of *being a veridical perception of a spider* is, like the property of being a bomb in an airport, a special property that is needed to explain why the *common* property has the explanatory potential it does. Whatever explanatory potential an indiscriminability property has in explaining why James behaves as he does is *inherited from* the explanatory potential of the associated case of real perception.

Martin therefore suggests that the screening off worry can be avoided by characterizing the hallucinatory state purely *negatively*. The disjunctivist should say that "when it comes to a mental characterization of the hallucinatory experience, nothing more can be said than the relational and epistemological claim that it is indiscriminable from the perception" (Martin 2004: 72).

Difficulties for negative disjunctivism

Given the negative disjunctivist's characterization of the hallucinatory state as a state that is simply indiscriminable from a perception of a certain kind, a lot hangs on the way in which the key notion of indiscriminability is understood. As we have seen, Martin claims that an experience will be indiscriminable from a perception of an *F* so long as it is "not possible to know through reflection" that it is not a perception of an *F*. Elements of this analysis of indiscriminability have been the source of objections. Both the restriction to the relevant knowledge being acquired "through reflection" and Martin's interpretation of the modality present in "not possible to know" have been challenged.

To take the "through reflection" clause first, one way of coming to know that your experience is not a perception of an *F* is by *testimony*. If I tell you that I slipped a drug in your coffee, you may on these grounds come to realize that your experience of pink elephants is nonveridical. In this way, we can see that it is possible for you to know that your experience is not a perception of pink elephants.

Even though you can know that your experience is not a perception of pink elephants *in this way*, we do not want this to preclude your experience's being indiscriminable from a perception of pink elephants. This is why Martin includes the "through reflection" clause in the definition of indiscriminability: in order to *rule out* the possibility of knowledge gained from testimony being relevant to the question of whether or not two experiences are indiscriminable.

Sturgeon, however, argues that this proposal cannot be made to work (2006). On the one hand, the "through reflection" restriction must be strong enough to rule out any of the routes by which hallucinating subjects might "figure out" that they are hallucinating. He suggests that it must therefore be taken to stipulate that the "information involved in background beliefs cannot be generally available to reflection . . . Otherwise the possibility of everyday knowledge of [hallucination] will slip through the net [and] count as knowledge obtainable by reflection" (Sturgeon 2006: 209).

On the other hand, when one hallucinates an *F*, one is thereby in a position to know a vast array of things. As a hallucination of an *F* is *discriminable* from perceptions of *G*s, *H*s, and *J*s, Martin's definition will require that, for each case, a subject hallucinating an *F* can know, by reflection alone, that his experience is not one of these cases of perception. Sturgeon suggests that this "is a huge amount of knowledge to be got solely by reflection . . . and *not* by reflection on the visual character of [the hallucination], recall . . . The only way that could be true, I submit, is if background beliefs were generally available to reflection on context" (2006: 210).

Sturgeon therefore presents Martin with a dilemma. On the one hand, to rule out the possibility we might simply use our background beliefs to figure out that we are hallucinating, the "through reflection" clause must restrict us from making use of background beliefs. On the other, to make sense of all the reflective knowledge Martin's theory allows that we are in a position to acquire when we hallucinate, the "through reflection" clause must *allow* us to make use of background beliefs. This, suggests Sturgeon, is just to say that Martin cannot give an adequate account of the "through reflection" restriction.

Another source of objections has stemmed from Martin's interpretation of the "not possibly knowable" condition. This condition is in the picture to enable the negative disjunctivist to acknowledge that creatures that lack the sophistication to *know* things might nonetheless have hallucinations. This is a *prima facie* problem because, if a creature cannot know things *at all*, then for any hallucination it might have, the creature will not know that it is not perceiving an *F*, or a *G*, or an *H*, and so on. As it stands, Martin's definition of indiscriminability threatens to count any creature hallucination as indiscriminable from each and every kind of creature perception.

To avoid this, Martin states that whilst a creature "might fail to discriminate one experience from another, making no judgment about them as identical or distinct at all, that is not to say that *we* cannot judge, in ascribing to them such experience, that there is an event which would or would not be judgeably different from another experience" (2004: 54; emphasis added).

In other words, Martin suggests that, when we talk about what it is or isn't "possible to know," we are not talking about what *the subject*—with the subject's idiosyncratic capacities—is or is not in a position to know. Rather, we are talking in an *impersonal* way. When we say that a hallucination is not possibly known to be distinct from a perception of a certain kind, we do not mean not possibly known *by the subject* but rather, not possibly known *in some impersonal sense*.

Siegel argues that this approach renders us unable to pick out the hallucinatory "experience"—the state or event that is reflected upon—in an appropriate yet nonquestion-begging manner (2008: 212). Given Martin's view, the hallucinatory experience cannot be identified by its having a certain robust property. This would conflict with Martin's insistence that nothing more can be said of the hallucination than that it is indiscriminable from the perception. Yet we cannot pick out the relevant state in virtue of its indiscriminability property either, because we are trying to explain what it is for a state of the creature's to have the indiscriminability property in the first place. This means that we cannot identify the experience we are talking about by appeal to its being the one that has the indiscriminability property.

I present an alternative version of negative disjunctivism in Fish (2009), where I depart from Martin on both of these issues. Where Martin endorses an impersonal sense of indiscriminability, I endorse a personal sense; where Martin rules out testimony, I rule it in. I argue that indiscriminability requires sameness of cognitive effects, where both behavior and (in conceptually sophisticated creatures) introspective beliefs qualify as species of cognitive effect. Where animals are concerned, a hallucination can therefore qualify as indiscriminable from a perception of a certain kind so long as it yields the kinds of behavior that a perception of that kind would have yielded. When it comes to known hallucinations, I ask what would be the effects of a perception in subjects who believed, through testimony, that they are hallucinating. I suggest that, in such a case, both the hallucination and the perception would yield the same kinds of belief. I therefore contend that in such a case the hallucination would have the same cognitive effects as a perception would have had, and thereby qualifies as indiscriminable from that perception. Siegel (2008) also raises objections to these claims.

Disjunctivism and illusion

We have seen two disjunctive approaches to hallucination: *positive disjunctivism*, which claims that a positive account can be given of hallucination, and *negative disjunctivism*, which claims that all that can be said of hallucination is that it is indiscriminable from a perception of a certain kind.

A further question for the disjunctivist is this. If perceptions and hallucinations are experiences of different kinds, what should we say about cases of illusion? These are similar to perceptions inasmuch as something is seen but similar to hallucinations inasmuch as we get things wrong. The two obvious possibilities are to place illusion into one of the two disjuncts that we already have: to treat illusions as either like hallucinations or like perceptions.

V vs. IH disjunctivism

The terminology of V vs. IH disjunctivism is taken from Byrne and Logue (2008). It indicates that illusion (I) is being treated along with hallucination (H) and against veridical perception (V).

McDowell seems to endorse this approach when he claims that "an appearance that such-and-such is the case can be *either* a mere appearance *or* the fact that such-and-such is the case making itself perceptually manifest to someone" (1998: 386–387). As McDowell's veridical disjunct contains cases in which a "fact" is made manifest then, as there is no such thing as a nonobtaining fact, any scenario in which it *appears* to the subject that such-and-such is the case when it is *not* could not be a case of a fact being made manifest. So illusions look to fall into the category of cases in which it merely *appears* as though a fact is made manifest along with hallucinations.

However, there are concerns with the attempt to treat illusions as hallucinations. Robinson protests that, "if all non-veridical perceptions were treated in the same way as hallucinations, then every case of something not looking exactly as it is would be a case in which one was aware of some kind of subjective content. Only perfectly veridical perceptions would be free of such subjective contents" (1994: 159). This leads A.D. Smith to ridicule the view: the "picture of our daily commerce with the world through perception that therefore emerges is one of a usually indirect awareness of physical objects occasionally interrupted by direct visions of them glimpsed in favoured positions" (2002: 28).

VI vs. H disjunctivism

Perhaps we would do better to bring illusion under the veridical, rather than the hallucinatory, disjunct. This gives us VI vs. H disjunctivism.

If illusion is treated as a special case of veridical perception, then the specific way in which illusion is treated will be dictated by the particular theory offered of the veridical cases. As one of the most significant motivations for disjunctivism is to make room for a naive realist account of the good cases, as we have seen, then this approach faces a problem. Illusions are cases in which objects look to be a way that they are not. As things stand, then, this approach to illusion would not be available to a disjunctivist who also wanted to be a naive realist about the good cases.

Having said this, one possibility is to insist that illusion is not, strictly speaking, a feature of experience but rather a feature of our cognitive *response* to our experiences (Brewer 2006; Fish 2009). On this view, as far as their *experiential* nature goes, illusions are perfectly veridical (hence VI vs. H disjunctivism). As Brewer puts it:

> The intuitive idea is that, in perceptual experience, a person is simply presented with the actual constituents of the physical world themselves. Any errors in her world view which result are the product of the subject's responses to this experience, however automatic, natural, or understandable in retrospect these responses may be. Error, strictly speaking, given how the world actually is, is never an essential feature of experience itself.
>
> (2006: 169)

Consider once again the Müller-Lyer illusion (see Figure 6.1). In this illusion, two lines, which are actually the same length, are given arrowheads, which mislead the subject into thinking that they differ in length.

All of the other theories we have considered attempt to accommodate this error within the visual experience itself. Thus, sense datum theorists would claim that, when subject to the illusion, we are aware of different length sense data; adverbialists that we sense different-length-ly, and intentionalists that our experience *represents* the presence of two different length lines.[11]

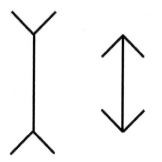

Figure 6.1

Brewer's alternative holds, in accord with naive realism, that the phenomenal character of our experience is in fact part-constituted by two *same length* lines but that, because of the arrowheads, we *take ourselves* to be confronted with two different length lines. Thus, the illusion is not a feature of experience, but a feature of the way we (cognitively) *take* that experience.

Two problems with this approach stand out. First, it is not obvious how to account for the fact that this illusion is *persistent*—that the lines continue to *appear* different lengths even though we *know* that the lines are the same length and hence do not *take* them to be different. Second, this approach seems unlikely to be applicable to all cases of illusion. Consider, in particular, familiar illusions of color, such as the observation that the colors of objects look different in different lighting conditions. A simple extension of this approach would be that the phenomenal character of our experience is part-constituted by the *same* color in all of these cases, it is just that we *take* this color differently. This seems phenomenologically implausible.[12]

Disjunctivism and the two hats

In this section, I will focus on discussing the successes and failings of disjunctivism about phenomenology employed in the service of defending naive realism about perception.

The phenomenological hat

Probably the most significant motivation for endorsing naive realism about perception is the thought that it is the best way of doing justice to the phenomenology of those experiences.[13] Yet naive realism does face some phenomenological objections.

For instance, consider the first pass claim that, on a naive realist view of perception, the presentational character of a perception is constituted by the scene that the subject is looking at. As it stands, this claim seems to be refuted by various considerations, including the everyday phenomenon of blurry vision. Two subjects standing in roughly the same place looking at the same scene could have experiences that are remarkably *different* in phenomenal character if one has normal vision whilst the other is short-sighted.

In addition to this concern is the thought that the same scene can be seen in different *ways* and that naive realism doesn't have the resources to account for this. One way in which this concern plays out is the thought, mentioned above in connection with illusion, that the same surface color can look different—can be seen in different *ways*—in different circumstances. In addition to this is the finding that different perceivers, all of whom qualify as "normal," will differ over precisely which surfaces are perceived as being a certain color. For example, perceiver A might claim that a surface that reflects light of 500 nanometers is unique green—green with no blue and no yellow component—whereas a surface that reflects light of 495 nanometers is a slightly blueish green. On the other hand, perceiver B, in the same observation conditions, might see the second (495 nanometers reflecting) surface as unique green and the first (500 nanometers reflecting) surface as a yellowish green! Again, this suggests that one and the same surface can be seen in different ways, a phenomenon that naive realists will need to account for.

A final point to make in connection with the naive realist's account of phenomenology concerns the time lag objection, discussed in Chapter 2. In this context, the time lag argument picks up on the naive realist's claim that the phenomenal character of one's perception is a matter of one's standing in a relation of acquaintance to external objects. As was highlighted by the time lag argument, however, we can have experiences of objects that no longer exist, as in the case of extinct stars, or experiences of the way objects *were* rather than the way objects *are*, as in the case of our experience of things happening on the surface of the sun. Both of these phenomena are explained by the finite speed of light and the vast distances separating us from the stars and sun.

One way for the naive realist to reply to this objection would be to deny that such experiences can be cases of perception proper, but this would seem desperate. An alternative response has therefore been to challenge the assumption that the objects that we are aware of have to coexist with the act of awareness. As Pitcher argues, time lag considerations

> [do] not entail that we do not directly see things and states of affairs in the "external world," but only that we must see them *as they were some time ago*. We see real physical things, properties, and events, all right, but we see them late, that is all. According to a [naive] realist, it is a mere prejudice of common sense—and one on which the time lag argument trades—that the events, and the states of objects, that we see must be simultaneous with our (act of) seeing them.
>
> (1971: 48)

Whether this response is adequate or not is open to further discussion.

The epistemological hat

Supposed epistemological advantages have also been cited as a significant motivation for disjunctivism. Consider a skeptical argument that runs as follows. When we hallucinate, the kind of experience we have clearly fails to put us in a position to know anything about the external world. The experience we have in the case of a perception indiscriminable from this hallucination is an experience of the same kind. As the bad case experience fails to put us in a position to acquire knowledge, having the same kind of experience in the good case cannot place us in a better epistemological position. According to this argument, then, even when we perceive, we are not in a position to know anything about the external world. (This objection develops the consideration touched on in the previous chapter, that if we could have a certain kind of visual experience when *p* was false, then having that visual experience could never justify us in believing that *p*.)

Disjunctivism offers to block this argument by denying the premise that the experience we have when we perceive is the same as the experience we have when we hallucinate. This would not, of course, prove that we *do* know anything about the external world, merely that such knowledge is not impossible. Yet it *would* block the skeptic from using the impossibility of knowledge as a premise in an argument for the conclusion that we do *not* know anything.

In response, the disjunctivist's opponent may point out that, given the acknowledged indiscriminability of perception and hallucination, we cannot know, on any given occasion, whether we are hallucinating or perceiving. For example, Wright (2002) has argued that, even if it is true that *seeing* O entails that O exists, if we don't have any reason to believe that we are seeing O rather than hallucinating O, we are not justified in believing that O exists. And as, of course, disjunctivists accept that hallucinations can be indiscriminable from perceptions, we could never have adequate reason to believe that we are seeing, rather than hallucinating, O. So we are never justified in believing that O exists. It is not after all clear that disjunctivism does provide any epistemological advantages.

The disjunctivist might reply that this misses the point. It is not that disjunctivism offers an argument to prove that we do have knowledge; rather, it offers a rebuttal to an argument that we cannot. To illustrate this, consider the familiar skeptical claim that all of our experiences might have been just as they are even if we were in the clutches of Descartes' demon. If the disjunctivist is correct, this is not actually possible. If any of my experiences are in fact perceptions, then, to be as they are, they have to be veridical. It is therefore not possible that they could have been as they are *and* misleading. Suppose, then, that the skeptic were to reformulate the skeptical hypothesis as follows: all of your experiences might have been of the misleading kind. Now we can ask, so what? As long as they are not misleading, then many of our empirical beliefs will be justified. As McDowell puts it, this leaves the door open for us to hold that "our knowledge that [the skeptical] possibilities do not obtain is sustained by the fact that we know a great deal about our environment" (2008: 379).

Questions

- Can the disjunctivist make plausible the claim that experiences can be indiscriminable despite not sharing phenomenal character?
- A premise of the restricted causal argument that the disjunctivist about phenomenology needs to reject is the claim that neural

replication would lead to replication of phenomenology. How might we go about determining whether or not this premise is true?

- How do cases of inherited or dependent explanatory potential aim to avoid the screening off problem?

Notes

1. Glossing over the fact, of course, that where Oscar's body is largely composed of H_2O, Twin Oscar's is largely composed of XYZ.
2. An alternative presentation of metaphysical disjunctivism might focus not on the *constituents* of the experiences but rather on their *supervenience bases*. So, whilst perceptions supervene on what is going on in the subject's brain and body *together with* elements of the environment, hallucinations supervene on what is going on in the subject's brain (and perhaps body) alone. This difference in supervenience bases yields a difference in kind of experience.
3. Of course, there could still be arguments between common factor theorists and metaphysical disjunctivists, thus understood. Perhaps, for example, there could be an argument over which principle of individuation makes best sense of the epistemological role of perception.
4. Should the addition of ball B have the consequence that the subject's experience now represents, falsely, that there is a ball off to the right, then a further ball (C) can be added to make this component of the content true as well. This can be iterated.
5. On the flip side, a defender of this approach wanting to *eschew* the disjunctivist label might argue that the mental states involved in perception and hallucination *are* the same in kind *despite* these differences in content (Burge 1991; Soteriou 2000). The defender of such an approach would therefore need to hold that such differences in content do not entail differences in experiential kind.
6. Naive realism is not always presented as involving the claim that subjects "sense" external objects. Other names for the key relationship are used, such as "acquaintance," "taking in," and "awareness or receptivity." These differences in terminology do not affect the substance of the proposal.
7. In the context of this chapter, it is also worth making clear that, because of this, Noë, like McDowell, takes conscious visual experiences to require its subject to possess certain cognitive capacities.
8. Noë's claim that certain parts of a tomato *cannot* be seen "strictly speaking" can make it look as though his theory has two stages: one that explains what seeing "strictly speaking" amounts to and a second that explains how seeing "in the full sense" is built on this basis. If this

were the right reading of Noë's project, then one might see the appeal to sensorimotor contingencies as relating to the second stage of the project, whilst the kind of traditional theories of perception we have been considering can be held up as responses to the first stage. On this way of looking at things, Noë's theory would not actually be in competition with the more traditional theories; instead it would be a supplement to them—a supplement that explains how, from the platform of such a theory, we can rightly be said to be aware of whole objects. Yet, because of claims such as "perceptual content is *virtual all the way in*" (Noë 2005: 193) I think that the reading given in the main text is the right reading.

9. Thau (2004: 195) suggests that this is the form of disjunctivism advocated by John McDowell. In presenting his disjunctive position, McDowell suggests that "an appearance that such-and-such is the case can be *either* a mere appearance *or* the fact that such-and-such is the case making itself perceptually manifest to someone" (1998: 472). Immediately following this presentation, McDowell goes on to say that "mere appearances" are the *objects* of deceptive experiences. So McDowell's complete picture looks to be one on which we have one kind of experiential relation to two different kinds of objects: "facts made manifest" in the perceptual case, and "mere appearances" in the hallucinatory ones.

10. Having said this, it is unclear whether or not Johnston's view really qualifies as a variant of disjunctivism for reasons that we will discuss below.

11. Brewer (2006) also contains a number of objections to the intentionalist account of this illusion.

12. Responses to these objections can be found in Brewer (2008) and Fish (2009).

13. Note that I am not claiming that this is a *good* motivation—see Hawthorne and Kovakovich (2006) for reasons to think it may not be—simply that it *is* a motivation.

Further reading

Many of the papers mentioned here can be found in:

- Haddock, A. and F. Macpherson (eds.) (2008) *Disjunctivism: Perception, Action, Knowledge* (Oxford: Oxford University Press) and in
- Byrne, A. and H. Logue (eds.) (2009) *Disjunctivism: Contemporary Readings* (Cambridge, Mass.: MIT Press).

Together these two texts contain almost all you could need to really get to understand disjunctivism and the various issues surrounding it.

For a good critical introduction to disjunctivism, see A. Byrne and H. Logue (2008) "Either/Or" in Haddock and Macpherson (2008) and their introduction to Byrne and Logue (2009).

Although a number of the elements of disjunctivism can be found in J.L. Austin's classic text, *Sense and Sensibilia*, the origin of disjunctivism in its contemporary form is the work of J.M. Hinton. See both his 1967 paper, "Visual Experiences" and his 1973 book, *Experiences*. The paper and extracts from the book can both be found in Byrne and Logue (2009).

On the pro-disjunctivism side, any student of disjunctivism should be familiar with Mike Martin's corpus. See particularly his "The Reality of Appearances" (1997) and "The Limits of Self-Awareness" (2004), both of which are reprinted in Byrne and Logue (2009), and his "The Transparency of Experience" (2002) and "On Being Alienated" (2006).

In addition, Mark Johnston's theory is presented in his "The Obscure Object of Hallucination," which is also reprinted in Byrne and Logue (2009); Alva Noë's theory is presented in his 2005 book *Action in Perception*; and William Fish's theory is developed in his *Perception, Hallucination, and Illusion* (2009).

Good general anti-disjunctivist material can be found in H. Robinson (1994) *Perception* and A.D. Smith (2002) *The Problem of Perception*.

For arguments for and against an epistemological advantage to disjunctivism, see John McDowell, "The Disjunctive Conception of Experience as Material for a Transcendental Argument" in Haddock and Macpherson (2008) (for) and Crispin Wright, "(Anti-) Skeptics Simple and Subtle: G.E. Moore and John McDowell" (against).

7   Perception and causation

Overview

This chapter focuses on the role of causal considerations in the philosophy of perception. The first half of the chapter considers different attempts to use a broadly causal criterion to distinguish the cases of visual experience that qualify as cases of seeing from those that do not. The second half of the chapter then looks in detail at the different components of the causal theory of perception: the claim that perception involves causation, the claim that the Common Factor Principle is true, and the claim that these two claims are conceptual truths.

In our discussions of the different philosophical theories of perception, we have presented a number of different *analyses* of the neutral category of *visual experience*.

Disjunctivism aside, each theory provided an analysis of what is involved in a subject having a *visual experience* of an *F*, where having a visual experience was *neutral* as to whether the experience was veridical, illusory or hallucinatory. For the subject to actually *see* an *F*, we noted that other conditions need to be met. What are these other conditions?

To enable us to discuss this in a way that is neutral as to which of the various theories of perception are correct, we can present the issue in the following way. (This is an analysis of object perception; a comparable analysis of property perception is a little more complex.)

A subject *S* sees object *O* if and only if:

- *S* has a visual experience as of *O*; and
- some other conditions are met.

The question then is, what is the nature of these "other conditions"? One suggestion is that *S*'s visual experience as of *O* needs to be satisfied.

To set the scene for this discussion, consider the discussion, within epistemology, about what distinguishes *mere belief* from *knowledge proper*.

A component of an influential response to this question has been that at least part of what distinguishes knowledge from mere belief is that, to know something, your belief has to be *true*.[1]

The claim that a visual experience constitutes a case of seeing if that experience is *satisfied* should be understood analogously. The analogy is strongest in the case of intentionalism: as with belief, a perceptual state will be satisfied if its content is *true*. Other theories will understand "satisfaction" differently. For example, the sense datum theory will take a visual experience to be satisfied if the external object or scene "matches" the subject's experience, where "matching" is a matter of resemblance between sense data and scene.

An initial worry with the appeal to satisfaction concerns precisely what is required for an experience to be satisfied. For instance, consider a visual experience as of a distant airplane. According to the intentionalist theory, this experience *represents* that there is a speck in the sky. But suppose there is an airplane off in the distance: is this content true? After all, an airplane is not a speck. The same problem arises for the sense datum theory. On this view, suppose my having that visual experience involves my sensing a speck-like sense datum. Does this *match* or *resemble* the world? The same concerns arise. So there is work to do to give an account of what kinds of relationships between experience and object or scene qualify as "matching."

Nevertheless, suppose this difficulty can be overcome. We can therefore supplement our analysis of *seeing* as follows.

Subject *S* sees *O* if and only if:

- *S* has a visual experience, *E*, as of *O*; and
- *E* is satisfied.

However, this analysis will not yet work. An appeal to satisfaction *alone* will not distinguish between those visual experiences that qualify as veridical and those that do not.

To see why, consider Grice's example of the clock on the shelf. In this example, a subject has a visual experience *as of* a clock on a shelf, so the first condition of our analysis of seeing is met. What is more, there *is* a suitable clock on a suitable shelf in front of the subject, so the second condition is met. As both conditions are met, our current analysis would count this as a case in which *S sees* the clock on the shelf. However, Grice argues that:

> it is logically conceivable that there should be some method by which an expert could make it look to X as if there were a clock on the shelf on occasions where the shelf was empty: there might be some apparatus by which X's cortex could be suitably stimulated, or some technique analogous to post-hypnotic suggestion. If such treatment were applied to X on an occasion when there actually was a clock on the shelf, and if X's impressions were found to continue unchanged when the clock was

removed or its position altered, then I think we should be inclined to say that X did not see the clock that was before his eyes.

(Grice 1961: 142)

In this way, straightforward satisfaction theories run into the problem of what Kim calls "fortuitous satisfaction," and he claims that "fortuitous satisfaction is the chief pitfall of all satisfaction theories" (1977: 611).[2]

Grice goes on to say that, "I think we should be inclined to say that X did not see the clock that was before his eyes just because we should regard the clock as playing no part in the origination of his impression" (Grice 1961: 142). In other words, Grice suggests that, for S to *see* the clock, the clock must be the *cause* of S's experience, E. Yet causation alone will also not provide a sufficient condition for seeing to take place. For one thing, there is the problem of picking out which component of the long causal chain is the component which is seen. An experience is causally dependent on numerous states of affairs—from states of our brains and eyes down to states of the electricity plant that generates the electricity that lights up the room—none of which are seen. For another, there is an issue with nonstandard experiences. For example, we might think that my hallucination was caused by my brain, but we do not want to say that, in having a hallucination, I *see* my brain.

Instead, a causal condition is usually *added* to the satisfaction condition, to get the following:

Subject S *sees* object O if and only if:

- S has a visual experience, E, as of O; and
- E is satisfied; and
- E was caused by O.

This analysis has also been criticized. Consider the following counter-examples (Lewis 1980):

The Brain before the Eyes: I hallucinate at random (thus the experience is caused by my brain) and seem to see a brain before my eyes which perfectly matches (purely accidentally) my own brain. However, my brain *is* before my eyes—it has been removed from my skull and all nerves (etc.) have been stretched somehow. In this case, the first condition of the analysis is met: I have a visual experience as of a brain before my eyes. So is the second condition: this experience is satisfied as there *is* a brain before my eyes. And so is the final condition: my having this experience was *caused by* the brain before my eyes. As all three conditions are met, our analysis would count this as a case in which I *see* the brain before my eyes. That doesn't seem right.

The Light Meter: I am blind, but electrodes have been implanted in my brain in such a way that when a light meter mounted on my head receives light over a certain threshold level, they will cause me to have an experience of a certain sort of landscape. By chance, just such a landscape is before my eyes, and its illumination is enough to turn on the electrodes. Once again, the first condition of the analysis is met: I have a visual experience as of a certain kind of landscape. So is the second condition: this experience is satisfied as there *is* just such a landscape in front of me. And so is the final condition: my having this experience was *caused by* the landscape. As all three conditions are met, our analysis would count this as a case in which I *see* the landscape. Again, that doesn't seem quite right.

As our analysis wrongly counts these situations as cases in which something is seen, this suggests that we need to augment our conditions to rule out such cases as counting as cases of seeing.[3]

Grice suggests that maybe what we need to do is to restrict the modes of causal mediation to the standard ones. Even if we can't spell out what they are (yet), we can nevertheless leave "a blank space to be filled in by the specialist" (1961).

With this modification made, our analysis of seeing would hold that subject *S sees* object *O* if and only if:

- *S* has a visual experience, *E*, as of *O*; and
- *E* is satisfied; and
- *E* was caused by *O* in the normal visual way.

The problem with this proposal, Lewis argues, is that it is too strong, and rules out cases of both *nonstandard* and *prosthetic* seeing. For instance, if some of us have visual systems that work on different principles to the rest of us, then their causal relation would be abnormal and hence they would not be said to see. As a more plausible version of this situation, it may be that scientists could develop a prosthetic eye which, when perfected, would produce effects just like a normal eye. Again, the causal relation in such subjects would be abnormal, and hence they would not see.

In both of these cases, Lewis suggests, we should not *rule out* the possibility that these subjects might really be said to *see*. The proposed modification should be rejected as it is too strong.

Lewis instead suggests that what is required is that the visual experience we have be *counterfactually dependent* upon the scene before the eyes. The underlying thought here is that if you really see an object or scene, then any changes in that object or scene would be reflected by changes in the visual experience.

With this modification made, our analysis of seeing holds that subject *S* *sees* object *O* if and only if:

- *S* has a visual experience, *E*, as of *O*; and
- *E* is satisfied; and
- *E* was caused by *O*; and
- the phenomenal character of *E* is counterfactually dependent upon *O*.[4]

This would rule out the original counterexamples as follows:

The Brain before the Eyes: As I am hallucinating, I would have had an experience as of a brain before my eyes even if the brain had not been there. The counterfactual dependence of experience on scene does not hold.

The Light Meter: Again, it doesn't matter what the scene in front of the subject is, so long as the illumination is adequate. You could change various aspects of the scene (so long as the overall illumination remained the same) without thereby changing the nature of the visual experience. The counterfactual dependence of experience on scene does not hold.

The addition of the counterfactual dependence clause would allow for nonstandard or prosthetic seeing, because in each of these cases if these alternative systems really worked, then if you changed the scene, the experience would change, and hence we would have a counterfactual dependence of experience on scene.

However, there is a further counterexample from Michael Tye which involves two robots, Tom and Tim (1982).

Although I cannot see it, I am standing facing a mirror angled so I see an area to my right. *Behind* the mirror, and therefore hidden from my view, stands robot Tim. Away to my right, hidden behind a wall, stands Tim's left–right inverted robot twin, Tom, who is facing the mirror. Robot Tom is therefore reflected in the mirror such that the image I see is of a robot which looks just like Tim would if the mirror were to be removed. Now, Tom is wired up so that all his movements are caused by Tim's movements—the only reason he is standing where he is is because Tim is standing where he is. And any movements Tim makes are copied (but left–right inverted)—if Tim waves his right hand, then Tom waves his left hand, and the mirror image of Tom "waves its right hand."

If I stand at the appropriate place in this set-up (Figure 7.1) and look (unknowingly) toward the mirror, I will have an experience as of a robot in front of me, so the first condition of Lewis's revised analysis will be met. As is the second condition: my experience is satisfied as there *is* just such a robot in front of me—robot Tim. As is the third condition: my having this

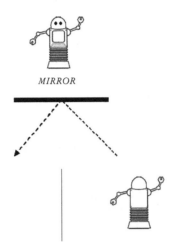

MIRROR

Figure 7.1

very experience is *caused by* the robot that is in front of me (Tim), as it is Tim being where he is that causes Tom to be where he is. And Lewis's final condition is also met. The phenomenological features of my experience are counterfactually dependent upon Tim—if he moves, Tom will move and my experience will change accordingly. As all four conditions are met, Lewis's revised analysis would count this as a case in which I *see* robot Tim. Yet although all the conditions of this analysis of seeing are met, our intuitions remain that it is Tom, not Tim, whom I see.

The causal theory of perception

The causal theory of perception is a generic name for the claim that causation is not only implicated in distinguishing between those visual experiences that are cases of successful perception and those that are not but that this is a conceptual truth about perception. To say that something is a *conceptual* truth is to say that it is something that would be "immediately acknowledgeable by any person, whatever their education, who can count as having the concept in question" (Snowdon 1981: 176).

In more detail, the causal theory of perception typically contains three distinct claims. These are characterized by Snowdon (1981: 175–6) as follows:

(I) The causal thesis: It is necessarily true that if a subject (*S*) sees a public object (*O*) then *O* causally affects *S*.

(II) The effect thesis: *O* must produce in *S* a state reportable in a sentence beginning "It looks to *S* as if . . . " [In our terminology, this means that

O must produce in *S* a visual experience, understood as a good case/bad case common factor].

(III) The conceptual thesis: This thesis amounts to a comment on the status of the other two. It says that theses (I) and (II) represent require-ments of our ordinary concept, or notion, of vision. For this claim to be correct, it must be the case that anyone who can be said to possess the concept of *seeing* would endorse both (I) and (II).[5]

Strawson argues for (III)—the claim that the causal theory is a conceptual truth—as follows:

The idea of the presence of the thing as accounting for, or being respon-sible for, our perceptual awareness of it is implicit in the pre-theoretical scheme from the very start. For we think of perception as a way, indeed the basic way, of informing ourselves about the world of independently existing things: we assume, that is to say, the general reliability of visual experiences; and that assumption is the same as the assumption of a gen-eral causal dependence of our visual experiences on the independently existing things we take them to be of.

(Strawson 1979: 51)

However, whilst this argument may provide reasons to think that (I) is a conceptual truth—that *O* must causally affect *S* in order for *S* to see *O*—it is entirely unclear how it bears on (II). There doesn't seem to be anything in the argument that gives us any reason to think that it is part of the concept of perception that whatever causal transactions are involved must be such as to cause a good case/bad case common factor in *S*.

In addition to this, Snowdon argues that the coherence of disjunctivism means that (II) cannot be a *conceptual* truth. He argues that, even if disjunc-tivism turns out to be false, it will only be "scientifically established facts about perceptual and hallucinatory processes" that disprove it (1990: 130). But these are results that the man on the street could not be expected to know merely in virtue of having the concept of perception.

Even if it does turn out to be false, then, disjunctivism is not a *conceptual* falsehood and therefore claim (II) of the causal theory—that the intrinsic nature of the experience a subject has when perceiving an object is inde-pendent of anything outside the subject—is not a conceptual truth as (III) claims.

Whilst there are reasons to doubt that claims (I) and (II) are *conceptual* truths, this doesn't mean that they are not *true*. The claims in question are these:

(I) The causal thesis: It is necessarily true that if a subject (*S*) sees a public object (*O*) then *O* causally affects *S*.

>(II) *The effect thesis:* O must produce in S a visual experience, understood as a good case/bad case common factor.

And as it happens, there are strong reasons to think that (I) might indeed be true.

For one thing, as Lewis notes, the phenomenal character of perception *does* seem to be counterfactually dependent upon objects in the world.[6] In addition to this, (I) offers a plausible explanation of why perception has the *defeaters* it does: why perception fails in the conditions in which it does fail. For instance, it explains why we don't see O if our eyes are closed, or other opaque objects are interposed between us and O, and so on (Child 1994). What these have in common is that, in each case, the causal link between the object and the subject is broken.

If we accept (I), then this can be used to argue for the truth of (II) as follows: how could the presence of causation be a *necessary condition* for perception to take place unless it was *also* the case that the seen object *causes* S to have an experience that is, in its intrinsic nature, independent of that object?

An important question, then, is whether or not we can argue from the truth of (I) to the truth of (II). Is it the case that, if object O causally affects subject S, it does so by producing in S a visual experience, conceived of as a good case/bad case common factor? Or is there another way in which we could accommodate the thesis that it is necessarily true that O must causally affect S in order for perception to take place?

William Child offers a way of accommodating causation without committing to (II)'s ontology of experiences by making use of a distinction between *personal* and *subpersonal* levels of explanation. This distinction separates out the level of talking about human beings *qua* minded agents from the level of talking about human beings *qua* physical systems or, as Dennett puts it, "the explanatory level of people and their sensations and activities . . . and . . . the *sub-personal* level of brains and events in the nervous system" (1969: 93).

With this distinction in mind, consider Lewis's account of the causal processes involved in perception.

>Ordinarily, when the scene before the eyes causes matching visual experience, it happens as follows. Parts of the scene reflect or emit light in a certain pattern; this light travels to the eye by a more or less straight path, and is focused by the lens to form an image on the retina; the retinal cells are stimulated . . . and the stimulations comprise a signal which propagates up the optic nerve into the brain; and finally there is a pattern of stimulation in the brain cells which either is or else causes the subject's visual experience.
>
>(Lewis 1980: 83–84)

Here we find that Lewis moves quite freely from talking about the causal processes at the subpersonal level to an effect—a visual experience—at the personal level. According to Lewis, processes in the subject's brain (subpersonal level) ultimately cause an experience (personal level).

Others, however, suggest that these levels of explanation ought to be kept separate:

> The mental state of affairs, *o*'s looking *F* to *S*, is not a state or event at the end of a causal chain initiated by *o*; it is, rather, a (larger-sized) event or state of affairs which itself consists in the whole chain of physical events (not merely events *within S*) by which *o* causally affects *S*. The experience is the complete state of affairs, *o* causally affecting *S*. The ultimate effect in this causal state of affairs—the state or event which lies at the end of the causal chain which starts with *o*—is something physical in *S*; but that ultimate effect is neither identical with nor constitutive of the experience itself.
>
> (Child 1994: 161–162)

Essentially, Child attempts to secure a role for causation at the *physical* (or subpersonal) level, whilst denying the common factor conception of mental states at the *mental* (or personal) level. This would enable him to both *endorse* (I) and *reject* (II). However, the availability of this response does depend, in part, on whether or not we *ought* to keep a strong distinction between the personal and subpersonal levels. Not everyone will agree that we should.

Questions

- Can you think of any ways in which the causal theory's analysis of seeing could be augmented to rule out Tim and Tom as a case of seeing?
- Can we both endorse a naive realist theory of veridical experience *and* secure a role for causation in perception?
- In thinking philosophically about perception, ought we distinguish between personal and subpersonal levels of explanation? What considerations ought we bring to bear in answering this question?

Notes

1. In these traditional theories, the mere truth of a belief is not taken to be *sufficient* for that belief to count as knowledge. We can imagine, the thought goes, that a belief might fortuitously happen to be true in situations where we would not want to say the subject has knowledge. Such analyses therefore hold that *other* conditions, such as the belief's being

justified, also need to be met. As we shall see, a similar process occurs in the perceptual case too.

2. Searle (1983) attempts to resurrect a satisfaction only account by actually including the causal component within the content. On his account, a visual experience of a yellow station wagon has the content, that there is a yellow station wagon there and the fact that there is a yellow station wagon there is causing this visual experience. This means that the content could only be satisfied if a suitable causal component is present, and hence remains a satisfaction only theory. As noted in Chapter 5, this proposal faces objections inasmuch as it doesn't seem like an accurate account of what visual experiences tell us. Moreover, it is also susceptible to the general concerns facing two component theories, discussed below.

3. It has been argued that the difficulties discussed in this section are not restricted to those who endorse the Common Factor Principle. Consider, therefore, the kind of theory of veridical experience discussed in the previous chapter. According to such a view, when we see, the seen object is actually a constituent of the experience. Coates argues that an equally problematic situation arises here. He asks *"what fact of the matter about my situation and the way I am placed in the world makes it the case that I am seeing, in a normal way, one particular object X, and not misperceiving some different object Y which happens also to be located somewhere in my surroundings?"* (2007: 73). So if a constitutive theory of experience claims that S sees O if and only if O is a constituent of S's experience, Coates's challenge is this: What fact of the matter makes it the case that it is O, and not some other object, P, that is a constituent of this experience?

4. Strictly speaking, for Lewis, the last two clauses are this analysis are not distinct. This is because Lewis endorses a *counterfactual theory of causation* according to which, to say that A caused B is to say *no more* than that the existence of B is counterfactually dependent on the existence of A—that had A not existed, then B would not have existed (Lewis 1986).

5. It is important to note that both (I) and (II) *can* be accepted without also accepting (III). To do so would be to hold that (I) and (II) are perhaps empirical truths without being conceptual truths. Moreover, as we shall see, it has been argued that (I) can be accepted without accepting either of (II) or (III).

6. Having said this, we should note that the fact of counterfactual dependence does not *entail* (I) as not all cases of counterfactual dependence are cases of causation. For example, my writing "Larry" is counterfactually dependent upon my writing "rr"—had I not done the latter I would not have done the former—but we do not want to say that my writing "rr" *caused* my writing "Larry". In light of this consideration, Lewis suggests that counterfactual dependence only constitutes a case of causation when

the two items in question are distinct existences and do not stand in a part–whole relation (1986: 259). Given this, in order to know whether or not the fact that there is counterfactual dependence of experience on world supports (I), we must first answer the following question: Are elements of the external world and our experiences of those elements distinct existences, or do they rather stand in a part–whole relation? But this is just the question at issue between disjunctivists and common factor theorists!

Further reading

Important early discussions of the causal theory of perception can be found in Grice, "The Causal Theory of Perception" (1961), Lewis, "Veridical Hallucination and Prosthetic Vision" (1980), and Strawson, "Perception and its Objects" (1979). All of these papers are reprinted in Dancy's *Perceptual Knowledge* (1988). Also see Strawson's 1974 paper, "Causation in Perception."

Snowdon's important discussions of the causal theory are his "Perception, Vision and Causation" (1981), which is also reprinted in Dancy's *Perceptual Knowledge*, and his "The Objects of Visual Experience" (1990). Both of these papers are reprinted in Byrne and Logue (eds.) *Disjunctivism: Contemporary Readings* (2009).

Tye's Tim and Tom example can be found in his "A Causal Analysis of Seeing" (1982) and Alva Noë's 2003 paper, "Causation and Perception: The Puzzle Unravelled" offers a way in which the Tim and Tom problems might be overcome.

Child's discussions on the compatibility of disjunctivism and the necessity of causation for perception can be found in Chapter 5 of his 1994 book, *Causality, Interpretation and the Mind*. A more recent discussion of the causal theory can be found in Gerald Vision's 1997 book, *Problems of Vision: Rethinking the Causal Theory of Perception*.

8   Perception and the sciences of the mind

Overview

This chapter focuses on the interplay between the philosophy of perception and the empirical sciences that investigate the mind.

The first section looks at ways in which philosophy can impact upon science by examining and critiquing certain of its foundational assumptions; the second section reciprocates, looking at how scientific results and findings can constrain philosophical theorizing. The third section then looks at a particular issue that has exercised both philosophers and empirical scientists—the relationship between the sensory aspects of our experiences and our capacity to cognitively access or report on our experiences. The final section then looks at more indirect ways in which science can impact upon philosophy, by looking at the argument that color realism can be refuted by considering the physiology of our visual systems.

At the outset of the book, I asked the question of what the role of the philosophy of perception was given that perception is also an object of study for the empirical sciences of the mind (a set of disciplines that I will bring together under the heading *cognitive science*).[1] There we noted that a critical role for philosophy was to consider perception in a somewhat wider context, taking into account its status as a paradigmatically conscious experience and its core epistemological role.

In the present chapter, we will look more closely at the interplay between philosophy and cognitive science. In the first section, we will consider one role for philosophy, which is to critique some of the foundational assumptions of the science. We will then go on to see how, reciprocally, science can help to keep philosophy grounded, by discovering and investigating phenomena that constrain philosophical explanations of perception. Following on from this, we will look at the question of the interplay between the conscious sensory aspects of experiences and their cognitive aspects, as this is an issue where philosophy and empirical science come together. The chapter will conclude with a discussion of how scientific findings can impact upon the philosophy of perception in other ways.

For reasons of space, this chapter will not be comprehensive. There are many more ways in which empirical science and the philosophy of perception will come together than those listed here. To pick some examples out of the air, phenomena such as attention, introspection, and our experience of time are further areas where I would expect philosophy and empirical science to interact. In addition to this restriction in scope, the discussions in this chapter will be unable to trace all the ins and outs of the topics we will cover. Instead, the goal is much more modest: to give a flavor of the way empirical and theoretical approaches to perception fit together, which will provide the reader with a platform from which to engage in further research on areas of interest.

Theoretical paradigms and their underlying assumptions

This section will focus on an assumption that continues to exert a great deal of influence in contemporary cognitive science. This is "the idea—widespread in both philosophy and science—that perception is a process *in the brain* whereby the perceptual system constructs an *internal representation* of the world" (Noë 2005: 2).

In his 1991 book, *Consciousness Explained*, Daniel Dennett challenged the assumption that the brain functions by continually creating a rich internal representation of the scene corresponding to the visual field. To illustrate this, he outlines an experiment you can perform for yourself.

> Take a deck of playing cards and remove a card face down, so that you do not yet know which it is. Hold it out at the left or right periphery of your visual field and turn its face to you, being careful to keep looking straight ahead (pick a target spot and keep looking right at it). You will find that you cannot tell even if it is red or black or a face card. Notice, though, that you are distinctly aware of any flicker or motion of the card. You are seeing motion without being able to see the shape or color of the thing that is moving. Now start moving the card toward the center of your visual field, again being careful not to shift your gaze. . . . You will probably be surprised at how close to center you can move the card and still be unable to identify it.
>
> (Dennett 1991: 53–54)

The moral Dennett draws from this experiment is that the perceptual system doesn't provide real-time rich color and shape information about the peripheries of the visual field. Of course, this doesn't *refute* the very idea—Dennett's opponent might claim that the representation is built up over time by piecing together the information from successive saccades (eye movements), for example—but it does raise a challenge.

In addition to this experiment, as part of this general program, Dennett also predicted that there would be cases in which subjects would fail to see some aspect of their immediate environment that, prior to the experiments, we would have felt confident that they would have seen (1991: 468).

For instance, consider the phenomenon known as *change blindness* (Simons and Levin 1997). In a well-known change blindness experiment, subjects view alternate presentations of a picture of a natural scene and a modified version of that picture. The kinds of modification include such things as significant objects appearing and disappearing, such as an airplane's engine or a garage, or significant portions of an object changing color. While these images are cycling, the visual system is prevented from seeing the change *happen* by techniques such as adding a *flicker*—a brief period of no image—between the presentations, or by ensuring that the changes take place during subject saccades. Even if viewing conditions are optimal, subjects are told that they are studying the images for a memory test (to ensure they are concentrating on features in the image) and are even told that the scenes depicted may change (so changes are expected), the changes can go undetected for a significant length of time.

Intriguingly, this phenomenon can also be found in real-world interactions. To demonstrate this, Simons and Levin set up two experiments in which a pedestrian was approached by an experimenter asking for directions. After these two individuals had interacted for 10–15 seconds, two people carrying a door passed between them and, whilst the conversation was thus interrupted, the experimenter who had initially asked for directions switched places with one of the experimenters carrying the door. Even though the two experimenters differed in height, voice, clothing, and so on, in 66 percent of trials (eight of twelve), subjects continued the conversation and, when asked if they had noticed anything unusual, did not report noticing the change (Simons and Levin 1998).

A closely related phenomenon is *inattentional blindness* (Mack and Rock 1998). In experiments studying this phenomenon, subjects are given an attention-demanding task to perform. In one example, participants are shown a recording of two intermingled teams of basketball players—one wearing black, one white—each team passing a ball to one another. Participants are then asked to count the number of passes made by members of the white team to one another. Then, whilst the subject's attention is occupied by this task, an unexpected event occurs; someone dressed in a (black) gorilla suit walks across the court, beating his chest midway. As with the change blindness experiments, if asked beforehand, we would probably expect such an event to be seen immediately. Because attention is otherwise engaged, almost half of the subjects of this experiment failed to see the gorilla cross the basketball court (Simons and Chabris 1999).

Noë argues that these results give us reason to think that perception is *not* "the process whereby a rich internal representation of experienced detail is built up" (2005: 50). Of course, as before, these findings do not *refute* the idea that perception involves the construction of internal representations. For one thing, Noë's interpretations of these results can be challenged—perhaps detailed representations are constructed but are not remembered (Pani 2000; but see Rensink 2000). For another, even if we accept that the findings show that the brain does not create *rich* internal representations, this is not to show that the brain does not create representations *at all*. Yet these examples illustrate a useful way in which philosophers can impact upon the practice of science.

Important phenomena

In the previous section, we looked at one way in which philosophy and empirical science interact: by philosophers examining and critiquing the things that scientists take for granted. In doing this, we also saw how empirical science discovers phenomena that have important ramifications for philosophical theorizing. This is another important point of contact: the scientists need to keep the philosophers grounded.

What I mean by this is that experimental researchers will often report important *results*—will provide accounts of what took place in various kinds of laboratory and/or real-life contexts—and/or discover important *phenomena*. Regardless of the theorists' particular theoretical backgrounds, unless there are reasons to think that these reports are suspect, then a philosophical theory of perception ought to be able to account for the existence of the phenomena and/or results discovered. So even if, as philosophers, we do not necessarily take on board the theoretical commitments of those working in cognitive science, we should nonetheless be aware of the phenomena that they discover, as our theorizing ought to be sensitive to this. In this section I will therefore briefly highlight a number of empirical findings that seem to be of importance to the philosopher of perception.

Pathologies of perception

A brief survey of the psychological and neuroscientific literature throws up numerous interesting pathologies of perception. Brief descriptions of some of these, together with indications of their philosophical relevance, follow.

Achromatopsia occurs when there has been damage to the area of a subject's brain—area V4—that supports the ability of humans to see color. Sufferers from achromatopsia lose the ability to see color but retain the abilities to see other features, such as shape, form, and motion. The existence of this condition therefore suggests that our ability to see certain properties can, in some sense, "come apart" from our ability to see other properties. Philosophical theories of perception therefore need to accommodate the possibility of this condition. In most cases, however, this looks to be straightforward: sense datum theorists could contend that the damage to V4 precludes the creation of colored sense data; adverbialists that it precludes the subject from sensing colorly; intentionalists that it precludes the representation of color; and naive realists, that it precludes the subject from being acquainted with worldly properties of color.

Akinetopsia, however, presents slightly more of a problem. This condition is due to damage to area MT—the area that supports our ability to see motion. Again, sufferers lose the ability to see movement whilst retaining their abilities to see other properties, such as color, form, and orientation. In this strange condition, sufferers report seeing people disappear from one place and reappear in another—they cannot see them moving from one place to another. When filling a teacup, sufferers see the liquid level jump from level to level rather than rise gently. Probably the closest experience for normal perceivers would be the experience of seeing moving objects under strobe lighting. However, such a parallel should not be taken too literally.

Once again, theories of perception should offer accounts of akinetopsia, but in all cases it is not clear how they should go about this. The problem is, most theories of perception have taken simple "still life" perception as their basic type of visual perception, with motion tacked on as somewhat of an afterthought. To put this point a different way, the difficulty is that motion is something that happens *across* time, whilst most theories of perception aim to give an account of what it is to have a certain kind of experience *at a time*. Theories of experience that focus on presenting an account of what it is to have an experience at a particular time have not given motion a central place.[2]

Having said this, I don't want to claim that extant theories of perception cannot provide some kind of explanation of akinetopsia. I do think, however, that it maybe indicates that, as philosophers of perception, our focus has been a little too tightly on experiences *at a time*, and that the temporally extended features of perception have been to some extent overlooked. So it is not so much that akinetopsia is a *problem*, more a gentle reminder that, when theorizing about perception, we also need to pay attention to the temporally extended aspects of visual experience.

A further interesting phenomenon is *unilateral neglect*, which usually results from damage to the right hemisphere of the brain. Although this damage doesn't seem to cause partial blindness of the left visual field—subjects can still have intact visual fields (Walker et al. 1991) and stimuli present to the left visual field can still produce priming effects (Berti and Rizzolatti 1992)—subjects with unilateral neglect nevertheless overlook what is presented there. For example, cases have been reported in which subjects only brush their hair on the right side, only shave or make up the right side of their face, or only eat the food on the right side of their plate and claim to be finished, despite insisting that they remain hungry! If such subjects are asked to cross out all the lines on a piece of paper, they will cross out the lines on the right-hand side and claim to be finished, despite unmarked lines being present on the left side of the paper. Do these subjects nonetheless *consciously experience* the neglected areas? This is an intriguing question to which we shall return shortly.

Achromatopsia, akinetopsia, and unilateral neglect can all be seen as types of *agnosia*. Generally speaking, agnosias occur when the subject loses the ability to know or be aware of something. So, achromatopsia has also been known as color agnosia, akinetopsia as motion agnosia, and unilateral neglect as hemiagnosia. But there are many other kinds of agnosia, which may also be of interest to the philosopher of perception. These include:

Apperceptive agnosia: Sufferers of apperceptive agnosia seem to be able to see well enough—their visual acuity, ability to see color, and so on remain intact, and they can successfully avoid obstacles—but they are unable to see the forms of objects, to recognize objects, to discriminate between different stimuli, to accurately copy a simple drawing, and so on.

Associative agnosia: Unlike apperceptive agnosics, sufferers of associative agnosia seem to have intact form perception and can do such things as accurately copy a drawing and match it to its original. Despite retaining these abilities, however, associative agnosics still fail to recognize what the drawing is a drawing of, even when it is their own copy. This nevertheless does seem to be some kind of visual defect inasmuch as, if the drawing is then verbally *described* to the subject, they will be able to identify it.

Prosopagnosia: Prosopagnosics have a very specific failure of recognition: they cannot recognize familiar faces. Even though prosopagnosics know the people well, can recognize them by their voices, or perhaps even by specific facial features (such as a mole or a chipped tooth), they cannot recognize them by their faces per se.

Simultanagnosia: Subjects with simultanagnosia retain the ability to recognize objects in their visual field but only one at a time. If more than one object is presented, the subject claims to only be able to see one. Because of this, simultanagnosic subjects are unable to see whole scenes.

Anton's syndrome (a form of anosognosia): Anosognosias are failures to recognize one's own illness or deficit, but one that is of particular interest to philosophers of perception is Anton's syndrome, in which subjects who have lost their sight will nevertheless claim that they can see and, on particular occasions, will also make quite specific claims about what they see or why they fail to see on those particular occasions.

The two visual systems hypothesis

The pathological conditions discussed in the previous section, together with findings from a variety of other sources, have led to the discovery of two different pathways in the brain that are both dedicated to the processing of visual information. All visual information begins on the same path: it is passed from the retinas, down the optic nerve to the lateral geniculate nucleus (LGN) and from there to the primary visual cortex V1 at the back of the head. From there, however, this information travels down two distinct anatomical pathways, each of which is dedicated to performing different processing tasks. On Ungerleider and Mishkin's classic presentation (1982), one of these pathways—the *what* pathway—travels along the base of the brain (the *ventral stream*) and the other—the *where* pathway—travels up and over the top of the brain (the *dorsal stream*).

Although the precise functions of these two pathways have continued to be discussed, their existence is now widely accepted. According to a more recent and highly influential treatment by Milner and Goodale (1995), the purpose of the ventral stream is to underpin object identification/recognition whereas the purpose of the dorsal stream is to enable real-time visual guidance of action (they therefore suggest the pathways subserve *what* and *how*, rather than what and where). Milner and Goodale contend (although this can be disputed) that conscious visual awareness is connected with only one of the two streams—the ventral (object identification and recognition) stream. This therefore predicts that subjects would not necessarily lose the capacity to act in appropriate ways to visually presented stimuli even if, due to localized damage, they failed to consciously *see* those stimuli.

A famous example of this is Milner and Goodale's patient D.F. This patient was presented with a vertically mounted disk with a slot cut into it, which was set at different angles for different trials, and D.F. was asked to report the orientation of the slot. However, Milner and Goodale found that her reports of the slot orientation were unaffected by its actual orientation—they were effectively random guesses. On their hypothesis, this showed that information about the slot was just not making it through to the ventral stream responsible for object identification and recognition. However, when asked to post a card *through* the slot, D.F. had no difficulty—her actions were accurate, smooth, and appropriate. So information about the slot's orientation clearly was making it through to the dorsal stream responsible for action.

Another interesting case, this time using normal subjects, is discussed by Haffenden and Goodale (1998). This experiment makes use of the Ebbinghaus illusion, in which a disk of a particular size surrounded by small circles is judged to be larger than a disk of the same size surrounded by big circles. Haffenden and Goodale discovered that, despite the presence of the illusion of size difference, if subjects were asked to *pick up* the central disks, they automatically moved their finger and thumb to the same distance apart in both cases. This suggests that, whilst the ventral pathway is subject to the illusion, the dorsal pathway is not.

Although these findings are fascinating in their own right, they are of particular significance for the philosophy of perception because they challenge something that can seem so obvious to us. For example, take your finger and place it slowly on this X. Naturally, it seems to us that any changes in the direction or angle or speed of our finger is made in response to our conscious awareness of the X, our finger, and the relationship between them. Yet, according to Milner and Goodale, conscious perceptual awareness does not play this role. Whilst it might play the role of singling out the X as something to put your finger on, once action begins it is guided by nonconscious processes.[3]

Synesthesia

A further interesting phenomenon for the philosopher of perception is *synesthesia*. In the majority of such cases, an otherwise unexceptional sensory experience in one modality automatically causes its subject to have a further experience in a distinct modality.[4] If we call the initial unexceptional experience the *triggering* experience and the experience that this yields the *synesthetic* experience, the most widespread form of synesthesia occurs when the triggering experience is the experience of hearing certain words or sounds, and the synesthetic experience is a visual experience of color (Harrison and Baron-Cohen 1997). However, intramodal forms of synesthesia have also been discovered. Most prominent is what is known is *grapheme–color* synesthesia, in which a visually experienced *black* grapheme—a numeral or letter written in black ink—yields an additional color experience. In laboratory testing, it has been shown fairly convincingly that synesthesia is a robust condition inasmuch as particular trigger/synesthetic experience pairings have been found to be extremely robust.

Although synesthetic experiences have been reported for well over 100 years, it is only relatively recently that scientists and philosophers have started taking the condition seriously. For many years, synesthetic reports were assumed to be either reports of memories that were associated with the things experienced, or perhaps even due to an overactive sense of metaphor—an extension of something we all do when we talk about, say, a wind as biting or a shirt as loud.

However, pop out experiments on grapheme–color synesthetes, conducted by Ramachandran and Hubbard (2001), seem to show that the phenomenon is not explained away so easily. The phenomenon of pop out is straightforward. If an image contains a triangle of red "2"s in an array of randomly placed green "5"s, the triangle formed by the red "2"s will "pop out": it will be easy for you to see (as can be seen in the monochrome version of this figure on the right of Figure 8.1). However, if you are a normal subject, then if an

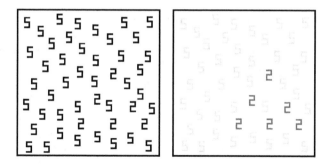

Figure 8.1

image contains a triangle formed by black "2"s in an array of randomly placed black "5"s, the triangle formed by the "2"s will not pop out (left).

Where subjects who synesthetically experience one color when they see a "5" and another color when they see a "2" are concerned, pop out actually occurs for the monochrome stimulus. This suggests that such synesthetes really do "see" the colors when they see the numbers rather than merely *associate* the colors with the numbers.

Here we have a case in which empirical research seems to have demonstrated the existence of a phenomenon. As noted above, it is therefore something that philosophers ought to take into account. How does it impact upon the philosophy of perception? Well, for one thing, standard cross-modal cases of synesthesia offer interesting challenges to theories of what makes an experience *belong* to a particular modality—makes it, say, a visual experience rather than an experience from a different modality, say an aural experience or a gustatory experience. We shall discuss this further in the next chapter.

As to the question of what relevance synesthesia has for theories of perception, that will depend in part on whether synesthetic experiences are truly perceptual or whether they are imaginary. Now, as it happens, when questioned about the nature of their synesthetic experiences, subjects typically place themselves into one of two classes: either *associators*, who experience the synesthetic colors as being "in their mind's eye," or *projectors*, who experience the synesthetic colors as being out there in the world. We might, therefore, think that the synesthetic experiences of projectors are likely to be of the same kind as visual experiences, which are also usually of things "out there in the world."

This claim—that at least some synesthetic experiences are truly perceptual—has also been the subject of empirical study. For example, Blake et al. (2005) argue that synesthetic experiences are perceptual because, like perceptions, they can lead a subject to have afterimages. Further evidence for the perceptual nature of synesthetic experiences derives from studies that show that the areas of the brain that are usually active during veridical color experiences are, in fact, active during synesthetic experiences.

What are the options for the philosopher of perception here? Well, if a projective synesthetic experience of color is agreed to be a truly *visual experience*, then as it takes place in the absence of corresponding worldly colors, such an experience would look to be a special kind of hallucination—special inasmuch as it is caused by another sensory experience. An adequate theory of perception had better be able to accommodate such cases within its theory of hallucination. If it cannot, then unless reasons can be given to think that the experiences are not, in fact, perceptual, it will constitute a significant problem for that theory.

However, there is a further feature of synesthetic reports that might be argued to show that they cannot be perceptual after all. This is that, whilst projective grapheme–color synesthetes do report that the grapheme in question looks to be colored, they also report that they can see the color of the ink. As one report states, "when probed about the locations of the two colors, [subject] A.D. reported that she didn't know how to explain it, but that both appeared on the shape in the same location at the same time" (Macpherson 2007: 76). Such an experience is difficult to imagine—seeing an object to be both red and black at the same time? This might be argued to be evidence that the experiences in question cannot be perceptual. On the other hand, if such an experience is nevertheless insisted to be perceptual, then once again an adequate theory of perception owes us an account of it.

Perception, cognition, and the phenomenal

Throughout the book thus far, I have taken the liberty of talking as though it is straightforward to distinguish between the sensory/phenomenal and conceptual/cognitive elements of visual experiences. In this section, I want to put some pressure on that distinction. In doing so, it will also provide an example of a way in which philosophy and empirical science can profitably interact with one another, whilst also highlighting some limitations to this interaction.

To enable us to focus on the issues, consider an ambiguous figure, such as the vase–face figure in Figure 8.2.

This figure can be seen as either two black faces looking at one another, or as a white goblet-like vase. What should we say, then, of the experience of seeing this figure as two faces as compared with the experience of seeing the figure as a vase? There are three options that present themselves.

[A] That the visual experiences are the same, it is just that the conceptual/ cognitive *consequences* of the two experiences differ.

[B] That the visual experiences are different, but that they nonetheless share phenomenal character (the differences between the experiences

Figure 8.2

being a matter of nonphenomenal conceptual/cognitive elements of the experiences).

[C] That the visual experiences actually have different *phenomenal character.*

There are empirical studies that have been taken to bear on which of these hypotheses is correct. For example, an array of studies have shown that words are more easily recognized than nonwords (the *word-superiority effect*); common or frequent words are more easily recognized than uncommon words (the *word-frequency effect*); repeated words are recognized more easily than novel words (*repetition effects*); and so on. Moreover, experiments with ambiguous figures have shown that, if subjects are presented with a disambiguated version of an ambiguous figure and then presented with the ambiguous one, subjects (unsurprisingly) interpret the figure in line with the previously seen disambiguation. In addition, Rock and Mitchener (1992) developed an experiment in which both *informed* and *uninformed* participants were shown ambiguous figures. They found that, whereas all of the informed subjects—who had been told that the figure they would see was ambiguous—reported being able to see both of the interpretations of the figure, only one in three of the uninformed subjects reported the figure reversing.

Altogether, these results look to show that knowledge and expectation—both of which are plausibly cognitive phenomena—have a significant effect on what subjects can see. For instance, Doyle and Leach (1988) present evidence to show that the word-frequency effect is a perceptual effect—in other words, that the words are literally *seen* more easily. This can look to give us reason to prefer one of [B] or [C] over [A].[5] If we accept this, then we accept that conceptual/cognitive differences can lead to differences in the experiences themselves. The question then becomes whether or not the cognitive/conceptual features have these effects by changing the phenomenal character of the two experiences of the vase–face figure, or whether they affect the experiences by simply being additional, nonphenomenal, elements of the experiences.

Which properties can be perceived?

For the purposes of this stage of the discussion, let us agree that phenomenal character *involves* what are often called "low-level" properties, such as color, shape, location, motion, and so on.[6] The question is whether or not phenomenal character involves any "higher-level" properties. "Conservatives" say no, claiming that phenomenal character is completely exhausted by low-level properties; "Liberals", on the other hand, insist that phenomenal character can involve one or more from the following list (this terminology is due to Bayne 2009).

Kind properties, such as the property of "being a house" or "being a tree" (Siegel 2006: 483; see also Bayne 2009). *Causal properties*, such as the property of a boulder's flattening a hut (Strawson 1985) or, more generally, one thing's causing another (see also Siegel 2009; Butterfill 2009). *Generic properties*, such as the property of being "five to ten rectangles arranged in a circle" (Block 2008: 307) or the property of being nonspecific text (Grush 2007: 504; Fish 2009: 64).[7]

How might we go about answering the question of whether or not the phenomenal character of a visual experience can involve these sorts of properties?

As Siegel points out, introspecting our experiences can only take us so far. When we see a bowl of fruit, introspection can tell us that the phenomenal character of this experience does not involve the property of being a blowfly or the property of being a bass guitar. But does it involve the property of being a banana? Introspection is ambivalent. In light of this, Siegel defends the claim that phenomenal character can involve kind properties by using what she calls the "method of phenomenal contrast" (2007). This operates as follows:

> Suppose you have never seen a pine tree before, and are hired to cut down all the pine trees in a grove containing trees of many different sorts. Someone points out to you which trees are pine trees. Some weeks pass, and your disposition to distinguish the pine trees from the others improves. Eventually, you can spot the pine trees immediately. They become visually salient to you.... Gaining this recognitional disposition is reflected in a phenomenological difference between the visual experiences you had before and after the recognitional disposition was fully developed.
>
> (Siegel 2006: 491)

In essence, the method of phenomenal contrast proceeds by finding two experiences that involve the same "low-level" properties and then asking whether or not there is a phenomenal difference between the two experiences. Here, the relevant experiences are (otherwise identical) experiences of a pine tree before and after gaining the capacity to pick them out by sight. Siegel's argument is that these two experiences differ in phenomenal character despite the fact that their phenomenal characters involve the same low-level properties. The best explanation for this difference is therefore that phenomenal characters *also* involve high-level properties, such as the property of being a pine tree.

As Siegel recognizes, this is at heart an appeal to intuition: it just seems right to say that there is a phenomenal difference between the two experiences before and after gaining the relevant capacity (she also gives an auditory example involving the experience of hearing words spoken in a language before and after learning that language). This has, however, been countered by another intuition. If I learn that the "lemon" I see is actually a bar of soap, I may insist that the phenomenal character of my experience hasn't changed, regardless (Byrne 2009: 449). If this is so, then either the property of being a lemon must still be involved in the phenomenal character of my experience even though I know it is not a lemon, or that property was not involved in the phenomenal character of my experience at the start.

To try to provide an alternative way of resolving this dispute, Tim Bayne presents a phenomenal contrast based argument using the phenomenon, discussed above, of associative agnosia. Recall that associative agnosics seem to be able to see perfectly well, but cannot recognize objects, even when the objects are drawings they have themselves copied. Bayne suggests that the effects of the condition are enough to make it "extremely plausible" that the phenomenal characters of the experiences of a patient with associative agnosia are not the same as the phenomenal characters of "normal" experiences. But, he argues, this is not because the patient's phenomenal characters no longer involve low-level properties: "those abilities that require the processing of only low-level [properties] remain intact. The patient's deficit is not one of *form* perception but of *category* perception" (Bayne 2009: 391). The conclusion of the argument is that the reason these agnosics have different phenomenal characters is because the phenomenal characters of their experiences (but not ours) cannot involve high-level properties.

One response available to those who think that phenomenal characters involve only low-level properties is to accept [C]—that the visual experiences actually have different phenomenal character—but to draw a distinction between two *variants* of [C]. [C1] agrees with [B] in the conservative claim that phenomenal character involves only low-level properties but nevertheless holds that conceptual/cognitive features *causally affect* the phenomenal character in such a way that the (low-level) phenomenal character of each experience differs (see Tye 1995: 140 for an explanation of this kind). The second, liberal, option, [C2], holds instead that phenomenal character is part-*constituted by* conceptual/cognitive features.

To see the difference between [C1] and [C2], consider the difference between a car driver and a railway points operator deciding whether the relevant vehicle is to go left or right. If the car driver wants to turn left, he has to turn the steering wheel that way. The driver's actions are naturally seen as *part of* the car's turning left—this is a constitutive view akin to [C2]. If the points operator wants the train to turn left, however, he just need set the points. This can happen a long time before the train gets there. Then, when the train does arrive, it simply follows the predetermined direction. In this case, the points operator's actions are not *part of* the train's turning left; rather they are something that is, strictly speaking, external to that process, yet which has causally influenced it. This is analogous to [C1], the claim that high-level processing merely causally affects which low-level properties are involved in phenomenal character.

Given these two hypotheses, the question becomes: How could we discover whether or not conceptual/cognitive activity partly constitutes phenomenal character?

Consciousness and reportability

Recently, Ned Block (2007b, 2008) has investigated the closely related question of whether activity in the mechanisms that underlie the *reportability of* and/or *cognitive access to* conscious experiences—both of which are, of course, conceptual/cognitive activities *par excellence*—are required for there to be phenomenally conscious experiences at all.

Again, this is a question to which intuition is ambivalent. On the one hand, a natural response to the change blindness and inattentional blindness experiments is to think that we must see the entire scene *in some sense*, even though we miss the changes or unattended objects. The claim that we literally do not see the thing that is changing, despite its taking up a large portion of our field of view, can be difficult to grasp. On the other hand, however, there is also a strong intuition that "the idea of phenomenal consciousness totally divorced from any access by the subject does not really seem like any kind of consciousness at all" (Levine 2007: 514).

Perhaps, then, this is a question for empirical science to answer. Yet as Block points out, the moment you think about how to *investigate* whether or not activity in the mechanisms that underlie cognitive access and reportability is required for consciousness, you run headlong into a methodological puzzle. As he says, a "natural methodology is to find the neural [activity that is taking place] in clear cases and apply it to the problem cases where for some reason there is no cognitive accessibility of the experience" (2008: 292). The difficulty arises when we ask how we know that a conscious experience is taking place. In the paradigmatic cases, it is because the subject *tells us* that they are. So we would expect to find neural activity in the areas underlying cognitive access and reportability.

Block illustrates this problem with an example involving a further pathological syndrome known as *visuo-spatial extinction*, which is brought on by brain injuries of certain kinds. If a subject suffering from visuo-spatial extinction sees an object on one or other side of his or her visual field, she can identify it and report its presence. Yet, if there are objects on *both* sides of the visual field, then the patient functions like a unilateral neglect patient: the patient can only identify and report one object, claiming to be unable to see the other. The first scenario clearly shows that such a patient has the *capacity* to be conscious of objects on both sides of the visual field. But, in the second case, is the subject *conscious* of the object on the unseen side yet unable to report it, or does the brain injury stop the subject from being conscious of it at all?[8]

Can science provide the answer to this question? Block reports studies by Nancy Kanwisher and colleagues that show that, in normal cases, there is activity in the area of the brain known as the "fusiform face area" when subjects report conscious experiences of faces. And experiments using magnetic resonance imaging (MRI) techniques on the brain of a subject with visuo-spatial extinction have indeed shown that, even in situations in which the subject claims not to see a face on the left of the visual field, the area of the brain responsible for recognition of faces on the left (the right half of the fusiform face area) is active, just as it is when the subject successfully sees the face.

As Block points out, this result could only show that the subject is conscious of the face but cannot report it if we have *already* assumed that activity in the fusiform face area alone supports the capacity to have conscious experience of faces and that activity in the areas underlying cognitive access and report are not required. This is the very question we are trying to answer. We want to know whether a subject can be conscious in the absence of any capacity for cognitive access or report, yet we have no (non-question-begging) way of determining whether a state is or is not conscious *other than* through the reports of the subject.

Some philosophers—Block (2007b: 486) cites Putnam (1981) and Dennett (1988, 1991)—have argued from this that the problem lies in the assumption that there must be a fact of the matter about whether subjects are conscious in these cases. In essence, they contend that the appearance of two distinct but unverifiable explanatory hypotheses shows that we are in fact operating with a problematic conception of consciousness.

Block, however, argues that we can resolve the problem by adopting the "method of inference to the best explanation, that is, the approach of looking for the framework that makes the most sense of all the data" (2008: 293). The bulk of his paper then contains arguments, based on this method, for the view that there can be consciousness without cognitive access/reportability.

At this point, however, I will leave readers to investigate these arguments for themselves.

What we must bear in mind, though, is that the method of inference to the best explanation functions as follows: a claim is supported if it is the best explanation of the evidence. Of course, this is entirely determined by what "evidence" we think needs explaining. As the sets of evidence that need explaining differ, so might our conclusion as to what constitutes the best explanation. In particular, if the relevant evidence set incorporates only the neuroscientific findings, the "best explanation" may indeed be, as Block suggests it is, that there can be conscious states that are unreportable/inaccessible. If, however, the evidence set is expanded to include such considerations as the epistemological role of perception, the best explanation of the conscious aspects of our experiences, and so on, then a different "best explanation" might be warranted. Yet this seems unsatisfactory: surely, we might think, there really is a fact of the matter here (or perhaps maybe Putnam and Dennett were right after all). At this point, it seems that it is *philosophy*, not science, that is needed to resolve this particular issue.

Color vision and color realism

The final potential interaction between empirical science and the philosophy of perception I shall consider concerns more "indirect" ways in which science can impact upon the philosophy of perception. For example, a number of the theories of perception we met in the first half of this book are committed to *realism* about color—committed to the view that colors are real, mind-independent properties.[9] Certainly the belief acquisition theorist, the content-first representationalist, and the naive realist are all so committed. However, over the years, color realism has itself been challenged by various empirical findings. If color realism is shown to be false, then of course any theory of perception that is committed to its truth will thereby also be shown to be false. In this section, we will spend some time looking at the empirical evidence for this claim.

An important discovery for the empirical argument against color realism was the discovery of the existence of *metameric pairs* (or simply *metamers*). It is well known that, generally speaking, objects that reflect *different* profiles of visible light look to be *different* in color. This suggests that the color realist might *identify* a particular color with a particular surface reflectance property might say that to have a certain color *just is* to have the property of reflecting a certain profile of visible light (alternatively, the property of reflecting a particular *color signal*). However, it has also been discovered that, in some cases, two surfaces that *look* the same in color (in particular viewing conditions) can nevertheless have markedly *different* reflective profiles. Such pairs of surfaces are known as metameric pairs, or metamers (if they look the same in *all* viewing conditions they are known as *isomeric pairs* or *isomers*).

Metamers

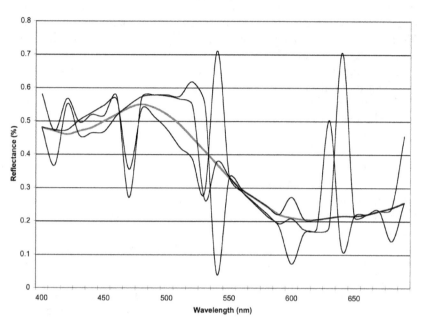

Figure 8.3

Figure 8.3 shows the different reflectance profiles of four different objects that are metamers.

The existence of metamers therefore has the consequence that the property of being green, say, cannot be identified with the property of reflecting such-and-such a color signal (as there exist green surfaces that lack this property). One possible response for the color realist would of course be to insist that one or other of these apparently green surfaces is not *really* green; another to identify color with a *disjunctive* surface reflectance property (and thus claim that the property of being green is the property of having surface reflectance property A *or* surface reflectance property B, and so on).

The most problematic feature of metamers, though, occurs when we ask *why* surfaces that differ in reflectance profile look the same in color. When we look at the physiology of color vision, we discover that metameric pairs *do* have a property in common after all. The only thing is, it is the property of affecting *us*—human perceivers—in the same way.

Let me explain. The physiology of color perception begins with the retina. The human retina comprises around 120 million rods, which only support achromatic (black, white and gray) vision, and around 7 million cones, which are required to support chromatic, or color, vision. Both rods and cones are *transducers*—they convert energy from one form (light) into energy in another (electrical). When light falls upon a cone (we shall focus on cones as the basis of color vision) it responds by *firing*: by sending an electrical signal to the neurons it is connected to. However, the electrical signal it sends is completely independent of the wavelength of light that stimulates the cone. No matter what wavelength the incoming light, if it stimulates the cone to fire, the signal it sends doesn't change. So, if all we have to go on are the signals being sent from the cone, we have no way of determining what the wavelength of light falling upon the retina is.

To overcome this, Mother Nature has given cones two critical features. First, she provides cones with a *sensitivity curve*. That is, cones are more likely to fire when stimulated by light of a particular wavelength (call that wavelength its peak sensitivity), and this likelihood of firing falls away as the wavelength of the incoming light departs from this peak sensitivity. The sensitivity of cones can therefore be represented with a bell curve (below). Second, in humans at least, Mother Nature equips us with three different *kinds* of cone, each of which has a different peak sensitivity. Roughly speaking, one type of cone is most sensitive to light of short wavelength (within the spectrum of visible light), another to medium wavelength light and the other to long wavelength light. Typical sensitivity curves of human cones are shown in Figure 8.4.

When light of a particular wavelength falls upon the retina, each type of cone will respond in a different way, and, from the different firing patterns of the cones, a great deal of information about the wavelength of incoming light can be recovered.

As powerful as this system is, however, it is not foolproof. In particular, it leaves room for there to be surfaces that reflect color signals that, whilst different, nevertheless cause the same overall patterns of activation in the cones. As these surfaces affect the eye in the same way, they cannot be distinguished—these are our metamers. This suggests that the existence of

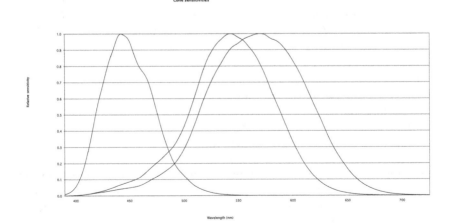

Figure 8.4

metamers is, in some sense, *subject relative*—the fact that there are metamers, and the particular metameric pairs that there are, seem to be a consequence not of the way the mind-independent world is but rather of the particular way our visual systems work. This has been argued to be evidence that colors are not mind-independent after all.

A further, related consideration is that certain features of our conscious experience of color seem to be likewise closely tied to the way our visual systems work. For instance, consider the distinction between *unique* and *binary hues*.

The unique hues are red, yellow, blue, and green—hues that are not experienced as being "made up" of other hues. Binary hues are, by contrast, experienced as being composite. So, for example, orange is experienced as a composite of yellow and red; purple as a composite of blue and red; and so on. (It is important to be clear that, despite superficial similarities, the division of hues into unique and binary is not the same as the division of colors into primary, secondary, and tertiary.)

When we investigate the physiology of color vision further, we discover that it also offers an explanation of *why* hues break down into unique and binary. Somewhat over-simplified, what we find is that the next stage of the visual system performs a number of *comparisons* of the outputs (firing rates) of the cones. These are represented in Figure 8.5.

In this diagram, the boxes L, M, and S represent the long, medium, and short wavelength cones, respectively. For our purposes, the two important computations that the visual system performs are, first, that it finds the difference between the output of the medium wavelength cones and the long wavelength cones and, second, that it finds the difference between the output of the short wavelength cones and that of the long and medium wavelength cones combined.

Focusing on the first computation first, if the output from the long wavelength cones is greater than that of the medium wavelength cones—if L > M—this signals *green*; if the output from the medium wavelength cones is

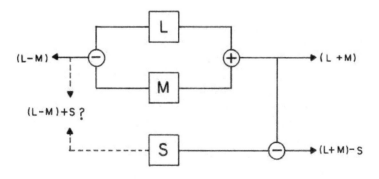

Figure 8.5

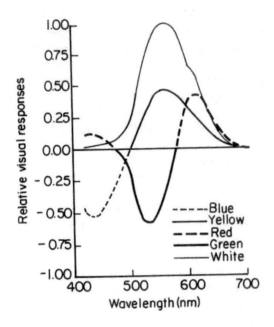

Figure 8.6

greater than that of the long wavelength cones—if L < M—this signals *red*; if the output of both types of cone is the same—if L = M—it signals neither. As for the second computation, if the long and medium wavelength cone output combined is greater than that of the short wavelength cones—if L + M > S—this signals *yellow*; if the other way round—if L + M < S—this signals *blue*. And again, if the output of the long and medium wavelength cones combined is roughly equal to the output from the short wavelength cones—if L + M = S—neither yellow nor blue is signaled. The way this *opponent-processing system* responds to incoming light of different wavelengths is represented in Figure 8.6.

With this graph in hand, we can see that if we were to show the subject a surface that reflects light of around 600 nanometers, the first (red–green) opponent processing system will signal red whilst the second (yellow–blue) system will signal yellow. And indeed, the subject will experience a combination of yellow and red—orange. The binary nature of orange is therefore accounted for, on this picture, by the fact that both elements of the opponent processing system signals a particular color: the orange color that the subject experiences is a composite of the colors—yellow and red—that are signaled. The same is true of the other binary hues.

Now, suppose we show the subject a surface that reflects a lot of short wavelength light—on our diagram, light of approximately 465 nanometers. In this case, as we can see from the graph, the first (red–green) opponent processing system will be in balance and will not signal either red or green. The second (yellow–blue) system, however, will signal blue and hence the subject will experience (unique) blue. Here, the unique nature of the hue experienced is accounted for by the fact that only one of the two elements of the opponent processing system is signaling. Again, the way phenomenological features of our color experiences turn out to correspond to features of the way we process color information has been taken as evidence for the claim that colors are a feature of the way we process visual information rather than a feature of the objective, mind-independent world.

Questions

- What kind of explanation could our different theories of perception offer of:
    - akinetopsia?
    - inattentional blindness?
    - the pop out experiments conducted on grapheme–color synesthetes?
- How should we go about addressing the question of whether there could be phenomenal experience in the absence of cognitive access or reportability?
- Do the findings from color physiology refute color realism?

Notes

1. Strictly speaking, cognitive science is actually a name for a collection of disciplines that study the mind and cognition, which includes not only psychology, neuroscience, artificial intelligence, linguistics, and anthropology, but also *philosophy*. So, setting up the issue as one of the interplay between philosophy and cognitive science is, strictly speaking, not quite right.
2. Perhaps intentionalists could claim that, at a given time, it still makes sense for an object to be *represented as* being in motion and that representation of this feature could explain the *experience* of motion. Possibly, but there is still a suspicion (in my mind at least) that this is still a failure to give motion its due as something that can be perceived.
3. Although Milner and Goodale (1995) do allow that the ventral system can control action in some circumstances, such as pointing at a previously seen target with closed eyes.
4. Sometimes, popular characterizations of synesthesia can be misleading. For instance, Richard Cytowic's influential 1993 book on the phenomenon was called *The Man Who Tasted Shapes*. Such a description suggests that, in synesthesia, objects or properties can be experienced via a

nonstandard sensory modality (it suggests that, in this subject, shapes can be experienced by the modality of taste). Sadly, however, this is not an accurate description—it is not that shapes are tasted but rather that experiencing certain tastes causes additional experiences of shape.

5. Having said this, I'm sure it would be possible to provide an interpretation of these results that was consistent with [A]. For example, Hochberg (1968) suggests that the word-frequency effect is judgmental—that unfamiliar words are equally easy to see, just more difficult to recognize.

6. "Involves" is to be read in a theory-neutral way. I use this term to accommodate the fact that different theories of perception will each frame this issue somewhat differently. For instance, a theorist who endorsed the existence of sense data might say that phenomenal character "involves" low-level properties in virtue of their being instantiated by sense data. A representationalist, on the other hand, would hold that phenomenal character "involves" such properties in virtue of their being represented, and a relationalist would hold that such properties are "involved" in phenomenal character in virtue of the subject's being acquainted with those properties.

7. Due to considerations of space, I won't discuss the arguments surrounding whether or not causal properties and generic properties can be involved in phenomenal characters. I will say, however, that thus far, these arguments have also had an important role for empirical results. For instance, the claim that causal properties can be involved in phenomenal character often appeals to empirical work by Michotte (1963). See, for example, Siegel 2009 and Butterfill 2009. The claim that generic properties can be involved in phenomenal character is also argued to be required to account for some of the change blindness and inattentional blindness results we discussed above (Grush 2007; Fish 2009).

8. There are clear parallels between the resolution to this question and the resolution to the question of whether or not subjects "see" the changed or unattended object in the change blindness and inattentional blindness paradigms discussed above. See Block (2008: 295–297) for discussion.

9. Strictly speaking, *colors*, as we normally conceive of them, have three dimensions—hue, saturation, and brightness. The best way to see what we are talking about when we talk about hue is to see it as what is *left* when we subtract saturation—the depth, density or intensity of a color—and brightness from a color. Moreover, there are colors, such as brown, that do not correspond to hues. All of the hues are represented in the color spectrum (the rainbow).

Further reading

Critiques of aspects of the representational paradigm can be found in Dennett's 1991 book, *Consciousness Explained*, Alva Noë's 2005 book,

Action in Perception, and William Ramsey's 2007 book, *Representation Reconsidered*.

Examples of the change blindness and inattentional blindness experiments can be found on the University of Illinois' Visual Cognition Lab website: http://viscog.beckman.illinois.edu/djs_lab/demos.html.

Semir Zeki has been at the forefront of research into perceptual pathologies, and a lot of this research appears in his very readable 1993 book, *A Vision of the Brain*. A good philosophical introduction to the phenomenon of synesthesia can be found in Fiona Macpherson's 2007 paper, "Synaesthesia."

Susanna Siegel's work has been prominent in discussions of the question of what properties can be perceived, see in particular her "How can we discover the contents of experience?" (2007) and her "Which Properties Are Represented in Perception?" (2006). A number of the other papers cited in this section can be found in a July 2009 special edition of the *Philosophical Quarterly*.

Ned Block's work should be the starting point for further research into the issues relating to consciousness and reportability. See his collection *Consciousness, Function and Representation* (2007a). His recent papers, "Consciousness, Accessibility and the Mesh between Psychology and Neuroscience" (2007b) and "Consciousness and Cognitive Access" (2008) are not included in this collection, but are both detailed, empirically savvy attempts to show how the methodological problems discussed in this section can be solved empirically.

Although it is getting on a bit, C.L. Hardin's 1988 book *Color for Philosophers: Unweaving the Rainbow* remains an excellent text on the scientific underpinnings of the philosophy of color and also contains key arguments against color realism.

9   Perception and other sense modalities

Overview

In virtue of what do the senses differ from one another? And how do we distinguish between seeing something, hearing something, feeling something, smelling something, and tasting something?

These questions are considered, before we attempt to extend the theories of visual perception, met in the previous chapters, to the non-visual modalities. We shall also discuss reasons to think that there can be experiences that are bimodal—experiences that we can only enjoy in virtue of the operation of *two* senses.

Our discussions thus far have focused exclusively on vision, but human beings have a number of other senses, too. When we consider all of our senses together, there are lots of interesting philosophical questions that arise. For one, how many senses do we have? The traditional view (which dates back to Aristotle—*De Anima*, 424b: 22–23) is that we have five: vision, hearing, touch, smell, and taste. Others have suggested that we have as many as *seventeen* different senses (Keeley 2002: 10). In this chapter we shall begin by asking what distinguishes the sense modalities from one another, before going on to ask what philosophers of perception have to say about the non-visual senses.

Individuating the senses

One interesting philosophical question turns on the question of by what criteria the different senses are distinguished from one another. In fact, this breaks down into two closely related questions:

- By what criteria are the senses distinguished from one another?
- How do *we*, as perceivers, distinguish between seeing something, as opposed to hearing it, feeling it, and so on?

The first of these questions is more metaphysical: it asks, what is it about the nature of the different senses that makes them distinct from one another? The second is more epistemological: it asks, when we have a sensory experience, how do we *know* which sense we are using? Suppose, for example, that as you are reading this, you smell coffee and hear the familiar whoosh of an espresso machine. How do you know that you smell the coffee and hear the coffeemaker rather than the other way round? In this section we shall consider three possible answers to these questions and the difficulties they face.

The sense organ view

One possible response to these two questions is to individuate sense modalities by appeal to their respective organs. This would be to answer the first question by claiming that seeing is what we do with the eyes, hearing with the ears, smelling with the nose, tasting with the tongue, and feeling with the skin. It answers the second question by claiming that we know which sense we are using because we know which sense *organ* we are using.

Of course, to try to individuate the senses by means of their respective organs means that we need to begin by individuating the organs themselves. This may seem obvious: the nose is the protuberance in the middle of the face; the eyes are the orbs located in the eye sockets; and so on.

However, things are not quite so straightforward. Consider, for example, that one can feel not only with the skin but also with the eyes, ears, nose, and tongue. If seeing is what is done with the eyes, then feeling something sharp poking one's eye would thereby be counted as a case of seeing; if hearing is what is done with the ears, then feeling the cold of ice water by having it dropped in the ear canal would count as hearing the coldness; and so on. This suggests that the basic attempt to individuate the senses by way of their respective organs will not work.

Two ways in which the sense organ view might be modified seem open to a significant objection. The first alternative is to say that, when we talk about "the organs of sight" we are not meaning to refer solely to the eyes but also to their downstream physiological and neural systems. Feeling something as sharp by pressing it into your eyeball would therefore *not* qualify as a case of seeing as the overall process would employ downstream physiological systems that are not used in standard cases of seeing. Alternatively, we might say that, by "the eyes," we mean the eyes *qua* organs that respond to light; by "the ears," organs that respond to sound waves; and so on. Feeling something as cold by dripping it into your ear canal would therefore not count as *hearing* coldness because, in such a case, the ears would not be functioning by responding to sound waves.

One difficulty with this proposal concerns the case of touch. Touch has both many downstream physiological systems—at least *fifteen* according to one estimate (Nudds 2003: 34)—and many different kinds of physical stimulus it responds to. In addition to this, these modifications of the proposal struggle to provide an adequate answer to the second, epistemological, question of how a normal perceiver might come to *know* that he is seeing or hearing. Suppose we have a perceiver who presses something sharp into his eye and denies that he *sees* the sharpness. The first response would seem to require this perceiver to *know* that nonstandard downstream physiological systems were being employed. Or suppose we have a perceiver who drips ice water into his ear and denies that he *hears* the coldness. The second response would seem to require the perceiver to *know* that in this case he was not responding to pressure waves in the atmosphere. Both of these responses therefore seem to require our perceiver to have specialized knowledge of a kind that, normally, we would not expect to be possessed by someone who could tell which sense they were using.

In addition to this concern, Roxbee-Cox (1970) asks why we group the two eyes together as organs of sight and the two ears together as organs of hearing? Why do we not, rather, group the left eye and the left ear together as organs of a certain kind? There must be, he suggests, something that is common to the eyes that explains and justifies our grouping them together; likewise for the ears.

What might this commonality be? Two possibilities, of course, would be that the two eyes respond to the same external energy source (light waves) or that they feed into the same physiological system. Again, though, this runs into problems when attempting to explain why *normal* perceivers class the eyes together as organs of sight as normal perceivers may well not possess this kind of specialized knowledge. Two other alternatives, that do not fall prey to this objection are: (1) that operation of the eyes yields a *characteristic kind of experience*; (2) that the eyes respond to a *characteristic set of properties*. If either of these two possibilities are what justifies us in grouping together the two eyes as organs of a particular sense (sight), then perhaps our answer to the questions above lies in one of them.

The characteristic experience view

The view that each sense corresponds with a particular kind of experience is tentatively supported by Grice, who outlines the suggestion as follows:

> It might be suggested that two senses, for example, seeing and smell-ing, are to be distinguished by the special introspectible character of the experiences of seeing and smelling; that is, disregarding the differences between the characteristics we learn about by sight and smell, we are entitled to say that seeing is itself different in character from smelling.
>
> (Grice 1962: 135)

What is important about this suggestion is that, to distinguish it from the alternative suggestion that sight and smell give us information about different properties (the characteristic properties view), Grice outlines it as claiming that seeing and smelling have a different character, *even when we disregard the differences between the properties we learn about.* In the terminology of earlier chapters, the suggestion is that the different senses have different associated *qualia* (for a similar suggestion, see Lowe 1992: 80).

When presented in these terms, we can see that the phenomenon of transparency, discussed in earlier chapters, may cause problems for the characteristic experience view. To claim that an experience is transparent, recall, is to say that, when we introspect, we "see through" the experience to the objects themselves; that we only find features of the *objects* of experience, not features of the experience *itself*. If this is so, then there is no additional "smelling character" and "seeing character" to the experiences—at least not one that we can discover through introspection. As Grice acknowledges, "the attempt to describe the differences between seeing and feeling seems to dissolve into a description of what we see and what we feel" (1962: 144).

In addition to this, a view that makes an ineliminable appeal to special modality-specific qualia runs into difficulty when it comes to accounting for the possibility of distinct sensory modalities in other animals. For instance, Nagel famously wondered what it is like to be a bat, given that bats have a sonar sense that humans lack (1979). Other animals also appear to have senses that we don't. For example, it is widely believed that sharks have the capacity to sense magnetic fields, that snakes have the capacity to sense infrared radiation, and that some fish can sense electric potential (Keeley 2002). If the characteristic experience view is correct, then this requires there to be distinct qualia associated with these distinct senses. Given the problems Nagel raises, claims that particular animals have senses that we lack would therefore have the status of "propositions to which one must subscribe without really understanding them" (1979: 447).

If an appeal to a special "seeing character" is problematic, we may be able to avoid this by appeal to the notion, discussed in detail in Chapter 6, that experiences can be *indiscriminable* from one another. To see how this might work, consider the relations *being exactly the same height as* and *looking as tall as*. Focusing on the first relation first, note that we can legitimately infer that, if Alice is exactly the same height as Barbara, and Barbara is exactly the same height as Carol, then Alice is exactly the same height as Carol. This inference is legitimate because the relation *being exactly the same height as* is a *transitive* relation. The relation *looking as tall as*, however, is *intransitive*. As this relation is intransitive, the following inference will be illegitimate: if Alice looks as tall as Barbara, and Barbara looks as tall as Carol, then Alice looks as tall as Carol. The reason this inference is illegitimate is because it leaves open the possibility that Alice and Barbara might be unnoticeably different in height, as might Barbara and Carol, but that when you stand Alice and Carol next to one another, you can just make out that they are not as tall as one another.

This provides a way of developing a characteristic experience view that does not appeal to special modality-specific qualia. The suggestion is this:

"Any two experiences belong to the same modality if and only if those experiences can stand at either end of a series of experiences that are connected at each stage by the indiscriminability relation" (Clark 1993: 141).

To see how this works, imagine three experiences: the first is an experience of an expanse of red; the second an experience of an expanse of green; the third an experience of C-sharp. In the case of the first two experiences, we could construct a series of experiences, such that the first experience is one of an expanse of red; the second is of a red with a hint of orange so slight as to be indiscriminable from the first; the third of a yet more orange-red indiscriminable from the second; and so on, through yellow to green. Our first two experiences could stand at either end of a series of experiences, where each pair of experiences in the series are indiscriminable from one another. They therefore qualify as experiences of the same modality. Yet we cannot construct such a sequence from *either* of the first two experiences to the experience of C-sharp. They therefore qualify as experiences from *different* modalities. In this way, it might be possible to separate out all experiences into modality-specific classes.

There are more generic concerns with the characteristic experience view, however. Grice, for example, worries that it leaves it a contingent matter that seeing is the kind of experience we have in response to colors and shapes, that smell is the kind of experience we have in response to odors and scents, and so on. This concern can be highlighted by asking the following question: Would it be possible to have the sight-characteristic experience—where this is either an experience with the introspectible "seeing character" or an experience from a particular indiscriminability-based class—in response to scents and odors, whilst having the smell-characteristic experience in response to colors and shapes? Our natural inclination is to answer this question in the negative, but it is not clear how this response justifies us in doing so.

More worryingly, though, is that the characteristic experience view rules out the possibility of nonconscious sensory modalities. Not only does this seem to be a coherent possibility, there is evidence to think that we might actually *have* such a modality (although of course, being nonconscious, this may come as news to us!) Keeley (2002) suggests that there is evidence that humans possess a *vomeronasal* sense modality, physically located in pits on either side of the nasal septum, which enable us to sense *pheromones*— chemical compounds that are involved in social sexual interactions. In other animals, damage to the vomeronasal system leads to reduced sexual behavior, whilst artificial stimulation of the system leads to *increases* in such behavior. According to Keeley, there is apparently a "growing list" of similar findings for humans, which is some evidence that humans have such a sense modality too (2002: 24). If there is indeed a vomeronasal sense modality, it is one which has *no* characteristic experiences associated with it. The characteristic experience view would be unable to distinguish this modality from others.

The characteristic property view

The characteristic property view aims to individuate the senses by means of the different external *properties* they give us access to. To adequately spell out this view, we need to begin with the sense-neutral claim that we *perceive*—have sensory access to—an array of properties. This claim is "sense-neutral" because it doesn't specify which sense we perceive these properties *by*, merely that they are perceived. Then, on this basis, we distinguish the senses from one another in terms of *which* of this array of properties each sense gives us access to. For example, *seeing* is the sense that gives us access to colors, shapes and sizes; *hearing* is the sense that gives us access to volume, pitch, and timbre; and so on.

An obvious initial difficulty with this approach turns on the fact that some properties can be perceived by more than one sense. For instance, we can both *see* and *feel* that things are warm, or smooth, or square. Likewise, we can both *see* and *hear* that someone is angry, or that the sea is rough. Or we can both *smell* and *taste* that something is sweet; or both *see* and *smell* the burnt toast; and so on.

In response to this, both Grice and Roxbee-Cox turn to the idea that some properties are perceived *directly*, whilst others are perceived *indirectly* or *in virtue of* the direct perception of distinct properties. The idea is that we can then deal with these problem cases by stipulating that the property in question is only perceived *directly* by (at most) one of the two senses. On this approach, we directly *feel* that something is warm but only *see* that it is warm *by* seeing other properties, such as its being red, perhaps. It is not clear that this response will work in all cases. Both smelling and tasting something as sweet, for example, or both seeing and feeling something to be square, seem to be cases in which both properties are perceived equally directly.

An alternative response is to appeal to the fact that, when we *see* an object to be square, we perceive far more properties than squareness alone; we see the object's squareness as a member of a set of properties that includes its size, color, direction of motion, and so on. When we *feel* squareness, however, we perceive squareness as a member of a *different* overall set of properties, including heft, texture, temperature, and so on. On this view, we distinguish between the senses by distinguishing between the *range* of properties that sense enables you to perceive.

As Grice points out, this proposal runs into a problem. "Suppose a man to be resting a half-crown on the palm of one hand and a penny on the palm of another: he might (perhaps truthfully) say, 'The half-crown looks to me larger than the penny, though they feel the same size'" (1962: 137–138).

According to the characteristic property view, this subject *perceives* an array of properties—where "perceives," recall, is sense-neutral—which includes properties from both the visual list (colors, shapes, etc.) and the tactual list (texture, temperature, etc.). Our subject also perceives one coin to be larger than the other *and* the two coins to be the same size. The problem is, nothing in the characteristic property view's presentation of the facts enables us to conclude that the perception of the coins as differing in size is through the sense of *sight* and that the perception of them as having the same size is through the sense of *touch*.

In light of this problem, Roxbee-Cox (1970) presents a *key feature* version of the characteristic property view, which is similar in spirit to Aristotle's claim that the senses can be individuated by their "special objects" (*De Anima*, 418a: 12). Where the straightforward characteristic property view collects together the array of properties that can be seen, and then claims that seeing just is the perception of those properties, the key feature view picks out *specific* properties *from* that collection and claims that seeing just is the perception of those *key* properties.

Roxbee-Cox (1970) suggests that the key feature for sight is the property of *having some color property*; the key feature for hearing is *having some loudness and timbre*; the key feature for taste is *having some taste*; the key feature for smell is *having some odor*; and the key feature for feeling is *having some feel to the touch*. The question of how a perceiver *knows* which sense he or she is using can then be answered by appeal to the perceiver's knowing that he or she is *hearing* something—say, by knowing that the thing perceived has some loudness or timbre—or would know that he or she is *smelling* something by knowing that the thing perceived has some odor, and so on.

In order to allow that other properties can be seen, heard, tasted, smelled, and felt, Roxbee-Cox presents the following suggestion. For non-key property, *p*, to be perceived by sense, *S*, the subject also needs to (directly) perceive that the object bearing *p* has *S*'s key feature. For instance, circularity is a non-key property. For it to be perceived by *sight*, this requires us to also directly perceive that the (circular) object has some color property. For it to be perceived by *touch*, this requires us to also directly perceive that the (circular) object has some feel to the touch.

Roxbee-Cox suggests that the key feature view can deal with Grice's coin case as follows. Recall that the characteristic property view claimed that the subject both perceived the half-crown to be larger than the penny *and* perceived the coins to be the same size but didn't have the resources to account for the fact that the subject *sees* the coins to differ in size whilst *feeling* them to be the same size. The key feature view, however, can say the following:

> the half-crown seems larger than the penny, and . . . the seeming-perception of this relationship involves the direct perception that the coins have some color property; while . . . the half-crown and the penny seem equal in size, and . . . the seeming-perception of this relationship involves the direct perception that the coins have some feel to the touch.
>
> (Roxbee-Cox 1970: 539)

There remain concerns with this approach, however. For one thing, the key feature for taste is the property of having some taste. Of course, for this to work, we have to know what tastes (*qua* properties of objects) are independently of them being defined as *whatever properties can be sensed by the modality of taste*. Given the statements of the key features listed above, it would seem that the same objection might also be made to smell and, given some of the concerns about color realism raised in the previous chapter, even to the case of vision.

In addition to this, we might also wonder whether the account of the perception of non-key properties is correct: is it really the case that perception of *any* non-key property at any time *requires* the subject to perceive the key property? For example, we saw in the previous chapter that subjects can suffer from *achromatopsia*—the inability to see colors—yet still have, and know that they have, visual experiences. Even where normal subjects are concerned, the change blindness experiments we discussed might be argued to show that, on some occasions, it is possible to see an object's shape, say, *without* seeing that object to have some color property.

The final objection to consider turns to the case of touch. What is the key feature that is associated with the sense of touch? Think of all the different kinds of feeling there are. There is an active kind of contact feeling, in which we probe the object to feel its shape, or the texture of its surface; there is a kind of passive feeling, when we feel an object press or push against us; there is feeling an object to be warm or cold, feeling the air to be warm or cold, feeling water in which we are immersed to be warm or cold, the feeling of cold when alcohol evaporates on the skin; there is feeling one's heart beating inside one's chest or an oyster slipping down one's throat; there is feeling the sun on your back and the wind on your face; there is feeling an itch or a tickle; there is feeling chemicals burning one's skin, and so on. When all of the different kinds of feeling are listed in this way, we can see how difficult it will be to identify one unique key feature for touch, especially when we recall that, on the key feature view, the perception of non-key properties *requires* the perception of the key feature.

Perhaps, in light of all of this, we should deny that touch is a single sense after all, and instead see touch as a catch-all name for a number of different skin-based senses. However, this also faces problems. For one thing, the list above actually took a while to spell out. Yet, whenever a new possibility suggested itself, it was clear to me whether or not it qualified as a case of feeling or not. This suggests that I have a good sense of when something qualifies as a case of feeling, which I *use* to determine whether or not a particular case qualifies. If the many-sense view of touch were correct, it would seem I ought to work in the other direction: that I determine whether or not a particular case qualifies as a case of (generic) feeling by considering my list of (specific) cases of feeling and seeing if that particular case appears.

Other approaches

Although each of these three approaches has appealing features, each picking out *something* that seems important for the question of what differentiates the senses, none of them has been generally accepted. What are the prospects for developing a more widely accepted method for individuating the senses? Well, there might be something to be gained by combining elements of the theories presented above, with the hope of thereby avoiding the problematic objections. Another possibility would be to reject the claim, implicit in the above, that our individuation process ought to answer *both* the metaphysical and epistemological questions together. Those questions, recall, asked what distinguished sensory modalities from one another and how we *know* that we are experiencing with one rather than another.

To see why this might be plausible, note that the very fact that there can be disagreement over whether or not humans have a vomeronasal sense relies on its being accepted that it is possible that there could be a sense organ that we are not conscious of using. If we have to know that we have a sense, then there can be no dispute. If we do accept that there could be sensory modalities we don't know we have, this suggests that the questions of what makes something a sense modality of a particular kind is importantly distinct from the question of how we might *know* which sense modality we are using on any given occasion. This would allow us to develop an account of what individuates the senses from one another on purely scientific grounds, say, without worrying about how a subject might *know* which sense they are using (Keeley 2002).

Touch, hearing, taste, and smell

Given that the majority of this book has been given over to discussing and evaluating theories of *visual* perception, we might think that we would be well placed to simply *extrapolate* theories of the nonvisual senses from these extant theories. Before we see whether this is the case, we need to consider what the other senses serve to make us aware of.

The objects of touch, hearing, taste, and smell

The question to ask here has the general form: *What* do we sense, *when* we sense? Thus, *what* do we touch, *when* we touch? *What* do we hear, *when* we hear? *What* do we taste, *when* we taste? And *what* do we smell, *when* we smell?

Everyday language might make us think we can offer the same theory of all of these cases: we touch, hear, smell, and taste *objects*. Thus I touch the book, hear the car, smell the coffee, and taste the pineapple. Yet, as is the case with vision, when we see an object, we don't *just* see that object—it is difficult to imagine what this would even be like—instead, seeing the object requires us to also see some of its properties.

If we follow this analogy through, then, we would say that, when I touch the book, I touch—sense—some of its properties, when I hear the car, I hear—sense—some of its properties, and so on. If this is the correct approach to take, then we can ask which *properties* the other senses make us aware of. When we discussed the characteristic property approach to individuating the senses, it was suggested that the characteristic properties of touch included properties such as shape, texture, and temperature. As these are indeed properties of objects, then the analogy works, thus far at least.

Things are not so simple when we consider the other senses. The characteristic properties of hearing, for instance, included pitch, loudness, and timbre. Unless we are speaking metaphorically, these are not properties of *objects* but of *sounds*, where here I am using "sound" to mean something objective rather than experiential. The property of the *object* that we are aware of in hearing, then, would have to be its *sound*—the sound it makes—and then hearing makes us aware of the pitch, loudness, and timbre *of this sound*. Likewise for smell and taste. If these senses do indeed make us aware of properties of objects, the properties they make us aware of would have to be the object's *odor* and *flavor* (we could call these the object's smell and taste, but that would have the potential for confusion).

There are, however, reasons to be suspicious of the claim that sounds and odors, at least, are properties of objects. In the case of sound, O'Callaghan (2007) points out that sounds have duration and can persist through changes in their pitch, loudness, and timbre. These features, he argues, are difficult to square with a view of sounds as properties. For odors, the difficult to accommodate features would be the fact that odors seem to occupy volumes of space and that (what we normally call) an object's odor can be detached from it and even survive the destruction of the object. For instance, cooking odors can pervade an entire room and persist long after the meal has been eaten and the pots and pans washed up. This is difficult to square with the claim that the odor is *a property of* the meal.

What are sounds and odors if they are not properties of objects? On the basis of his phenomenological observations, O'Callaghan goes on to suggest that the best theory of the nature of sounds is that they are event-like particulars that are spatially located at or near their sources (2007: 30). Likewise, to account for the fact that they can be disconnected from their sources, odors would also need to be treated as a kind of particular that has the capacity to fill a volume of space. Even if such claims can be motivated by the phenomenology of auditory and olfactory experience, we do need to keep in mind that the phenomenological hat is not the only hat a theory of perception has to wear. There is also the epistemological hat. Treating sounds and odors as distinct particulars does raise the question of how the perception of, say, the rough, barking sound made by a car with a cracked muffler could, given that it is a distinct particular, justify us in having beliefs *about the car*.

Theories of touch, hearing, taste, and smell

Once we have a fix on what the objects of our different senses are, we can then ask how these senses function. This is the call for a philosophical theory of those senses. Perhaps, one might think, we can develop a theory of each sense by simply extrapolating our preferred theory of vision. Of course, things are not that simple.

Consider sense datum theories first. A sense datum theory of hearing would hold that, when we (as we would normally say) hear a sound, we directly sense a sense datum with properties of loudness, pitch, and timbre. Likewise for the other senses: when we feel the texture of a surface, we directly sense a sense datum with that texture; when we smell a spicy odor, we directly sense a spicy sense datum; when we taste a bitter taste, we directly sense a bitter sense datum.

Many of these claims seem strange. The Phenomenal Principle, which, recall, is a significant motivator for the sense datum theory of vision, doesn't have quite the force in the nonvisual cases. When we taste something bitter, for example, why should we think that there has to be some*thing* bitter that we taste? Sometimes one can just have a bitter taste in one's mouth without there being anything bitter that one tastes. A number of philosophers of perception have also contended that the phenomenology of the sense of *touch* cannot be adequately explained by a sense datum theory, even by philosophers who endorse that theory for vision. Brian O'Shaughnessy, for example, suggests that touch "involves the use of no mediating field of sensation. There is in touch no analogue of the visual field of visual sensations which mediates the perception of the environment" (1989: 38). Here, O'Shaughnessy makes clear his adherence to a sense datum theory for the case of *vision* in *denying* that the same theory is true of *touch*.

Other philosophers of perception have been led to the same conclusion. A.D. Smith, for example, focuses on the particular tactile case of the *Anstoss*: the experience of there being "a check or impediment to our active move-ment: an experienced obstacle to our animal striving, as when we push or pull against things" (2002: 154). Smith argues that the "unique non-sensory nature of the *Anstoss*" alone serves to refute the claim that we are always directly aware of mediating sense data. "In the case of the *Anstoss* . . . it is just such focal sensations that are absent. There is simply no such sensuous item to interpose itself between us and the external physical force that we experience" (2002: 165).

How would an adverbialist deal with the nonvisual senses? Well, there are two ways an adverbialist might go. One way would be to have a mode of sensing that corresponds to each sense and then distinguish between experiences *within* that mode adverbially. This approach would hold that we *taste sourly* when we eat a grapefruit, *taste sweetly* when we eat a peach, and *smell sweetly* when we smell that same peach. The difference between the experience of tasting something sweet and smelling something sweet would thus be a matter of the different *modes* of sensing, rather than the different adverbially modified ways in which the sensing takes place.

Another way to develop an adverbial theory—the way that corresponds most closely to the qualia theory—would be to hold to only *one* mode of sensing and to distinguish between *all* experiences from *all* modalities by the adverbs alone. Thus we sense *sweet-smell-ly* when we smell the peach and sense *sweet-taste-ly* when we eat it. In this case, the difference between the experience of tasting something sweet and smelling something sweet is not a matter of different modes of sensing but rather of different ways in which that mode is modified—there is a *sweet-smell-ly* way of sensing *and* a *sweet-taste-ly* way.

In the terminology of the qualia theory, the claim would be that the *gustatory qualia* possessed by the experience of eating a peach would differ from the *olfactory qualia* possessed by the experience of smelling a peach, and so on. The same would go for the other senses—the differences between what it is like to, say, feel a plush toy, feel a glass, and hear a car door slam would be differences between the tactual and auditory qualia possessed by each of those experiences. The concern with this approach is that to say that the difference between the experiences of smelling coffee and tasting pineapple is a difference in their qualia seems more like a restatement of the problem than a solution.

Intentionalists can also extrapolate reasonably straightforwardly. Exactly what is represented will depend, in part, upon what the objects of nonvisual sensory experiences are taken to be. To give a sense of the way intentionalist theories of the nonvisual senses might look, we might say that touch experiences represent objects as having certain tactile properties, auditory experiences represent sounds as having loudness, timbre, pitch, and possibly location properties, and smell and taste represent odors and flavors as having certain gustatory and olfactory properties.

Of course, phenomenology-first intentionalists would then couple this kind of claim with a qualia theory to account for the phenomenological aspects of experience. Inasmuch as that is the case, it faces the same question about its explanatory force. Representationalists, on the other hand, have an explanation of *why* an experience has the phenomenology it does—it is because of what it represents. Representationalism faces a problem in that it needs to claim that any property an experience can represent is a mind-*independent* property. In some cases, this might seem implausible. For instance, the way sugar tastes to me is quite naturally seen to be a feature of the way *I respond to* sugar rather than a mind-independent property of the substance. An argument for this claim is that if I have a cold, sugar may taste bitter to me (Locke 1961: 124). If this is correct, then the (normal) taste of sugar is arguably not, as the realist about taste would have to claim, a property *of sugar itself.*

Naive realist theories of the nonvisual senses also run up against this difficulty. The naive realist would claim that tactual experiences are episodes of being *acquainted with* surface textures, temperatures, shapes, and so on, that auditory experiences are episodes of being acquainted with sounds and their properties, that smell experiences are episodes of being acquainted with odors and their properties, and that taste experiences are episodes of being acquainted with the flavor properties of objects. It must also, therefore, allow that the taste of sugar is a *real* property of sugar. Not only can this be difficult to square with the intuition that tastes are a feature of how things affect us, it also runs into difficulties when it comes to explaining how one and the same thing can taste different in different circumstances.

How distinct are the senses?

Our discussions thus far have treated the senses as relatively distinct from one another. There is an underlying assumption that, for example, visual experiences do not depend, in any important way, on our experiences in other modalities.[1] To illustrate this, we haven't been given any reason to doubt that, were we to suddenly become deaf, for example, our visual experiences would continue much as they are. Yet one might wonder whether this really is the case. Perhaps, instead, some of our experiences are actually *multi-modal*—requiring the operation of *more than one* sense.

We are actually very familiar with one seemingly multi-modal experience—the everyday experience of taste. As it happens, the taste buds on the tongue only respond to fairly broad categories of taste—roughly: bitter, salty, sweet and sour—not nearly enough to account for the variety of different flavors we can taste. Our rich palette of tastes is in fact explained by the fact that, when food is placed in the mouth, some odor molecules travel through the passage at the back of the mouth to *olfactory* receptor cells at the top of the nasal cavity. It is this interaction of smell and taste that accounts for the rich variety of flavors we can perceive. This is why, when you have a cold, food tastes much more bland—not because anything different is happening with your taste receptors, but because your cold blocks the odor molecules from stimulating your sense of smell.

Although the senses of smell and taste are both involved in our perception of flavor, it would be phenomenologically inapt to treat the experience as merely additive—like tasting the sweet, salty, sour or bitter components of food *plus* smelling the food's odor. Tasting food does not *seem* to us, phenomenologically, to involve *smelling* at all—in particular, the act of inhaling through the nose, which seems so important to the experience of smelling, does not take place. Instead, these two senses intertwine to yield a homogenous experience that involves both the taste and smell modalities.

Matthew Nudds (2001) has argued that such bimodal experiences also occur in the case of vision and hearing. Consider the effect of listening to someone "throw their voice," an effect known as the *ventriloquism effect*. This occurs when the ventriloquist—the voice thrower—speaks, whilst moving the mouth of a dummy and keeping his or her own mouth and lips still. This leads the audience to experience the voice as emanating from the *dummy*. Even though the voice does not actually come from the dummy's direction, it is nonetheless experienced as so doing.

Nudds argues that:

> when one experiences the ventriloquism effect, the voice one hears appears to be *produced by* the dummy; it's not just that one hears the voice as coming from the same place as one sees the dummy to be, one experiences the dummy and its mouth movements as responsible for what one hears.
>
> (Nudds 2001: 218; my emphasis)

As evidence for this, he points to the experience of watching a film when the soundtrack is slightly out of sync. Even though the sounds and pictures are experienced as coming from the same place, what is missing, he claims, is the experience of hearing the sounds *as being produced by* what is seen. If this is right, then experiencing a sound *being produced by* something that you can see is an essentially multi-modal experience—it is an experience that requires the joint operation of two different senses.

Altogether, these considerations suggest that there is still much important work to be done in the philosophy of perception. Although the vast majority of philosophical work has focused on vision, there remains no widely accepted theory of *sight*. What is more, we have also seen that there are reasons to think that theories of the other senses may follow a different pattern. So, even if a theory of vision does gain wide acceptance, there is no guarantee that adequate theories of hearing, touch, smell, and taste will follow. Finally, we have seen reason to question the assumption that the right way to think about perception is by breaking it down into distinct senses and dealing with them separately. Perhaps, instead, a thorough philosophical understanding of our capacity to perceive the world will require a united theory of all our senses. How all of this plays out remains to be seen.

Questions

- What do you think is the key difference between the different senses?
- What are the advantages and disadvantages of attempting to develop a theory of perception that covers all five senses?
- As philosophers of perception, how should we begin thinking about sense perception?

Note

1. Often, philosophical discussions of the relationship between the senses have focused on *Molyneux's Question*, which was first stated in a letter from William Molyneux to John Locke in 1688. It asks whether a blind man, who had learned to distinguish between a cube and a sphere by touch could, upon restoration of his sight, recognize which was the cube and which was the sphere without touching them. Molyneux's question has a number of intriguing aspects. For instance, it might be taken to be a question about the phenomenological similarities and differences between visual and tactual experiences of shape. Or it might be taken to be asking whether we have distinct shape concepts for each sense or whether the same shape concepts are employed on the basis of both sight and touch.

Further reading

Two important early discussions of the issue of how we individuate the senses are H.P. Grice's paper, "Some Remarks on the Senses" (1962) and J.W. Roxbee-Cox's, "Distinguishing the Senses" (1970).

Good discussions of the phenomenology of touch, and the differences between touch and vision, are Brian O'Shaughnessy's "The Sense of Touch" (1989) and M.G.F. Martin's 1992 paper, "Sight and Touch." A.D. Smith's *The Problem of Perception* (2002) also contains typically astute discussions of the nonvisual senses, and Casey O'Callaghan's recent book *Sounds* (2007) is an excellent discussion of auditory perception (although it maybe focuses on phenomenological issues to the exclusion of the epistemological role of auditory experience).

Matthew Nudds defends the existence of bimodal visual/auditory experiences in his 2001 paper, "Experiencing the Production of Sounds."

References

Aristotle (1984) *De Anima*, in J. Barnes (ed.), *The Complete Works of Aristotle*, Vol. I, (Princeton, NJ: Princeton University Press), pp. 641–692.

Armstrong, D.M. (1961) *Perception and the Physical World* (London: Routledge & Kegan Paul).

—— (1968) *A Materialist Theory of the Mind* (London: Routledge & Kegan Paul).

—— (1973) *Belief, Truth and Knowledge* (Cambridge: Cambridge University Press).

Austin, J.L. (1962) *Sense and Sensibilia* (Oxford: Clarendon Press).

Barnes, W. (1965) "The Myth of Sense-Data," in R.J. Swartz (ed.), *Perceiving, Sensing and Knowing* (Berkeley, Calif.: University of California Press), pp. 138–167.

Bayne, T. (2009) "Perception and the Reach of Phenomenal Content," *The Philosophical Quarterly* 59(236): 385–404.

Bennett, J. (1971) *Locke, Berkeley, Hume: Central Themes* (New York: Oxford University Press).

Berkeley, G. (1910) *A New Theory of Vision and Other Writings* (London: J.M. Dent & Sons Ltd.).

Berti, A. and G. Rizzolatti (1992) "Visual Processing without Awareness: Evidence from Unilateral Neglect," *Journal of Cognitive Neuroscience* 4: 345–351.

Blake, R., T.J. Palmeri, R. Marois, and C.-Y. Kim (2005) "On the Perceptual Reality of Synaesthetic Color," in L.C. Robertson and N. Sagiv (eds.), *Synaesthesia: Perspectives from Cognitive Neuroscience* (New York: Oxford University Press).

Block, N. (1990) "Inverted Earth," in J.E. Tomberlin (ed.), *Philosophical Perspectives Volume 4: Action Theory and Philosophy of Mind* (Atascadero, Calif.: Ridgeview), pp. 53–79.

—— (2007a) *Consciousness, Function and Representation* (Cambridge, Mass.: MIT Press).

—— (2007b) "Consciousness, Accessibility and the Mesh between Psychology and Neuroscience," *Behavioral and Brain Sciences* 30: 481–548.

—— (2008) "Consciousness and Cognitive Access," *Proceedings of the Aristotelian Society* 108(3): 289–317.

Brentano, F. (1995) *Psychology from an Empirical Standpoint* (London: Routledge).

Brewer, B. (2005) "Perceptual Experience Has Conceptual Content," in E. Sosa and M. Steup (eds.), *Contemporary Debates in Epistemology* (Oxford: Blackwell), pp. 217–230.

—— (2006) "Perception and Content," *European Journal of Philosophy* 14(2): 165–181.

—— (2008) "How to Account for Illusion," in A. Haddock and F. Macpherson (eds.), *Disjunctivism: Perception, Action, Knowledge* (Oxford: Oxford University Press), pp. 168–180.

Burge, T. (1991) "Vision and Intentional Content," in E. LePore and R. vanGulick (eds.), *John Searle and His Critics* (Oxford: Basil Blackwell), pp. 195–214.

—— (2007a) "Individualism and the Mental," in T. Burge, *Foundations of Mind* (Oxford: Clarendon Press), pp. 100–150.

—— (2007b) "Cartesian Error and the Objectivity of Perception," in T. Burge, *Foundations of Mind* (Oxford: Clarendon Press), pp. 192–207.

Butchvarov, P. (1980) "Adverbial Theories of Consciousness," *Midwest Studies in Philosophy* 5(3): 261–280.

Butterfill, S. (2009) "Seeing Causes and Hearing Gestures," *The Philosophical Quarterly* 59(236): 405–428.

Byrne, A. (1997) "Some Like It HOT: Consciousness and Higher-Order Thoughts," *Philosophical Studies* 86(2): 103–129.

—— (2001) "Intentionalism Defended," *The Philosophical Review* 110: 199–240.

—— (2002) "DON'T PANIC: Tye's Intentionalist Theory of Consciousness," *A Field Guide to the Philosophy of Mind* symposium on Tye's *Consciousness, Color, and Content*. Available online at http://host.uniroma3.it/progetti/kant/field/tye-symp_byrne.htm. (Accessed October 6, 2009.)

—— (2009) "Experience and Content," *The Philosophical Quarterly* 59(236): 429–451.

Byrne, A. and H. Logue (2008) "Either/Or" in A. Haddock and F. Macpherson (eds.), *Disjunctivism: Perception, Action, Knowledge* (Oxford: Oxford University Press), pp. 57–94.

—— (2009) *Disjunctivism: Contemporary Readings* (Cambridge, Mass.: MIT Press).

Campbell, J. (2002) *Reference and Consciousness* (Oxford: Clarendon Press).

Casullo, A. (1983) "Adverbial Theories of Sensing and the Many-Property Problem," *Philosophical Studies* 44(2): 143–160.

Chalmers, D.J. (1994) "Facing Up to the Problem of Consciousness," in J. Shear (ed.) (1997), *Explaining Consciousness: The Hard Problem* (Cambridge, Mass.: MIT Press.

—— (1996) *The Conscious Mind* (New York: Oxford University Press).

—— (2004) "The Representational Character of Experience," in B. Leiter (ed.), *The Future of Philosophy* (Oxford: Oxford University Press), pp. 153–181.

—— (2006) "Perception and the Fall from Eden," in T.S. Gendler and J. Hawthorne (eds.), *Perceptual Experience* (Oxford: Oxford University Press), pp. 49–125.

Child, W. (1994) *Causality, Interpretation and the Mind* (Oxford: Oxford University Press).

Chisholm, R.M. (1942) "The Problem of the Speckled Hen," *Mind* 51(204): 368–373.

Clark, Andy (2001) "Visual Experience and Motor Action: Are the Bonds Too Tight?" *Philosophical Review* 110(4): 495–519.

—— (2002) "Is Seeing All It Seems? Action, Reason and the Grand Illusion," in A. Noë (ed.), *Is the Visual World a Grand Illusion?* (Thorverton: Imprint Academic), pp. 181–202.

Clark, Austen (1993) *Sensory Qualities* (Oxford: Clarendon Press).

Coates, P. (2007) *The Metaphysics of Perception: Wilfrid Sellars, Perceptual Consciousness and Critical Realism* (New York: Routledge).

Cornman, J.W. (1971) *Materialism and Sensations* (New Haven, Conn.: Yale University Press).

Crane, T. (1992) "The Nonconceptual Content of Experience," in T. Crane (ed.), *The Contents of Experience: Essays on Perception* (Cambridge: Cambridge University Press), pp. 136–157.

—— (1998) "Intentionality as the Mark of the Mental," in A. O'Hear (ed.), *Contemporary Issues in the Philosophy of Mind* (Cambridge: Cambridge University Press), pp. 229–251.

—— (2000) "The Origins of Qualia" in T. Crane and S. Patterson (eds.), *The History of the Mind-Body Problem* (London: Routledge), pp. 169–194.

—— (2003) "The Intentional Structure of Consciousness," in Q. Smith and A. Jokic (eds.), *Consciousness: New Philosophical Perspectives* (Oxford: Clarendon Press), pp. 33–56.

Cytowic, R.E. (1993) *The Man Who Tasted Shapes* (London: Abacus).

Dancy, J. (1985) *Introduction to Contemporary Epistemology* (Oxford: Blackwell).

—— (1988) *Perceptual Knowledge* (Oxford: Oxford University Press).

Davidson, D. (1980) "The Logical Form of Action Sentences," in *Essays on Actions and Events* (Oxford: Clarendon Press), pp. 105–122.

Davies, M. (1991) "Individualism and Perceptual Content," *Mind* 100: 461–484.

Dennett, D.C. (1969) *Content and Consciousness* (London: Routledge).

—— (1981) "True Believers: The Intentional Strategy and Why it Works," in A.F. Heath (ed.), *Scientific Explanation* (Oxford: Oxford University Press), pp. 53–78.

—— (1988) "Quining Qualia," in A. J. Marcel and E. Bisiach (eds.), *Consciousness in Contemporary Science* (Oxford: Oxford University Press), pp. 42–77.

—— (1991) *Consciousness Explained* (London: Penguin).

Doyle, J.R. and C. Leach (1988) "Word Superiority in Signal Detection: Barely a Glimpse, Yet Reading Nonetheless," *Cognitive Psychology* 20(3): 283–318.

Dretske, F. (1969) *Seeing and Knowing* (London: Routledge & Kegan Paul).

—— (1981) *Knowledge and the Flow of Information* (Cambridge, Mass.: MIT Press).

—— (1995) *Naturalizing the Mind* (Cambridge, Mass.: MIT Press).

—— (2003) "Experience as Representation" in E. Villanueva (ed.), *Philosophical Issues 13: Philosophy of Mind* (Atascadero, Calif.: Ridgeview), pp. 67–82.

Ducasse, C.J. (1942) "Moore's Refutation of Idealism," in P.A. Schlipp (ed.), *The Philosophy of G.E. Moore*, Vol. I (La Salle, Ill.: Open Court), pp. 225–251.

Elugardo, R. (1982) "Cornman, Adverbial Materialism and Phenomenal Properties," *Philosophical Studies* 41: 33–50.

Evans, G. (1982) *The Varieties of Reference* (Oxford: Oxford University Press).

Firth, R. (1965) "Sense-Data and the Percept Theory," in R.J. Swartz (ed.), *Perceiving, Sensing and Knowing* (Berkeley, Calif.: University of California Press), pp. 204–270.

Fish, W.J. (2009) *Perception, Hallucination, and Illusion* (New York: Oxford University Press).

Fodor, J. (1992) "A Theory of Content II: The Theory" in *A Theory of Content and Other Essays* (Cambridge, Mass.: MIT Press), pp. 89–136.

Foster, J. (2000) *The Nature of Perception* (Oxford: Oxford University Press).

Gibson, J.J. (1966) *The Senses Considered as Perceptual Systems* (Boston, Mass.: Houghton Mifflin).

Goldman, A.H. (1976) "Appearing as Irreducible in Perception," *Philosophy and Phenomenological Research* 37(2): 147–164.

Grice, H.P. (1961) "The Causal Theory of Perception," *Proceedings of the Aristotelian Society* 35: 121–152.

—— (1962) "Some Remarks about the Senses," in R.J. Butler (ed.), *Analytical Philosophy* (Oxford: Basil Blackwell), pp. 133–153.

Grush, R. (2007) "A Plug for Generic Phenomenology," *Behavioral and Brain Sciences* 30(3): 504–505.

Haddock, A. and F. Macpherson (2008) *Disjunctivism: Perception, Action, Knowledge* (Oxford: Oxford University Press).

Haffenden, A.M. and M.A. Goodale (1998) "The Effect of Pictorial Illusion on Prehension and Perception," *Journal of Cognitive Neuroscience* 10(1): 122–136.

Hardin, C.L. (1988) *Color for Philosophers: Unweaving the Rainbow* (Indianapolis, Ind.: Hackett Publishing Co.).

Harman, G. (1987) "(Non-Solipsistic) Conceptual Role Semantics," in E. LePore (ed.), *New Directions in Semantics* (London: Academic Press), pp. 55–81.

—— (1990) "The Intrinsic Quality of Experience" in J.E. Tomberlin (ed.), *Philosophical Perspectives 4: Action Theory and the Philosophy of Mind* (Atascadero, Calif.: Ridgeview), pp. 31–52.

Harrison, J.E. and S. Baron-Cohen (1997) "Synaesthesia: An Introduction," in S. Baron-Cohen and J.E. Harrison (eds.), *Synaesthesia: Classic and Contemporary Readings* (Oxford: Blackwell), pp. 3–16.

Hawthorne, J. and K. Kovakovich (2006) "Disjunctivism," *Proceedings of the Aristotelian Society, Supplementary Volume* 80(1): 145–183.

Heck, R.G. (2000) "Nonconceptual Content and the 'Space of Reasons,'" *The Philosophical Review* 109(4): 483–523.

Hinton, J.M. (1967) "Visual Experiences," *Mind* 76(302): 217–227.

——(1973) *Experiences: An Inquiry into Some Ambiguities* (Oxford: Clarendon Press).

Hochberg, J.E. (1968) "In the Mind's Eye" in R.N. Haber (ed.), *Contemporary Theory and Research in Visual Perception* (New York: Holt, Reinhart & Winston), pp. 99–124.

Horgan, T.E. and J.L. Tienson (2002) "The Intentionality of Phenomenology and the Phenomenology of Intentionality" in D.J. Chalmers (ed.), *Philosophy of Mind: Classical and Contemporary Readings* (Oxford: Oxford University Press), pp. 520–533.

Hurley, S. (1998) *Consciousness in Action* (Cambridge, Mass.: Harvard University Press).

Jackson, F. (1975) "On the Adverbial Analysis of Visual Experience," *Metaphilosophy* 6(2): 127–135.

—— (1977) *Perception: A Representative Theory* (Cambridge, Mass.: Cambridge University Press).

—— (1982) "Epiphenomenal Qualia," *The Philosophical Quarterly* 6(2): 127–135.

—— (1994) "Representative Realism" in J. Dancy and E. Sosa (ed.), *A Companion to Epistemology* (Oxford: Blackwell), pp. 445–448.

Johnston, M. (2004) "The Obscure Object of Hallucination," *Philosophical Studies* 120(1–3): 113–183.

Keeley, B.L. (2002) "Making Sense of the Senses: Individuating Modalities in Humans and Other Animals," *Journal of Philosophy* 99(1): 5–28.

Kim, J. (1977) "Perception and Reference without Causality," *The Journal of Philosophy* 74(10): 606–620.

Kriegel, U. (2002) "PANIC Theory and the Prospects for a Representational Theory of Phenomenal Consciousness," *Philosophical Psychology* 15(1): 55–64.

—— (2007) "Intentional Inexistence and Phenomenal Intentionality," *Philosophical Perspectives* 21(1): 307–340.

—— (2008) "The Dispensibility of (Merely) Intentional Objects," *Philosophical Studies* 141(1): 79–95.

Levine, J. (1983) "Materialism and Qualia: The Explanatory Gap," *Pacific Philosophical Quarterly* 64: 354–361.

—— (2001) *Purple Haze: The Puzzle of Consciousness* (New York: Oxford University Press).

—— (2007) "Two Kinds of Access," *Behavioral and Brain Sciences* 30(3): 514–515.

Lewis, C.I. (1929) *Mind and the World Order: An Outline of a Theory of Knowledge* (New York: Charles Scribner's Sons).

—— (1952) "The Given Element in Empirical Knowledge," *Philosophical Review* 61(2): 168–175.

Lewis, D. (1980) "Veridical Hallucination and Prosthetic Vision," *Australasian Journal of Philosophy* 58(3): 239–249.

—— (1986) "Causation," in D. Lewis *Philosophical Papers*, Vol. II (New York: Oxford University Press).

Locke, D. (1975) "Review of Hinton's *Experiences*," *Mind* 84(1): 466–468.

Locke, J. (1961) *An Essay Concerning Human Understanding* (London: J.M. Dent and Sons).

Loewer, B. (1997) "A Guide to Naturalizing Semantics" in C. Wright and B. Hale (eds.), *A Companion to the Philosophy of Language* (Oxford: Blackwell), pp. 108–126.

Lowe, E.J. (1992) "Experience and its Objects," in T. Crane (ed.), *The Contents of Experience: Essays on Perception* (Cambridge: Cambridge University Press), pp. 79–104.

Lycan, W. (1996) *Consciousness and Experience* (Cambridge, Mass.: MIT Press).

Macdonald, G. (1979) *Perception and Identity* (London: Macmillan).

Mack, A. and I. Rock (1998) *Inattentional Blindness* (Cambridge, Mass.: MIT Press).

Macpherson, F. (2007) "Synaesthesia, Functionalism and Phenomenology," in M. Marraffa, M. De Caro and F. Ferretti (eds.), *Cartographies of the Mind: Philosophy and Psychology in Intersection* (Dordrecht: Kluwer), pp. 65–80.

Martin, M.G.F. (1992) "Sight and Touch," in T. Crane (ed.), *The Contents of Experience: Essays on Perception* (Cambridge: Cambridge University Press), pp. 196–215.

—— (1994) "Perceptual Content," in S. Guttenplan (ed.), *A Companion to the Philosophy of Mind* (Oxford: Blackwell), pp. 463–471.

—— (1997) "The Reality of Appearances" in M. Sainsbury (ed.), *Thought and Ontology* (Milan: FrancoAngeli), pp. 81–106.

—— (2002) "The Transparency of Experience," *Mind and Language* 17(4): 376–425.

—— (2004) "The Limits of Self–Awareness," *Philosophical Studies* 120(13): 37–89.

—— (2006) "On Being Alienated," in T.S. Gendler and J. Hawthorne (eds.), *Perceptual Experience* (Oxford: Oxford University Press), pp. 354–410.

McCulloch, G. (1995) *The Mind and its World* (London: Routledge).

McDowell, J. (1994) *Mind and World* (Cambridge, Mass.: Harvard University Press).

—— (1998) "Criteria Defeasibility and Knowledge," in *Meaning, Knowledge and Reality* (Cambridge, Mass.: Harvard University Press), pp. 369–394. First published 1982.

—— (2008) "The Disjunctive Conception of Experience as Material for a Transcendental Argument," in A. Haddock and F. Macpherson (eds.), *Disjunctivism: Perception, Action, Knowledge* (Oxford: Oxford University Press), pp. 376–389.

McGinn, C. (1982) *The Character of Mind* (Oxford: Oxford University Press).

Michotte, A. (1963) *The Perception of Causality* (London: Methuen).

Milner, A.D. and M.A. Goodale (1995) *The Visual Brain in Action* (Oxford: Oxford University Press).

Moore, G.E. (1942) "A Reply to My Critics," in P.A. Schlipp (ed.), *The Philosophy of G.E. Moore*, Vol. II (La Salle, Ill.: Open Court), pp. 553–677.

Nagel, T. (1979) "What Is It Like to Be a Bat?" in *Mortal Questions* (Cambridge: Canto), pp. 165–180.

Neisser, U. (1967) *Cognitive Psychology* (New York: Appleton Century Crofts).

Noë, A. (2001) "Experience and the Active Mind," *Synthese* 129(1): 41–60.

—— (2003) "Causation and Perception: the Puzzle Unravelled," *Analysis* 63(2): 93–100.

——(2005) *Action in Perception* (Cambridge, Mass.: MIT Press).

Nudds, M. (2001) "Experiencing the Production of Sounds," *European Journal of Philosophy* 9(2): 210–229.

—— (2003) "The Significance of the Senses," *Proceedings of the Aristotelian Society* 104(1): 31–51.

O'Callaghan, C. (2007) *Sounds* (New York: Oxford University Press).

O'Regan, J.K. (1992) "Solving the 'Real' Mysteries of Visual Perception: The World as an Outside Memory," *Canadian Journal of Philosophy* 46(3): 461–488.

O'Regan, J.K. and A. Noë (2001) "A Sensorimotor Account of Vision and Visual Consciousness," *Behavioral and Brain Sciences* 24(5): 939–73.

O'Shaughnessy, B. (1989) "The Sense of Touch," *Australasian Journal of Philosophy* 67(1): 37–58.

Pani, J.R. (2000) "Cognitive Description and Change Blindness," *Visual Cognition* 7(1–3): 107–126.

Peacocke, C. (1983) *Sense and Content* (Oxford: Oxford University Press).

—— (1992) *A Study of Concepts* (Oxford: Oxford University Press).

Pitcher, G. (1971) *A Theory of Perception* (Princeton, NJ: Princeton University Press).

Price, H.H. (1932) *Perception* (London: Methuen).

Price, R. (2009) "Aspect Switching and Visual Phenomenal Character," *The Philosophical Quarterly* 59(236), 508–518.

Putnam, H. (1975) "The Meaning of 'Meaning,'" in K. Gunderson (ed.), *Language, Mind and Knowledge: Minnesota Studies in the Philosophy of Science, VII* (Minneapolis, Minn.: University of Minnesota Press).

—— (1981) *Reason, Truth and History* (Cambridge: Cambridge University Press).

Ramachandran, V.S. and E.M. Hubbard (2001) "Synaesthesia: A Window into Perception, Thought and Language," *Journal of Consciousness Studies* 8(12): 3–34.

Ramsey, W.M. (2007) *Representation Reconsidered* (Cambridge: Cambridge University Press).

Reid, T. (2002) *Essays on the Intellectual Powers of Man*, ed. by D. Brookes (University Park, Penn.: Pennsylvania State University Press).

Rensink, R. (2000) "The Dynamic Representation of Scenes," *Visual Cognition* 7: 17–42.

Robinson, H. (1994) *Perception* (London: Routledge).

Rock, I. and K. Mitchener (1992) "Further Evidence of Failure of Reversal of Ambiguous Figures by Uninformed Subjects," *Perception* 21: 39–45.

Rosenthal, D. (1990) "A Theory of Consciousness," in N. Block, O. Flanagan, and G. Güzeldere (eds.), *The Nature of Consciousness* (Cambridge, Mass.: MIT Press), pp. 773–788.

Roxbee-Cox, J.W. (1970) "Distinguishing the Senses," *Mind* 79: 530–550.

Russell, B. (1927) *The Analysis of Matter* (London: Kegan Paul).

—— (1948) *Human Knowledge: Its Scope and Limits* (London: George Allen & Unwin).

—— (1967) *The Problems of Philosophy* (Oxford: Oxford University Press).

Ryle, G. (1990) *The Concept of Mind* (London: Penguin).

Schellenberg, S. (forthcoming) "Ontological Minimalism about Phenomenology," *Philosophy and Phenomenological Research*.

Searle, J. (1983) *Intentionality: An Essay in the Philosophy of Mind* (Cambridge, Mass.: Cambridge University Press).

Segal, G. (1989) "Seeing What is Not There," *Philosophical Review* 97(2): 189–214.

——(1991) "In Defence of a Reasonable Individualism," *Mind* 100(1): 485–494.

Sellars, W. (1956) "Empiricism and the Philosophy of Mind," in H. Feigl (ed.), *Minnesota Studies in the Philosophy of Science*, Vol. I (Minneapolis, Minn.: University of Minnesota Press), pp. 307–329.

——(1975) "The Adverbial Theory of the Objects of Sensation," *Metaphilosophy* 6(2): 144–160.

Shear, J. (1997) *Explaining Consciousness: The Hard Problem* (Cambridge, Mass.: MIT Press).

Siegel, S. (2004) "Indiscriminability and the Phenomenal," *Philosophical Studies* 120(1–3): 90–112.

—— (2006) "Which Properties are Represented in Perception?" In T.S. Gendler and J. Hawthorne (eds.), *Perceptual Experience* (Oxford: Oxford University Press), pp. 481–503.

—— (2007) "How can we Discover the Contents of Experience?" *Southern Journal of Philosophy* 45: 127–142.

—— (2008) "The Epistemic Conception of Hallucination," in A. Haddock and F. Macpherson (eds.), *Disjunctivism: Perception, Action, Knowledge* (Oxford: Oxford University Press), pp. 205–224.

—— (2009) "The Visual Experience of Causation," *The Philosophical Quarterly* 59(236): 519–540.

Siewert, C.P. (1998) *The Significance of Consciousness* (Princeton, NJ: Princeton University Press).

Simons, D.J. and C.F. Chabris (1999) "Gorillas in Our Midst: Sustained Inattentional Blindness for Dynamic Events," *Perception* 28: 1059–1074.

Simons, D.J. and D.T. Levin (1997) "Change Blindness," *Trends in Cognitive Science* 1(7): 261–267.

—— (1998) "Failure to Detect Changes to People during a Real-world Interaction," *Psychonomic Bulletin and Review* 5(4): 644–649.

Smart, J.J.C. (1959) "Sensations and Brain Processes," *The Philosophical Review* 68(2): 141–156.

Smith, A.D. (2002) *The Problem of Perception* (Cambridge, Mass.: Harvard University Press).

Snowdon, P. (1981) "Perception, Vision and Causation," *Proceedings of the Aristotelian Society* 81: 175–192.

—— (1990) "The Objects of Perceptual Experience," *Proceedings of the Aristotelian Society* Supp. Vol. 64: 121–150.

—— (2005) "The Formulation of Disjunctivism: A Response to Fish," *Proceedings of the Aristotelian Society* 105(1): 129–141.

Soteriou, M. (2000) "The Particularity of Visual Perception," *European Journal of Philosophy* 8(2): 173–189.

Strawson, P.F. (1974) "Causation in Perception," in *Freedom and Resentment and Other Essays* (London: Methuen), pp. 73–93.

—— (1979) "Perception and its Objects," in G.F. Macdonald (ed.), *Perception and Identity: Essays Presented to A.J. Ayer* (London: Macmillan), pp. 41–60.

—— (1985) "Causation and Explanation," in B. Vermazen and J. Hintikka (eds.), *Essays on Davidson* (Oxford: Oxford University Press), pp. 115–135.

Sturgeon, S. (2006) "Reflective Disjunctivism," *Proceedings of the Aristotelian Society, Supplementary Volume* 80(1): 185–216.

Swartz, R.J. (1965) *Perceiving, Sensing, and Knowing* (Berkeley, Calif.: University of California Press).

Thagard, P. (2005) *Mind: Introduction to Cognitive Science*, 2nd edn (Cambridge, Mass.: MIT Press).

Thau, M. (2004) "What is Disjunctivism?" *Philosophical Studies* 120(1–3): 193–253.

Thomas, A. (2003) "An Adverbial Theory of Consciousness," *Phenomenology and the Cognitive Sciences* 2(3): 161–185.

Travis, C. (2004) "The Silence of the Senses," *Mind* 113(449): 57–94.

Tye, M. (1975) "The Adverbial Theory: A Defence of Sellars against Jackson," *Metaphilosophy* 6(2): 136–143.

—— (1982) "A Causal Analysis of Seeing," *Philosophy and Phenomenological Research* 42(3): 311–325.

—— (1984) "The Adverbial Approach to Visual Experience," *The Philosophical Review* 93(2): 195–225.

—— (1992) "Visual Qualia and Visual Content," in T. Crane (ed.), *The Contents of Experience: Essays on Perception* (Cambridge: Cambridge University Press), pp. 158–176.

—— (1995) *Ten Problems of Consciousness: A Representational Theory of the Phenomenal Mind* (Cambridge, Mass.: MIT Press).

—— (2000) *Consciousness, Color and Content* (Cambridge, Mass.: MIT Press).

—— (2003) "Blurry Images, Double Vision, and Other Oddities: New Problems for Representationalism?" in Q. Smith and A. Jokic (eds.), *Consciousness: New Philosophical Perspectives* (Oxford: Clarendon Press), pp. 7–32.

—— (2009) "The Admissible Contents of Visual Experience," *The Philosophical Quarterly* 59(236): 541–562.

Ungerleider, L.G. and M. Mishkin (1982) "Two Cortical Visual Systems," in D.J. Ingle, M.A. Goodale and R.J.W. Mansfield (eds.), *Analysis of Visual Behavior* (Cambridge, Mass.: MIT Press), pp. 549–586.

Vision, G. (1997) *Problems of Vision: Rethinking the Causal Theory of Perception* (New York: Oxford University Press).

Walker, R., J.M. Findlay, A.W. Young, and J. Welch (1991) "Disentangling Neglect and Hemianopia," *Neuropsychologia* 29: 1019–1027.

Warnock, G.J. (1987) *The Philosophy of Perception* (Oxford: Oxford University Press).

Weiskrantz, L. (1986) *Blindsight: A Case Study and Implications* (Oxford: Oxford University Press).

Weiskrantz, L., E.K. Warrington, M.D. Sanders, and J. Marshall (1974) "Visual Capacity in the Hemianopic Field Following a Restricted Occipital Ablation," *Brain* 97(4): 709–728.

Whyte, J.T. (1990) "Success Semantics," *Analysis* 50(3): 149–157.

Wittgenstein, L. (1953) *Philosophical Investigations* (Oxford: Blackwell).

Wright, C. (2002) "(Anti-)Sceptics Simple and Subtle: G.E. Moore and John McDowell," *Philosophy and Phenomenological Research* 65(2): 330–348.

—— (2008) "Comment on John McDowell's 'The Disjunctive Conception of Experience as Material for a Transcendental Argument'," in A. Haddock and F. Macpherson (eds.), *Disjunctivism: Perception, Action, Knowledge* (Oxford: Oxford University Press).

Zeki, S. (1993) *A Vision of the Brain* (London: Blackwell Scientific Publications).

Index

achromatopsia 128–9, 156
act-object theory 16
admissible contents 136–8
adverbialism 33–7; analyses of 37–9
afterimages 6, 35, 39
agnosia, types of 130
akinetopsia 129
Anstoss, the 159
argument from hallucination, the 11–15
argument from illusion, the 11–15
Armstrong, D. 22, 30, 51–61, 81
Austin, J. 14, 97–9

Barnes, W. 29
Bayne, T. 136–7
belief acquisition theory 51–64
Berkeley 19
blindsight 63
Block, N. 70–1, 136, 138–40
Brewer, B. 82, 105
Burge, T. 73–4, 82
Butchvarov, P. 46
Byrne, A. 17, 66, 67–8, 104, 137

Campbell, J. 96
causal objection, the 89–91; the revised
    94–5
causal theory of perception, the 118–21
Chalmers, D. 38, 56, 70
change blindness 83, 127, 138, 146, 156
characteristic experience view, the 151–3
characteristic property view, the 154–6
Child, W. 4, 88, 120–1
Clark, A. 152–3
cognitive science 125, 145
coherentism 54–5
Common Factor Principle, the 3–5,
    13–15, 36–7, 52, 66–7, 72, 87–9
complement objection, the 43–4
concepts: acquiring new 61–2; basic 60–
    1; belief and 59–61; demonstrative 83

content 7–8, 65–6; conceptual/
    nonconceptual 74–7; Fregean theory
    of 72, 83, 84; internalism/externalism
    about 73–4, 83; naturalistic theories
    of 77–8, 82–4; possible world theory
    of 72; singular theory of 72–3, 82–3,
    84, 92–3
continuity, perception to illusion 14
Cornman, J. 36, 38–9
Crane, T. 8, 38, 66, 76, 79, 81

Dancy, J. 19
Davidson, D. 47
Dennett, D. 60, 120, 126–7, 139
disjunctivism 87–9; about content
    92–4; epistemological 91; about
    metaphysics 91–2; negative 100–3;
    about phenomenology 94–6, 98,
    106–8; positive 98–100
disjunctivism and illusion: V vs. IH 104;
    VI vs. H 104–6
doxastic theory *see* belief acquisition
    theory
Dretske, F. 59, 61–2, 75, 77
Ducasse, C. 36

epistemological hat, the 2; adverbialism
    and 46–7; belief acquisition theory
    and 54–6; disjunctivism and 107–8;
    intentionalism and 80–2; other senses
    and 158; sense datum theory and
    19–22; sensory core theory and 27–8
*ex*ing 66, 81
externalism: about content 73–4, 83;
    about justification 54–5, 83; about
    phenomenology 83

Firth, R. 25–7
Fish, W. 95, 103, 105, 136, 146
Foster, J. 22, 58
foundationalism 20–2, 47, 54–5

Goldman, A. 59, 61
Grice, H. 114–6, 151–5

hallucination: definition of 3; disjunctive theories of 98–103
Harman, G. 8, 45–6, 77
Heck, R.G. 81
Hinton, J. 89
hues, unique and binary 143–5

Idealism 22
illusion: definition of 3; disjunctive theories of 104–6
inattentional blindness 83, 127–8, 138, 146
inclination to believe 58–9
Indirect Realism 19, 46, 154
indiscriminability 3–5, 14, 66, 72, 79, 82, 94–6, 100–4, 152–3
indistinguishability *see* indiscriminability
intentional strategy 60
intentionalism 65–6; first-order 69–70, 80; higher-order 68–9, 80; strong content-first 68–70, 75, 77–80, 83, 84, 140, 160; strong phenomenology-first 67–8, 77, 84, 160; weak 70–1
internalism: about content 73–4, 83; about justification 55, 83; about phenomenology 83
Inverted Earth 70–1

Jackson, F. 2, 19–20, 39–44
Johnston, M. 98–100

Keeley, B. 149, 152, 153, 157
Kim, J. 115
Kriegel, U. 80

Levine, J. 138
Lewis, C.I. 20, 29
Lewis, D. 10, 115–18, 120–1, 122
Locke, D. 89
Locke, J. 160
Lycan, W. 69, 77

many property problem, the 39–43
Martin, M.G.F. 8, 66, 89, 91, 95–6, 99, 100–3
McCulloch, G. 64
McDowell, J. 83, 104, 108
McGinn, C. 72, 82
metamers 140–3

method of phenomenal contrast, the 136–7
Mirroring Thesis, the 67, 78
misrepresentation 8, 73, 74
modesty 95–6
Moore, G.E. 19–20
multimodal experiences 161–2

Nagel, T. 2, 152
naive realism 96–8, 105–7
Noë, A. 48, 64, 97–8, 109–10, 126, 128
Nudds, M. 150, 161–2

O'Callaghan, C. 158
O'Shaughnessy, B. 159

PANIC 69, 75, 84–5
particularity 92–3
Peacocke, C. 7–8, 70, 75–6, 81
percept theory 24–9
perception, definition of veridical 3
phenomenal character 17; according to adverbialism 38–9; according to belief acquisition theory 56; and the cognitive aspects of experience 134–40; and disjunctivism 94–6; according to intentionalism 68; according to naive realism 96–8, 107; according to representationalism 79, 84–5; according to sense datum theory 17–18
Phenomenal Principle, the 5–6, 11–13, 15, 28, 33–7, 52, 79, 96–7, 159
phenomenological hat, the 2; adverbialism and 44–6; belief acquisition theory and 56; naive realism and 106–7; other senses and 158; percept theory and 28–9; representationalism and 78–80; sense datum theory and 18–19
Pitcher, G. 53–4, 57–8, 59–60, 64, 107
presentational character 17; according to adverbialism 38, 48; according to belief acquisition theory 56; according to naive realism 97, 106; according to representationalism 79, 84–5; according to sense datum theory 17–18, 28
Price, H.H. 5, 14, 22, 23, 24
Putnam, H. 83, 90, 139

qualia 38, 39, 45–6, 48, 68, 78–9, 82, 84, 151–2, 160

relationalism *see* naive realism
Representational Principle, the 7–9, 23–7, 47, 52, 65–6, 67, 92–3, 97
representationalism 69, 78–82, 97, 160
Robinson, H. 5–6, 16, 19, 24–6, 30, 34, 95, 99, 104
Rosenthal, D. 69
Roxbee-Cox, J. 151, 154–5
Russell, B. 15–16, 72
Ryle, G. 17, 22, 29

satisfaction 113–4
scenario content 75–6, 81
Schellenberg, S. 83
screening off problem, the 99–101
Searle, J. 93, 122
Segal, G. 74
Sellars, W. 42
sense datum theory 16–18
sense organ view, the 150–1
senses: individuating the 149–57; number of 149; theories of nonvisual 157–61;
sensing, the relation of 16–17, 97–8
sensory core theory 23–4
sensory/cognitive distinction, the 24–5, 29, 105–6, 134–40
Siegel, S. 103, 136–7
Siewert, C. 67
skepticism 107–8

Smart, J.J.C. 39
Smith, A.D. 14, 104, 159
Snowdon, P. 91, 118–19
Soteriou, M. 92–3
Strawson, P.F. 18, 44, 119, 136
Sturgeon, S. 102
synesthesia 132–4

teleosemantics 77–8, 84
thermometer view, the 54–5
time lag argument, the 15–16, 107
Tom and Tim 117–18
transparency 45–6, 78–80, 84, 152
Twin Earth 73–4, 83, 90
two visual systems hypothesis, the 131–2
Tye, M. 17, 38–9, 42–3, 44–5, 69, 75–6, 77, 78–80, 84, 117, 137

unilateral neglect 129–30

veil of perception doctrine, the 19–20, 46–7, 54
ventriloquism effect, the 161–2
veridical perception, definition of 3
visuo–spatial extinction 139

Weiskrantz, L. 63
Whyte, J. 77
Wittgenstein, L. 17

zombies 56

CPSIA information can be obtained
at www.ICGtesting.com
Printed in the USA
LVHW081228211121
704028LV00004B/141